PRAGMATICS
IMPLICATURE, PRESUPPOSITION, AND LOGICAL FORM

PRAGMATICS
IMPLICATURE, PRESUPPOSITION, AND LOGICAL FORM

Gerald Gazdar
School of Social Sciences
University of Sussex
Brighton, England

ACADEMIC PRESS
New York   San Francisco   London
A Subsidiary of Harcourt Brace Jovanovich, Publishers

ACADEMIC PRESS, INC.
111 Fifth Avenue, New York, New York 10003

United Kingdom Edition published by
ACADEMIC PRESS, INC. (LONDON) LTD.
24/28 Oval Road, London NW1 7DX

LIBRARY OF CONGRESS CATALOG CARD NUMBER: 78–4817

ISBN 0–12–278450–2

PRINTED IN THE UNITED STATES OF AMERICA
79 80 81 82 83 84   9 8 7 6 5 4 3 2 1

For
Raoul Duke and the Brown Buffalo

CONTENTS

PREFACE

This preface is intended to give the prospective reader an indication of the issues this book has the most to say about and the issues it has the least to say about. It also includes a thumbnail sketch of the position taken with respect to the relation between semantics and pragmatics.

Following Grice, there is a treatment of CONVERSATIONAL IMPLICA-TURE, but, unlike Grice's treatment, it is one which attempts a partial formalization. Implicatures due to the MAXIM OF QUALITY are treated, in effect, as epistemic implications in the sense of Hintikka. Two sorts of implicature due to the MAXIM OF QUANTITY are identified: A modified version of Horn's theory is used to handle SCALAR IMPLICATURES and an original treatment of CLAUSAL IMPLICATURES is given. Following Gazdar and Pullum, certain universals are proposed respecting the LOGICAL FUNCTORS that can be employed by a natural language. These universals are motivated by a combination of (*i*) Gricean maxims, (*ii*) psycholinguistic work on negation, and (*iii*) recent syntactic work on linear order in underlying representation. The major original contribution of the book lies in its treatment of PRESUPPOSITION. A definition is given, as is a fully worked out solution to the PROJECTION PROBLEM, a solution that handles the numerous counterexamples to which other putative solutions are shown to fall prey. The formal framework within which the theories of implicature and presupposition are elaborated is Hamblin's "commitment store" model of dialogue, and it is shown that this allows an inductive definition of CONTEXT and, following Stalnaker, a pragmatic definition of SENTENCE MEANING.

The major lacuna in the book is the absence of any detailed proposals concerning ILLOCUTIONARY FORCE. Although Chapter 2 is devoted to showing that the only extant linguistic theory of illocutionary force cannot be maintained, nothing is offered to replace it. The argument for a pragmatic theory is negative in character: Since illocutionary force cannot be handled within semantic representation (i.e., with the performative hypothesis), then it must be handled within the pragmatic component of the overall linguistic theory. There are two main problems in this area: One is to give a formal account of the way the illocutionary force of an utterance relates to, and changes, the context of utterance; the other is the problem of stating explicitly the relation between the various distinct forces and the syntax of a language. The most promising approach to the first problem is to be found in Hamblin's work on dialogue, Stalnaker's work on assertion, and in recent related (but largely unpublished) work of Kamp. The situation with respect to the second problem is depressing at the present time. Despite the fact that much interesting data has been noted (e.g., in Sadock's work) and the fact that the muddled beginnings of a solution to a part of the problem is available (i.e., the Gordon and Lakoff–Heringer–Forman line), little if any progress has been made for a number of years (Heringer 1977 is an exception). Since this book is neither a survey of the field nor a textbook, no chapter on "the pragmatics of illocutionary force" is included.

Semantics, by which I mean a recursive truth definition, is the *éminence grise* of this book. Chapter 1 defines pragmatics as meaning minus semantics. That chapter also argues for a formalist methodology for pragmatics, a methodology which is attractive precisely because of its achievements, in Montague's hands, in semantics. The attack on the performative hypothesis in Chapter 2 is partly motivated by semantic considerations—a compelling *argumentum ab inconvenienti* is always lurking in the wings. Chapters 3 and 4 attend, inter alia, to the resolution of the meaning discrepancies between logical functors and their putative natural language counterparts. Although the analysis itself is pragmatic, the motivation is again a semantic one: the preservation of truth-functionality. Chapters 5 and 6 develop a pragmatic theory of presupposition, an aspect of meaning with which even the most esoteric semantic theories are demonstrably unable to cope. The provision of a pragmatic theory of presupposition relieves the semantics of the need for nonbivalent interpretations, ambiguous negation, and counterintuitive connective definitions, among other things. Chapter 6 concludes with a pragmatic definition of sentence meaning that accounts for one of the standard problems for (truth-conditional) semantics: the fact that tautologous sentences can mean different things. Finally, in Chapter 7, the relation between semantics and pragmatics is addressed directly. The first half of the chapter uses a memorable claim of Lakoff's as a pretext for elaborating on the points made above. The second half addresses itself briefly to a crucial issue that has hardly begun to be studied: the question whether the semantics of a natural language is autonomous with respect to the pragmatics.

The present work is a radical, although essentially structure-preserving, transformation of my 1976 doctoral dissertation. For the latter I am massively indebted to Hans Kamp and Ed Keenan for indispensable supervision, and to Ewan Klein and Geoff Pullum, who went through it chapter by chapter before I submitted it. The many additions, excisions, and revisions that have led to the pages that follow, were provoked, in large part, by the detailed comments and criticism I have had from Derek Bickerton, Alice Davison, Lauri Karttunen, George Lakoff, Steve Levinson, John Lyons, Stan Peters, and Arnold Zwicky, to all of whom I am extremely grateful. Thanks finally to Jerry Sadock for waving a magic wand at the publishers, and to Jackie Ford, Judith Dennison, and Alison Mudd for uncomplainingly converting waste paper into a manuscript.

LIST OF SYMBOLS AND
TYPOGRAPHICAL CONVENTIONS

1. Double quotation marks
   1.1 quotation
   1.2 naming nonsymbolic metalinguistic expressions, for example, "pre-supposition" is the name of a relation that holds between sentences
   1.3 "scare" quotation
2. Single quotation marks—quotation within quotation
3. Symbolic expressions are treated as autonymous
4. Italics distinguish nonsymbolic object language expressions that
   4.1 occur in the text, for example, *and* and *or*
   4.2 are combined with symbolic expressions, for example, $[\phi\,{}^\frown and\,{}^\frown \psi] \subseteq [\phi\,{}^\frown or\,{}^\frown \psi]$
5. ϕ, ψ, χ, π—metalinguistic variables ranging over sentences of the object language
6. α, β, γ—metalinguistic variables ranging over words, strings, or expressions of the object language
7. X, Y, Z
   7.1 same as 6 but used for arbitrary and potentially null expressions, for example let $X\,{}^\frown \alpha\,{}^\frown Y$ be a sentence where X and Y are any expressions, possibly null, . . .
   7.2 metalinguistic variables ranging over sets of propositions
8. Γ—metalinguistic variable ranging over sets of sentences

9. x, y, z

    9.1 metalinguistic variables ranging over propositions

    9.2 object language variables ranging over individuals, for example, in discussion of definite descriptions

10. $\neg$, $\wedge$, $\vee$, $\overline{\vee}$, $\rightarrow$, $\leftrightarrow$—used standardly with assumed bivalent interpretation

11. $\exists$, $(\ )$—used standardly for existential and universal quantification respectively

12. $\in$, $\cup$, $\cap$, $\subseteq$, $\subset$, $\times$, $\mathscr{P}$, $\sim$, $\{,\}$, $<,>$—used standardly as in, for example, Suppes (1960) (*Note:* $\mathscr{P}$ is also used as a presupposition-set notation in Chapter 5)

13. Λ, λ—the empty set and the abstraction operator, respectively

14. $\cdot$—conjoins within set-definitions to obviate the need for bracketing, so we get $\{\phi : \phi = X^\frown\psi^\frown Y \cdot \psi\rightarrow\phi\}$ instead of $\{\phi : (\phi = X^\frown\psi^\frown Y)\wedge(\psi\rightarrow\phi)\}$

15. μ

    15.1 used as a deontic operator in Chapter 3

    15.2 used for Hintikka's (1962) model sets in proofs

16. A,B,C,D,E,F,G,H,I,J,K,L,M,N,O,P,Q,T,V,X
Polish notation (after Lukasiewicz) for truth-functional operators and connectives in Chapter 4

17. A*, D*, E*, J*, K*, O*, V*, X*—ad hoc notation used for set-taking truth-functions in Chapter 4 (also used in Gazdar and Pullum 1976)

18. $\square$ $\square$—$\square\phi\square$ denotes the truth value of ϕ

19. [ ]

    19.1 brackets, usually after quantifiers, for example, $(\phi)[\phi\rightarrow\phi]$

    19.2 a function from sentences into propositions, $[\phi]$ is the proposition (i.e., set of possible worlds) denoted by the sentence ϕ. We can say that ϕ entails ψ if and only if $[\phi]\subseteq[\psi]$. See the first section of Chapter 6.

20. ⟦ ⟧—a function from sentences into functions from contexts into propositions, defined in the last section of Chapter 6

21. K, P

    21.1 Polish notation for conjunction connective and invariant-truth operator respectively (only in Chapter 4)

    21.2 Unsubscripted K is used as an abbreviation for the string *speaker knows that*. Unsubscripted P is used as an abbreviation for the string *for all the speaker knows* and for *it is compatible with all the speaker knows that*. It is assumed that K and P have exactly the properties ascribed to them in Hintikka (1962), thus, for example, $K\phi\leftrightarrow\neg P\neg\phi$ is assumed to hold for all values of ϕ.

Formal proofs involving K and P will be done in the same way that Hintikka does them and reference to Hintikka (1962) will be necessary if the proofs are to be checked. Hintikka's logic may be regarded, to all intents and purposes, as a notational variant of Lewis's S4.

22. Example numbers

All examples drawn from other authors have been renumbered, without comment, to fit the present text.

(20)   *Caesar lives.*
(21)   *Brutus dies.*

In addition to the standard use of (20) to refer to the sentence *Caesar lives*, we employ a number of abbreviatory conventions:

⌐20 or ⌐(20) for *Caesar does not live.*
K(20) for *Speaker knows that Caesar lives.*
P(20) for *For all the speaker knows, Caesar lives.*
[20] for [*Caesar lives.*]

These conventions are generative and compound expressions like [K⌐P(20)] occur frequently in Chapter 6. Although [20] always denotes the proposition that Caesar lives, expressions like (20) and K(20) are sometimes used with systematic utterance/sentence/proposition ambiguity:
Thus

(20) neither pre-supposes nor presupposes K(21)

abbreviates

It is not the case either that the sentence (20) pre-supposes the sentence K(21) or that utterance of (20) ever presupposes the proposition [K(21)]

23. In general, notation used by other authors has been changed to fit the present conventions. Exceptions to this generalization include Lakoff's "meaning postulates," Horn's definition of scalar implicature, and the definitions of pragmatic presupposition given in Chapter 5.

PRAGMATICS
IMPLICATURE, PRESUPPOSITION, AND LOGICAL FORM

1

INTRODUCTION

Pragmatics

> Although an increasing number of linguists are now beginning to
> use the term "pragmatics" in contrast with "semantics," most of
> them do so without associating themselves with the view that
> linguistics is, or should be, a branch of semiotics. This is also true
> of the majority of logicians and philosophers who draw a distinc-
> tion between semantics and pragmatics. Indeed, it is arguable
> that, by now, the origins of the tripartite distinction in Peirce's
> conception of an overall science of semiotics are more or less irrele-
> vant to the way in which this distinction is currently drawn by
> either linguists or philosophers. Even less relevant is the connex-
> ion, in Peirce's work, between pragmatics as a subdivision of
> semiotics and the philosophical movement known as pragmatism
> [Lyons 1977:119].

The present work provides no exception to the trend described by
Lyons in the preceding quotation. The syntax–semantics–pragmatics
trichotomy has been familiar since the work of Morris (1938). Although
the domains of syntax and semantics have remained fairly clear cut, the
domain of pragmatics has never been very precisely delimited. Morris
wanted it to subsume psycholinguistics, neurolinguistics, and sociolinguistics: "It is a sufficiently accurate characterization of pragmatics to say
that it deals with the biotic aspects of semiosis, that is, with all the
psychological, biological, and sociological phenomena which occur in

the functioning of signs [Morris 1938:108]." Carnap sometimes seems to equate pragmatics with what is now called "sociolinguistics": "We may study the preferences of different social groups, age groups, or geographical groups in the choice of expressions. We investigate the role of language in various social relations, etc. . . . . Pragmatics . . . consists of all these and similar investigations [Carnap 1938:148]." But Carnap (1955) equates pragmatics with a discipline concerned with such notions as *acceptance, intension,* and *utterance.* An even more restricted domain for the subject is offered by Kalish (1967): "Pragmatics, so conceived, is simply the extension of the semantical truth-definition to formal languages containing indexical terms [p. 356]." Sayward (1974) has argued persuasively that the original Carnap–Morris distinction was defective in various respects and he has gone on to argue, in Sayward (1975), that Kalish's reformulation will not do either. Those interested in a critical history of the terminological issue will find it in these two papers. I shall not elaborate further on it here.

Probably the single most important reason for this unclarity about the proper domain of pragmatics is that in the 30 years that elapsed between Morris's original monograph and Montague's "Pragmatics" (reprinted in Montague 1974) hardly anyone studied anything which they themselves called "pragmatics."[1] Montague, of course, shares Kalish's view of pragmatics.

In this book I shall adopt a view of the domain of pragmatics which is much more restricted than that of Morris, but one which does not coincide with that of Kalish. The view I shall adopt is one which is implicit in much recent linguistic theorizing. Close relatives of the view can be found stated explicitly in the works of Karttunen, Stalnaker, and Thomason. Pragmatics has as its topic those aspects of the meaning of utterances which cannot be accounted for by straightforward reference to the truth conditions of the sentences uttered.[2] Put crudely: PRAGMATICS = MEANING − TRUTH CONDITIONS. Since indexical expressions are standardly and naturally handled with truth-conditional apparatus, it follows that this domain excludes that proposed by Kalish. As has become increasingly obvious in recent years, indexical expressions permeate natural language. If we adopt Kalish's terminological suggestion then it appears that natural languages will only have a syntax and a pragmatics. It seems altogether more sensible to refer to the domain indicated by Kalish,

---

[1] Notable exceptions are Bar-Hillel (e.g., Bar-Hillel 1954) and Martin (1959, 1963).

[2] The "straightforward" qualification is necessary because some Gricean implicatures (see Chapter 3) rely crucially, though indirectly, on truth–conditional properties of the sentence. See also Chapter 7 for data that make any clear-cut semantics–pragmatics distinction problematic.

and developed by Montague and others, as "semantics" and reserve the term "pragmatics" for the topic delimited above.

Others working recently on the same general area as the present book have cut the cake of meaning in somewhat different ways. It is worth pausing a moment to examine their dichotomies with a view to reducing terminological confusion. Wilson (1975) equates semantics with those aspects of the meaning of words and constructions which are CONVEN-TIONALLY associated with them. She argues that truth-conditional aspects of meaning form only a proper subpart of this domain. Pragmatics is then equated with those aspects of meaning that are arrived at by general principles of preferred interpretation. Kempson (1975) makes a simialr division but is unwilling to allow that there are any aspects of conventional meaning that cannot be handled truth-conditionally. She further regards pragmatic theories as performance theories (the present work, by contrast, is unrepentantly competencist). The question of whether there are conventional, but non-truth-conditional, aspects of meaning is an empirical one: Our terminological decision to identify pragmatics with the set of non-truth-conditional aspects of meaning permits agnosticism in this regard.

Like Kempson, Katz (1977) regards pragmatics as a part of performance but he cuts the cake with an "anonymous letter" criterion:

> The anonymous letter situation is the case where an ideal speaker of a language receives an anonymous letter containing just one sentence of that language, with no clue whatever about the motive, circumstances of transmission, or any other factor relevant to understanding the sentence on the basis of its context of utterance. . . . We intended to draw a theoretical line between semantic interpretation and pragmatic interpretation by taking the semantic component to properly represent only those aspects of the meaning of the sentence that an ideal speaker–hearer of the language would know in such an anonymous letter situation [p. 14].

It is not clear to me from Katz's discussion how one applies this criterion. Consider the following two anonymous letters:

(1)   *Tom's doggie killed Jane's bunny.*
(2)   *Tom's dog killed Jane's rabbit.*

Although (1) and (2) are truth-conditionally synonymous, it seems to me that Katz's criterion renders them semantically nonsynonymous, despite his claim (1977:21) to the contrary. On receipt of such letters, the ideal speaker–hearer of English will naturally infer that the author of (1) is either a child, someone posing as a child, someone who thinks that they are addressing a child, or someone posing as someone who thinks that they are addressing a child. This disjunctive inference can be made in the complete absence of any contextually given information about the author, the intended recipient, the animals or Tom and Jane. No such inference can be derived from (2). To the extent that the criterion can be used to distinguish semantics from pragmatics, it appears to do it in a manner which is at variance with Katz's own intentions.

Given our own terminological decision about "pragmatics," how should a pragmatic theory best be formulated and what should its goals be? To facilitate discussion of alternative answers let me introduce some abbreviatory notation. Let D be the set of sentences of some natural language, J the set of propositions, M the set of contexts and E the set $D \times M$. One goal often advanced for pragmatics is the identification, in effect, of a set $U \subset E$, namely the set of possible utterances (the strategy of treating utterances as sentence-context pairs is widespread and, I think, uncontroversial). Although this goal strikes me as legitimate and of some interest, it is not one that will be pursued, except incidentally, in the course of the present work. Accordingly, I shall assume, counterfactually, that E is the set of possible utterances.

If we have some function that maps D into J then we have done the semantics of sentences: What we need in addition is some function that tells us about the meaning of utterances. Clearly such a function must have E as its domain but it is less clear what we ought to have as the range. Suppose we choose D (or J—it does not matter which for the remarks that follow). Then to each utterance will be assigned some sentence, the sentence which denotes the meaning of the utterance (this is, to all intents and purposes, the strategy adopted by Katz 1977:16). This way of doing things presents us with a problem—a problem connected with the fact that utterances change the context. How do we ascertain what the new context is? A simple-minded solution goes as follows: to get the new context augment the old context with the sentence which denotes the meaning of the utterance just made. This solution could be made to work for quantity implicatures (see Chapters 3 and 6), for presuppositions (see Chapters 5 and 6), and most varieties of speech act. But not for all. There exists a class of speech acts, described by such verbs as *abolish, countermand, downgrade, exempt, permit, renounce, rescind, resign, retract,* and *revoke,* whose effect on context cannot be handled by augmentation.[3] What these acts have in common is that they require there to be something in the context when the act takes place, something which is not there afterward. Take the case of PERMISSION: If I permit $\mathcal{F}$ then it must be the case that $\mathcal{F}$ is prohibited at the time I do the act of

---

[3] These verbs are taken from Fraser (1974:147). They all fall into his category of "verbs of legitimizing." Not all members of that category have the requisite property, but no members of any other of his categories appear to have it.

permitting. As a result of that act $\mathscr{F}$ is no longer prohibited. The act of permission has the effect of removing or deleting an existing prohibition.[4] If we attempt to simply add the permission to the context which includes the prohibition then we end up with an inconsistent context, one in which $\mathscr{F}$ is both prohibited and permitted. Our putative solution to the context-change problem must therefore be rejected.

We can solve the problem by formulating our function so that it has M as its range. For each utterance, then, our function will return as value a new context—the context as changed by the sentence uttered (this way of proceeding is due, essentially, to Hamblin 1971). And we can treat the meaning of the utterance as the difference between the original context and the context arrived at by uttering the sentence. A reasonable goal for pragmatics is thus the provision of a function that will map E into M. A function that appears to achieve this for a restricted subset of pragmatic aspects of meaning can be found in Chapter 6 of this volume.

Formalism

> Anyone who doubts the advantages of symbols (in their proper place) is invited to solve the equation $x^2 + 3x - 2 = 0$ by completing the square (as taught in high school), BUT doing all the work in words. We start him off by stating the equation in words: The square of the unknown, increased by three times the unknown, and diminished by two, is equal to zero.
>
> Anyone who doubts that APT choices of mathematical symbolism have played a major role in the modern development of mathematics and science is invited to multiply 416 by 144, BUT doing all the manipulations in Roman numerals. His problem is thus to multiply CDXVI by CXLIV [Kleene 1967:5].

This book contains a number of empirical theories about implicature, presupposition and logical form in natural language. These theories are expounded in a language which contains formal set theory among its resources and often makes use of this resource to describe aspects of natural language use in set-theoretical terms. As the quotation from Kleene suggests, full prose exposition can sometimes reduce, rather than increase, intelligibility, so the nature of the theories presented must be deduced in part from the formal definitions given.

Set-theoretic notation is uncommon in linguistics and some explanation for its use here seems due. In the first place set-theory is the most

---

[4] This view of PERMISSION, and of its significance, is due to Kamp (1973), a similar analysis of RETRACTION is to be found in Hamblin (1971).

basic and the best understood formal system available. Secondly, the pragmatic theories provided make essential reference to a model-theoretic semantic interpretation function and such functions return sets, or their characteristic functions, as values. It may be that if one assumes this kind of semantics then one does not have too much choice about the format in which one does one's pragmatics. The use of set-theoretical notation in the present context has an additional advantage in that it eliminates the risk of readers interpreting sentences of the metalanguage as "underlying pragmatic representations" by analogy with the sentences of semantic representation. It is quite contrary to the spirit of this book to hypostatize "underlying pragmatic representations."

An issue familiar to transformationalist linguists concerns the power of their formal apparatus. One who was concerned about such matters might note my use of set-theory, recollect that anything expressible is expressible set-theoretically, and conclude that theoretical claims made within it must be vacuous and nonempirical. To argue this way is to miss the distinction between a theory and the way that theory is expressed. This distinction is not often made in transformational grammar because Chomsky's writings implied that (3) makes an empirical claim:

(3)　　The syntax of any natural language can be expressed as
　　　　a transformational grammar.

If we have already made the methodological assumption that the well-formed sentences of any natural language are recursively enumerable then (3) is NOT an empirical claim—that is it does not tell us anything that we have not already assumed (see Peters and Ritchie 1973a,b). But, of course, the fact that (3) cannot be held to be an empirical claim does not invalidate transformational grammar as an enterprise. Likewise (4) makes no kind of empirical claim but that does not mean that you cannot EXPRESS empirical pragmatic theories in set-theoretic notation.

(4)　　The pragmatics of natural language can be described
　　　　set-theoretically.

The failure to see this very obvious distinction between a theory and its mode of expression has led to some curious consequences in the literature. The conclusions to be drawn are as follows: I assume (4) to be true, but this is a methodological assumption, not an empirical claim. The set-theoretic systems found in this book are held to capture at least some of the properties that any system would have to capture if it were to approximate generation of the relevant phenomena. The expressive power of one's formalism is a subsidiary matter and can be decided retrospectively—it would be misleading to formulate something in Montague's intensional logic when one could just as well do it in the propositional calculus, but it would be no more than misleading.

Formalization[5]

> *The gains that have resulted from conceiving of syntax and semantics as mathematical sciences justify us in requiring the same of pragmatics* [Thomason 1977:164].

If this book were about phonology or syntax, then explicit adoption of a formalist methodology would be redundant and misplaced. It would be redundant because, despite areas of vagueness, both these topics in linguistics have been conducted in a fairly well–defined manner for some years now. It would be misplaced because demands for excessive formal rigor merely waste energy at the expense of the data. Once one has a formal system and a terminology defined on it one can discuss informally, in natural language augmented with the terminology, most issues that arise within the system. But this book is not about syntax or phonology— it is about semantics and pragmatics (largely the latter) and, despite their current popularity, the formal status of these areas within linguistics is problematical. In transformational grammar, semantics and pragmatics are not well-defined domains. GENERATIVE SEMANTICS provided semanticopragmatic representations and rules which mapped those representations into surface structures, but the well-formedness conditions on the representations were unclear, the rules of inference which applied to them were unclear, and no semantic interpretation was ever given for them. EXTENDED STANDARD THEORY or TRACE THEORY postulates, but rarely provides semantic representations and rules linking them to surface structures: There is no attempt at interpretation, no well-formedness conditions, no rules of inference and no provision for pragmatics. The only major body of formal work on natural language semantics is that done within the paradigm which has come to be known as "Montague Grammar" (see, e.g., Groenendijk and Stokhof 1976; Montague 1974; Partee 1976; Rodman 1972). There is almost no formal work on natural language pragmatics. The most influential work on pragmatics, that of Grice and Searle, is self-consciously informal. Thomason (1973:4) has commented that "Grice's patterns of explanation have much more in common with the best and most rigorous literary criticism than with mathematical logic." Searle (1975:82) explicitly rejects approaches

---

[5] Schachter (1973:48) also argues for a return to formal rule writing.

to pragmatics, such as the one to be found in this book, that postulate sets of necessary and sufficient conditions or sets of structural rules. And Katz and Langendoen (1976:11) have asserted that "It is not important or possible to specify the nature of the rules comprising PRAG [PRAG = pragmatic theory]." In this situation a formalist methodology stands in need of defence. Formalization has a number of more or less obvious methodological virtues which I shall list and discuss in what follows.

Formalization forces the theorist to list his primitives and expose his ontology. For example, the model of implicature and presuppposition assignment given in Chapter 6 of this book contains a set W of possible worlds. Persons having Quinean qualms about the existence of such entities are provided with prima facie grounds for queasiness, they can, however, also inspect the rest of the system to see if the theory it expresses crucially depends on this primitive or whether it is replaceable by something which they may find ontologically more digestible.

Formalization both allows and demands standards of rigor and exactitude in the expression of theories, standards which are beyond the scope of informal statements. For example, in a theory of illocutionary force assignment in which "questioning" is not a well-defined operation, it is unclear whether any or all of the following examples should count as questioning the proposition expressed by the sentence *Addressee wants a drink*:

(5)   *You want a drink.*
(6)   *Do you want a drink.*
(7)   *What do you want to drink.*

It is even unclear whether the notion "questioning a proposition" is meaningful (cf. footnote 11 to Chapter 2, page 26).

Formalization permits proofs, which in turn exhibit the limits of one's theory. I can give equally plausible informal explanations for why neither (8) nor (9) presuppose (10), but the theory of presupposition given in Chapter 6 below can be shown to fail, in common with all other theories of presupposition, to predict the absence of presupposition in (9).

(8)   *If Dixon waited for boys in the restroom of the YMCA then*
        everybody knew that he did.
(9)   *John dreamed that Dixon was a homosexual and that*
        everyone knew that he waited for boys in the restroom of the
        YMCA
(10)   *Dixon waited for boys in the restroom of the YMCA.*

Formalization of theoretical claims allows their properties to be critically studied by the powerful techniques made available by mathematical logic. These techniques are simply not applicable to informal theories. For example, Karttunen (1971) suggested defining presupposition along the lines of (11):

(11) ϕ **presupposes** ψ iff $\Diamond\phi$ entails ψ and $\Diamond\neg\phi$ entails ψ.

This definition was quickly shown to be semantically incoherent (Herzberger 1971), given any of the more plausible assumptions concerning the properties of the possibility operator and the entailment relation. Subsequent work (Martin 1975) has shown that it can be rendered coherent given a four-valued two-dimensional model theory. Another example is the mathematical work done on the empirical status of the universal base hypothesis in transformational grammar (see e.g., Peters and Ritchie 1969). This work would not have been possible if Chomsky had not formalized the concepts involved.

The logical properties of formalized systems are independent of their interpretation. An informal descriptive or explanatory system typically requires of those that consult it that they "fill in" for it on the basis of their knowledge of the domain that it is intended to apply to. Since what is "filled in" will be peculiar to that domain, the informal system will not extend beyond it. Thus, for example, complex structural universals of language are unlikely to be readily derivable from a set of informal grammars for different languages. The type of description inherent in each informal grammar will be restricted in application to the language it was devised for. Given formal grammars,[6] however, one can rapidly see whether or not all the languages can be said to have a rule of CLEFTING or whether EQUI can always be allowed to precede PASSIVE, say.[7] Informal systems require a charitable interpretation of their terminology (cf., e.g., the discussion of Kempson's extension to Grice's maxim of relevance and of Kroch's critique of Grice, in Chapter 3). Counterexamples to informal systems often seem perverse, as if their progenitor had deliberately sought to misread or misrepresent the author of the system. Formal systems churn out their predictions regardless. Informal systems allow, and sometimes exploit, equivocation. For example, existing informal theories of illocutionary force assignment (e.g., Gordon and Lakoff 1971; Forman 1974) equivocate on the word *question*: Part of the time this is used to refer to the act of using an interrogative sentence and part of the time it is

---

[6] Clearly the formal grammars have to be of the same general type. In the absence of detailed mathematical work, stratificational, systemic, and transformational grammars are not comparable. Some of the necessary work has been done for Montague grammar, generative semantics, and extended standard theory (see Cooper and Parsons 1976).

[7] I am NOT making any implicit assumptions about the need for parochial rule ordering in transformational grammar (see Pullum 1976a:Chapter 1).

used to refer to the act of requesting the addressee for information. A formal approach would force one either to explicitly claim an identity between these acts or else to define them as distinct.

Formalization has heuristic value:

> Precisely constrained models for linguistic structure can play an important role, both negative and positive, in the process of discovery itself. By pushing a precise, but inadequate formulation to an unacceptable conclusion, we can often expose the exact source of this inadequacy and, consequently, gain a deeper understanding of the linguistic data. More positively, a formalized theory may automatically provide solutions for many problems other than those for which it was explicitly designed. Obscure and intuition-bound notions can neither lead to absurd conclusions nor provide new and correct ones, and hence they fail to be useful in two important respects [Chomsky 1957:5].

> The attempt to characterize exactly models of an empirical theory almost inevitably yields a more precise and clearer understanding of the theory. . . . The effort to make it exact will at the same time reveal the weakness of the theory [Suppes 1961:172].

It might be objected that formalization of theories within such a relatively new field as pragmatics is premature. This objection is misplaced in principle because formalization of a THEORY is never premature: If the theory is trivial or incoherent, then formalization will rapidly make the fact evident [see Gazdar (1977) for a demonstration of this with respect to a theory of Bernstein's]. If the theory is only weakly predictive, then that too will become apparent [see Hurford (1976) for a demonstration of this with respect to certain abbreviatory notations in transformational grammar]. If the theory is strongly and wrongly predictive then that too will become obvious. Of course, if one thinks that no theory should ever be formalized until it is right then all linguistic formalization is premature. The same goes for quantum mechanics—but in that case the theory would not even exist without the formalization.

Formalization has a paradoxical role in the investigation of new areas. Once you have it you may no longer need it. As was pointed out earlier, as soon as such expressions as "Equi," "precede," and "Passive" are defined on the formal theory one can begin to ask and answer such questions as, "Can Equi precede Passive?" without ever exhibiting the formalism.[8] Even if all the empirical claims Chomsky ever makes turn out to be wrong, we could still justifiably ascribe to him a decisive role in linguistics on the grounds that he was the first linguist to provide a proper formalism on which to define the terminology necessary for the discussion of the syntax of natural languages. An analogous claim could be made with respect to the relation between Montague and the semantics of natural languages.

---

[8] Cf. Postal (1977:152–154).

In this book I hope, along with Stalnaker,

> to defend, by example, the claim that the concepts of pragmatics can be made as
> mathematically precise as any of the concepts of syntax and formal semantics; to show
> that one can recognize and incorporate into abstract theory the extreme context depen-
> dence which is obviously present in natural language without any sacrifice to standards of
> rigor [1975: 281–282].

Data

For all linguists, the data base contains some subset D of the free monoid T^* defined on the terminal vocabulary T used for description.[9] This terminal vocabulary T will consist, for example, of words or morphemes if the linguist is a syntactician. Thus the data base contains a set of strings D: So much—and just so much—is uncontroversial. Most linguists in the last couple of decades have allowed the data base to contain, in addition, various intuitive or introspective judgments associated with individual members of D. Once you allow that such judgments constitute data then you allow also an enormous increase in the number of strings available to you as data: In addition to OCCURRENT strings one now has available an infinite number of strings which may not have occurred. Those strings which are coupled with a positive acceptability judgment will be regarded as SENTENCES of the language regardless of whether they are strings of which tokens have appeared. The legitimacy of this enlargement of the data base was much discussed in the early days of transformational grammar and I see no point in repeating the debate here. In common with most other linguists, I shall assume throughout this book that invented strings and certain intuitive judgments about them constitute legitimate data for linguistic research. Note that as soon as one extends the data base beyond OCCURRENT sentences one has automatically introduced intuitive judgments—otherwise one would have no way of telling that one's additions were not arbitrary strings. A generative linguistic theory compels one to employ intuitive judgments. How one employs them is a topic I shall discuss briefly below.

Linguists are concerned in the first place with the ACCEPTABILITY of strings. Given an acceptable string one may then ask whether or not it exhibits an AMBIGUITY. And given two acceptable strings we may ask whether an IMPLICATION or SYNONYMY relation holds between them. That seems to me to be about as much as one can expect one's intuitions to reliably provide.[10]

[9] For the notation and terminology, see Wall (1972:165–166). As Wall notes, strictly speaking the monoid is $<T,^*{}^\frown>$ rather than the set T^*.

[10] This is not to say that we have no way of deciding whether some intuitive judgment reflects a syntactic, semantic or pragmatic fact. Our overall theoretical framework should provide us with criteria which bear on the decisions. Thus Zwicky and Sadock (1975) list a

(12) *The police think who the FBI discovered that Bill shot.[11]

(13) *When did Tom leave, I don't want to know.[12]

(14) Everyone speaks one language.[13]

(15) Bill managed to open the door.

(16) Bill tried to open the door.

(17) I allowed the doctor to examine John.

(18) I allowed John to be examined by the doctor.[14]

Thus we can rely on our intuitions to tell us that (12) and (13) are UNACCEPTABLE, that (14) is AMBIGUOUS, that (15) IMPLIES (16), and that (17) and (18) are NOT SYNONYMOUS, but we cannot rely on them to tell us whether (12) is bad for syntactic or semantic reasons, whether (13) is bad for syntactic or pragmatic reasons, whether the ambiguity in (14) is semantic or pragmatic, whether (15) entails (16) rather than merely presupposing it, or whether (17) and (18) are semantically or pragmatically distinct.

Our position on this is a generalization of that described by Partee (1971:308–309) in the quotation that follows.

> While certain sentences will be judged in some way deviant or unacceptable by native speakers, the classification of deviance into SYNTACTIC and SEMANTIC is not part of the raw data of speaker intuitions, but will simply be a product of whatever theory attains the greatest overall simplicity. Therefore, if the simplest overall theory deems the sentence *I saw himself* to be syntactically well-formed but semantically ill-formed, so be it; we have no pre-theoretic notions of syntax vs. semantics to falsify such a claim. What a linguist might take as intuitions to the contrary are just prejudices born of habit. Notice how easily *colorless green ideas sleep furiously* slid over the fence and back again— grammatical in SYNTACTIC STRUCTURES, ungrammatical in ASPECTS, grammatical again once McCawley showed what should have been obvious—that selection restrictions must be semantic and not syntactic.

---

large number of tests for discriminating between semantic and pragmatic ambiguity and Moore (1976:28ff) offers a criterion for distinguishing syntactic from semantic unacceptability. Unfortunately, as Zwicky and Sadock point out, the criteria they discuss often break down on crucial examples.

[11] Chomsky (1976:95) writes as follows concerning Example (12): "Suppose that someone claims to have a very refined sort of "grammatical intuition" that tells him whether the deviance of (12) is "syntactic" or "semantic". Such a person, then, will have an answer to the question left open here. Personally, I have no such intuitions. I can make the judgment that certain sentences are fine and others deviant . . . but have no further intuitions that provide me, in such cases as these, with the basis for these judgments. I am therefore skeptical that others have such intuitions. I suspect that they are adhering to certain traditional explanations, which may or may not be correct."

[12] The example is from Ross (1975:253).

[13] The question of whether (14) is semantically or pragmatically ambiguous is usefully discussed in Sadock (1975).

[14] Schmerling (1978) argues convincingly that the meaning difference between (17) and (18) is pragmatic rather than semantic.

Bach (1974:252) explicitly espouses the more general position:

> Without some ideas about what an adequate theory of semantics might look like, AS WELL AS AN ADEQUATE THEORY OF LANGUAGE USE, we simply have no idea whether a particular judgment of acceptability, say, is to be accounted for in a syntactic way [emphasis added].

And Thomason (1977:164) adds an important caveat:

> Suppose, to take only one type of example, that a sentence is judged anomalous. Its anomaly may be evident, but the proper interpretation of this fact will in general be a more complicated matter. Often the data itself will give us no way of telling whether, for instance, the anomaly is syntactic or semantic, and the best explanation is the one that is easiest—the one that leads to the simplest combined theory. And as long as the anomaly is explained in one place or the other, there has been no evasion of the duty to explain it. On the other hand it would be less satisfactory to pass the explanation on to a discipline that isn't well enough developed so that its theories are clearly compatible with some evidence, and incompatible with other evidence. This is the trouble with pragmatics. Even if the phenomenon in question were best dealt with at the pragmatic level—a syntactic or semantic explanation would be much messier—there is as yet no way to separate this case from the one where it has simply been discarded, labeled "pragmatic" because it is recalcitrant. In other words, no way of keeping honest.

Even if it achieves nothing else, this book at least takes an honest look at some of the data which has been thrown into the "pragmatic waste-basket."[15]

---

[15] This felicitous phrase is due to Bar–Hillel (1971:405).

2

ILLOCUTIONARY FORCE: THE PERFORMATIVE HYPOTHESIS

The only school of contemporary linguistics that has had anything substantive to say about pragmatic phenomena is generative semantics. A recurrent feature of work done within this school has been an attempt to conflate pragmatics and semantics by putting relevant pragmatic information into the semantic representations of sentences. The rationale for this move is cogently expressed in the following, somewhat premature, claim of Lakoff's (1972:655): "What we have done is to largely, if not entirely, eliminate pragmatics, reducing it to garden variety semantics." Thus, "from the generative semantic point of view, illocutionary force is an aspect of sentence meaning [Sadock 1977:67]," an aspect that is encoded as an abstract verb in semantic representation. This theory of illocutionary force has come to be known as "the performative hypothesis" (PH, hereafter). The PH is, in fact, the ONLY well-developed theory of illocutionary force in contemporary linguistics[1]. This chapter will show that the PH is seriously inadequate. So inadequate, in fact, that it requires replacement rather than repair. All that can be salvaged from it is a completely trivial claim that no one would want to object to except on terminological grounds [see (80), page 35]. We proceed by briefly noting the precursors and ontogenesis of the PH. Next we follow standard linguistic practice [classically exemplified in, for example, the Chomsky–Halle attack on the phoneme (Chomsky, 1964), or G. Lakoff's attack on

[1] For the standard account of ILLOCUTIONARY FORCE, see Austin (1962).

15

deep structure, Lakoff (1968)] by defining the position to be attacked in terms of a set of subclaims and then showing that none of these subclaims can be satisfactorily maintained.

In Chomsky (1957) the problem of how to account for the syntactic well-formedness of the content-related declarative, imperative, and interrogative sentences is solved by deriving the imperative and interrogative from an underlying declarative by means of optional transformations.

Katz and Postal (1964) claimed that (1) was ambiguous between an imperative and a declarative reading but that this ambiguity was not captured in Chomsky (1957):

(1)   *You will go home.*

Accordingly they proposed that (1) had two underlying structures, one declarative and one containing an imperative morpheme. Interrogatives were also given an underlying morpheme to trigger the relevant transformation. Katz and Postal (1964:76) suggested that their imperative morpheme should be assigned "a dictionary entry that represented it as having roughly the sense of *the speaker requests (asks, demands, insists, etc.) that.*' " This was to allow them to capture the suggested paraphrase relation in (2) and (3) and the anomaly felt in both (4) and (5).

(2)   *I request that you go home.*
(3)   *Go home.*
(4)   **I request that you want more money.*
(5)   **Want more money.*

The motivation for the introduction of imperative and interrogative morphemes was that it allowed Katz and Postal, and subsequently Chomsky (1965), to make the "empirical" claim that transformations were "meaning-preserving." Although proponents of the PH have latterly referred to these abstract morphemes as ad hoc, Katz and Postal explicitly intended them to embody many of the defining characteristics of the later PH: surface syntactic form was to be derived from a SINGLE DELETABLE UNDERLYING marker or ILLOCUTIONARY FORCE in the TOPMOST S and this marker was primarily a SEMANTIC, rather than syntactic or pragmatic, entity. It is these characteristics, and not the more technical ones such as whether or not the underlying morphemes are verbs, which make the PH untenable as will shortly be shown. Indeed it was in a footnote to Katz and Postal (1964:149) that the PH makes its first public appearance:[2]

> A case can be made for deriving imperatives syntactically from sentences of the form I $Verb_{request}$ *that you will Main Verb* by dropping at least the first three elements . . . .

[2] George Lakoff (personal communication, August 1977) drew this to my attention.

Such a derivation would permit dispensing with I [the imperative morpheme] and its reading RIM and would simplify the semantic component by eliminating one entry. It would also eliminate from the syntax all the necessary heavy selectional restrictions on I and the rules that must introduce this element. Although we do not adopt this description here, it certainly deserves further study. Either the derivation with I or the one just suggested supports our main point that the underlying P-markers of imperatives are different from those of declaratives in the semantically relevant ways.

Four or 5 years later a number of linguists explicitly adopted and argued for the PH: Versions of it are to be found in Boyd and Thorne (1969), R. Lakoff (1968), Ross (1970), and Sadock (1969a). Of these Ross (1970) is the best known and most influential, so I shall direct most of my remarks either to his discussion or to the most up-to-date statements of the PH, which are due to G. Lakoff (1975) and Sadock (1974).[3]

Ross proposed that a declarative sentence like (6) had the deep structure given as (7):

(6)   *Prices slumped.*

(7) $(_S(_{NP}I) (_{VP}(_V V) (_{NP}you) (_{NP}(_S(_{NP}prices) (_{VP}slumped)))))$

$$\begin{bmatrix} +V \\ +\text{performative} \\ +\text{communication} \\ +\text{linguistic} \\ +\text{declarative} \end{bmatrix}$$

Ross's hypothesis differs from that of Katz and Postal in that declaratives also have an abstract morpheme in underlying structure. Furthermore, this morpheme is a verb which has a pronoun referring to speaker as subject and a pronoun referring to addressee as indirect object.

I do not propose to consider the syntactic evidence for and against the PH in any great detail. Partly this is because the topic is well-covered elsewhere (see the works by Anderson, Dahl, Fraser, Matthews, and Mittwoch cited below) and partly for a reason noted by Dahl (cf. Matthews 1976).

If one looks close to the arguments that are given for the hypothesis, it often turns out that they are of the form "construction-type A and construction-type B both obey constraint C; thus, if they are derived from the same source, we need not state C twice." Now, if we take for example the class of imperative sentences and the class of sentences of the type *x orders y to S*, it is not very astonishing a priori that they have some properties in common, since they are both connected with commands: imperative sentences express commands, the second type of sentences report them. For example, if the sentence *Be sixty years old:* is odd because this is a very strange thing to order

---

[3] There are a number of differences between these three versions of the PH, but I shall not address them directly here.

someone, one can also expect the sentence *John ordered Bill to be sixty years old* to be odd. A really good argument for performatives should be one that does not refer to such correspondences in meaning but rather on some unequivocally formal property of the sentences in question. Very few of the arguments given so far have been of that type, however [Dahl 1972:4].

It seems to me to be preferable, in the present context, to devote more time to semantic and pragmatic arguments for the PH which have received relatively little critical attention, and semantic and pragmatic arguments against it, which have received almost none. The latter seem to me sufficiently persuasive to make it mandatory to find alternative ways of dealing with the syntactic evidence fot the PH. Semantic or pragmatic explanans for syntactic phenomena must meet semantic and pragmatic standards of adequacy. I shall argue that the PH fails to meet such standards. Ross (1970:261) himself allowed for this: "The interconnection between syntax and pragmatics should be investigated in detail. Possibly when they have been clarified, a reason for choosing either a performative analysis or a pragmatic analysis of all sentence types will emerge." Claim (8) makes explicit what the strongest possible performative hypothesis requires. After each subclaim I have given a reference to the source for the subclaim (numbers refer to the quotations following the claims. It is important to realize that (8) does not represent a position which any particular proponent of the PH has ever attempted to defend as a whole. G. Lakoff, for example, has never maintained (b), and (d) makes little sense in grammars that allow transderivational constraints.

(8)   For Ξ sentences S, in all natural languages, the deep structure of S

(a)   has a clause containing a PERFORMATIVE verb (9).
(b)   the subject of this clause is *I* and the indirect object is *you*. Ross (1970:passim)
(c)   this clause is the HIGHEST clause in the deep structure (9).
(d)   this clause is DELETABLE when the verb is marked to allow this (Ross 1970:249), and the deletion transformation is MEANING-PRESERVING (early generative semantics assumption).
(e)   the verb in the clause is the ONLY verb in the sentence which is performative (9).
(f)   the verb represents the ILLOCUTIONARY FORCE of the sentence (10), (12).
(g)   illocutionary force is SEMANTIC (11), (12).
(h) Ξ is the UNIVERSAL quantifier (9).

(9)   "Every deep structure contains one and only one
        performative sentence as its highest clause [Ross 1970:261]."
(10)   "Illocutionary force . . . is to be represented in logical form
        by the presence of a performative verb [G. Lakoff 1972:561]."
(11)   "There will be a uniform deep structure configuration on
        which to base the semantic notion Speech Act [Ross
        1970:248]."
(12)   The illocutionary force of an uttered sentence is that aspect
        of its meaning which is represented by the performative
        clause in the semantic structure of the sentence [Sadock
        1977:67]."

In what follows, I shall show, or refer to works that show, that NONE of
the subclaims (a)–(h) of (8), are supported by the data, and that, in some
cases, there is strong evidence against maintaining the claims. All of
them, with the exception of (a), have already been omitted or abandoned
by one or another proponent of the PH. Curiously enough, (a) was, by
Ross's own admission, the claim for which he had least evidence.

(a)   The verb is performative

> The one fact for which I have least support is the claim that the
> verb of the deleted higher clause has the feature [+performative]
> and is in fact a performative [Ross 1970:248].

Ross (1970) only provides one "rather weak argument [ibid.: 248]"
for (a), which is based on his claim that "performative verbs cannot be
used performatively in complements [ibid.: 252]." The argument collapses because this claim cannot be maintained in the light of examples
like (20), (35), and (36). The motivation for (a) relies on the plausibility of
(f) and (g), if neither of those can be maintained then there is no point in
attempting to defend (a).

(b)   The clause contains *I* and *you*
Most of the arguments in Ross (1970) address themselves to (b) and
counterexamples to all of them can be found in Anderson (1971), Fraser
(1971), and Matthews (1972). A more recent work, Sadock (1974), which
devotes over 150 pages to the defence and elaboration of the PH, attempts
to rebut only one or two of the classes of counterexample advanced by
these authors against (a) and (b) and so I think we are entitled to assume
that the others go through.[4]

---

[4] Sadock (1974) mentions Fraser (1971), but Anderson (1971) and Matthews (1972) are
not discussed, nor do they occur in the bibliography. Davison (1973) replies to Fraser and
establishes that some of his counterarguments do not go through. Others, she admits, do.

The acceptability judgments on the remaining data proposed as support for (b) are in dispute, especially where REFLEXIVE PRONOUNS are concerned. Sadock (1974:24), in his defense of the PH, notes this fact as follows:

> I should point out that, unfortunately for the [performative] theory, it is not always the same idiolect that disallows both second-person spurious reflexives and spurious reflexives whose antecedent is the indirect object of a higher clause. Such mixed idiolects are very difficult for orthodox generative grammar, and particularly for the theory under scrutiny here.

Both Anderson (1971) and Matthews (1972) note that performative verbs can take singular OR plural subjects and indirect objects. The latter remarks that if the PH is modified to allow this then (1) becomes four ways ambiguous. G. Lakoff (1972)[5] omits (b) and uses variables for subject and indirect object of the performative; this has the effect of substituting indeterminacy for Matthews's putative multiple ambiguity. These variables will be specified as first and second person respectively by a rule of grammar.[6] However, as Dahl (1972:5) shows, there are performative sentences in which the subject is not first person, and others in which the indirect object is not second person. So even Lakoff's alternative to (b) cannot be maintained. Lakoff has claimed that his alternative has the effect of simplifying the overall grammar since, in his view, it allows one to remove the speaker and hearer coordinates from the model theory one applies to semantic representation: "Given a uniform performative analysis, the treatment of indexicals in natural language does not require that additional coordinates for speaker, hearer, and time and place of utterance be added to points of reference [Lakoff 1975:276]." G. Lakoff's (1972) suggestion is to allow an assignment coordinate (for which see Lewis 1972) to specify the value of the variables standing for speaker, addressee, etc. and not have such items listed in the n-tuple to which the semantic interpretation is relativised. Dahl (1972:11) has argued that Lakoff's suggestion is incoherent: "It is absurd to eliminate the contextual coordinates for the assignment coordinate; the assignment coordinate is, on the contrary, determined by the contextual coordinates."

(c)   The performative clause is the highest clause in SR

---

[5] This paper contains a number of additional arguments for the PH. They are critically evaluated, with negative result, in Fraser (1971) and Dahl (1972).

[6] The PH presupposes a simple–minded theory of personal pronominalization in which *I* always refers to the speaker and *you* always refers to the addressee. Such theories are shown to be untenable in Watson (1975) and Sacks (1976). Note also, in this connection, that Comrie (1976) has demonstrated that the PH is neither necessary nor sufficient for handling honorific distribution in those languages which manifest honorifics.

Unfortunately for the simplicity of the PH, some of the pronominal evidence which points to the existence of a deleted higher verb also points to such an entity when the performative is NOT deleted (cf. Sadock 1974:69–71; Fraser 1971:23; Anderson 1971:8). Thus if (13) is evidence for a higher verb, then so is (14)[7]:

(13)   As for myself, these matters are beyond my ken.
(14)   As for myself, I declare these matters are
          beyond my ken.

One response to (14) would be to abandon (13) as evidence for the PH on the grounds that the *myself* involved is not a reflexive pronoun at all, but merely an homophonous emphatic pronoun (relevant evidence includes stress, and translation). Another response would be to say that since (13) is evidence for one higher verb, then (14) MUST be evidence for yet another. Sadock's and Ross's[8] response is of the latter variety, and so Sadock (1969b) proposes an abstract DO verb dominating the performative clause. Even if Occam's razor did not lead one to have methodological qualms about this move, example (15) might.

(15)   As for myself, I do declare that these matters are beyond my
          ken.

Although a potentially infinite regress of superordinate abstract verbs for every sentence has a certain metaphysical appeal, considerations of linguistic parsimony weigh heavily against it.

Ross (1970: 255–257) treats *as for me/myself* examples as decisive between the PH and a pragmatic analysis of the syntactic facts he discusses. Thus he says—of a set of examples of which (16) is the first member—that "if even one such sentence is grammatical, the performative analysis must be rejected [p. 257]" (Ross rates (16) as ?* and (17) as ?).

(16)   As for myself, I authorize the purchase of a rodent.

On the other hand, he says that, if (17) is ungrammatical, then this fact "does constitute counterevidence to the pragmatic analysis [p.257]."

(17)   As for me, I promise that Tom will be there.

I will not go into why Ross thinks these examples should be so decisive, but I think it worth demonstrating that, if we make Ross's assumptions,

---

[7] A similar example is to be found in Ross (1970:255).

[8] In unpublished work cited in Sadock (1974:70). In Ross (1970), however, Ross proposes to derive sentences like (14) by preposing *as for myself* from the complement. Anderson (1971:9) shows this to be unworkable since such phrases can occur when the performative has no complement.

then this evidence points decisively towards a pragmatic analysis and not a PH (cf. Kuno 1972 who provides an alternative analysis for this data). Consider the following dialogues:

(18) X: *Professor Zingwall, I want each member of your*
department to authorize the purchase of a rodent
immediately.

Z: *As for myself, I authorize the purchase of a rodent (but*
naturally I cannot speak for my colleagues).

(19) A: *Hey you two, I want you both to guarantee that Tom*
comes to the meeting tomorrow. Bill?

B: *I'll try but . . . .*

A: *Clara, c'mon you are his wife, huh?*

C: *As for me, I promise that Tom will be there.*

If the two last utterances in these two dialogues are acceptable then, in Ross's own view, the PH must be rejected and a pragmatic analysis preferred.

By introducing the DO verb, proponents of the PH have abandoned (c) in favor of a slightly weaker hypothesis, namely that the performative occurs in a fixed position in deep structure. Fraser (1971) notes many counterexamples to (c), all of which would count equally against this weaker hypothesis. One of these examples is taken up by Sadock (1974:61–66), who devoted several pages to discussion of it.

(20) *I regret to inform you of the death of your goldfish.*

Regret is not a performative verb, *inform* is, and, both Fraser and Sadock would claim, (20) has the illocutionary force of INFORMING. Any straightforward version of the PH will require *inform* to be in a higher clause than *regret* in DS but no known transformation is available to map such a DS into (20). Sadock (1974:64), with slight understatement, proposes the "fairly wild transformation" whose details are "fairly obscure," sketched in (21).

(21) *(I* INFORM *you (S AND (I regret S)))*
⇓
(I regret (I inform you S))

Quite apart from methodological qualms and the complete absence of syntactic motivation, there is even syntactic evidence which counts AGAINST such a transformation; namely the arguments for Ross's Coordinate Structure Constraint, Ross (1967), which is violated by (21), so far as I can tell. As Sadock (1974:64) remarks, "the necessity for such an enormously powerful and unique transformation is a serious drawback to the proposal [i.e., the PH] under consideration." Put more straightforwardly, (20) constitutes an apparently irremediable counterexample to anything approaching claim (c) of the PH. And without something like condition (c) it is hard to see how the PH could be formulated at all, since it would no longer be possible to write a general syntactico-semantic rule which would pick out THE performative clause. In the absence of the PH there is a perfectly simple solution for this particular example: since affirmative *regret* sentences entail their complements (see Chapter 5), it follows that (20) entails (22).

(22)   *I inform you of the death of your goldfish.*

If (20) is true then (22) must also be true. And if (22) is true then we need look no further for the source of the illocutionary force of (20). Note that (23), the past tense counterpart of (20), does not entail (22) and does not have the illocutionary force of *informing:*

(23)   *I regretted informing you of the death of your goldfish.*

Not all cases can be handled as simply as (20) and ENTAILMENT does not unfortunately, of itself, provide a general solution to the problem of embedded performatives contributing to illocutionary force (cf. Thompson and Wright 1975). See also, in this connection, Anderson's (1971:13–14) discussion of how Ross's (1970) restrictions on *lurk* apply equally when the first person ascriptions appear as factive complements.[9] A similar explanation to that just given for (20) applies.

Carden (1977) has drawn attention to sentences like (24) and (25):

(24)   *I hereby sentence each of you to 10 years in the federal penitentiary.*
(25)   *I hereby sentence you to be hanged and order the sentence to be carried out immediately.*

If we make the generative semantics assumption that quantifiers and conjunctions are higher predicates, then the relative scope of performative to quantifier or conjunction in these examples shows conclusively that (c) cannot be maintained.

(d)   The performative clause is deletable when the verb is marked to allow this and the deletion is meaning-preserving

The first conjunct of (d), namely that the performative clause is deletable when the verb is marked to allow it, is true by definition.

___

[9] Harnish (1975) has provided a pragmatic explanation for the restrictions on *lurk*. This accounts for Ross's observation, as well as those of Anderson and Fraser.

Anderson (1971:5) expresses this view when he remarks that the only syntactic characteristic of performatives "is their ability to disappear when unneeded, and their existence remains to be demonstrated before this can be considered." Let us assume, therefore, that the performative is deletable if it is deletable.

The serious question is whether the deletion transformation is meaning-preserving. The claim that it is has a certain plausibility if we restrict ourselves to consideration of pairs like (2) and (3) above, although even here one might want to argue that (2) will be true or false on an occasion of utterance whereas neither of those ascriptions may ever be applied to (3). Ergo they differ in meaning. The claim has less immediate plausibility if we apply it to examples (26) and (27) below, (given in Fraser 1971:28).

(26)   *I promise you that I will be home at 5 o'clock.*
(27)   *I will be home at 5 o'clock.*

Clearly, (27) is falsified by the truth of (28), but (26) is not thus falsified. From the fact that I fail to keep a promise it does not follow that no promise was made.

(28)   *Speaker was not home at 5 o'clock.*

Such examples are by no means conclusive counterexamples to (d), however. The PH advocate might mark *promise* as [–deletable] and say that the "promise" interpretation of (27) was perlocutionary or due to some complex indirect speech act apparatus such as that discussed in Forman (1974), Gordon and Lakoff (1971), and Heringer (1972). Or he might argue that (27) could indeed be derived from (26) but that that was only one of several sources for this sentence. The falsity of (28) would not then automatically falsify (27)—but would only falsify it when (27) was derived from a higher sentence of *stating*, say. Both these responses are open to the charge of question–begging: In the first case, whenever there is a meaning change, mark the verb [-deletable], then no verbs undergoing deletion will involve meaning change. Only if there is an independent criterion for assigning the feature [±deletable] can the circularity charge be rebutted. In the second case, whenever the truth conditions of the simple and performative sentences differ, then describe the former as ambiguous. Only if the sentence passes at least some independent tests for regarding sentences as ambiguous (e.g., those described in Zwicky and Sadock 1975) can the circularity charge be rebutted.[10]

Consider (29) and (30):

[10] Sadock (1972) DOES employ ambiguity tests, but not for examples like (27).

(29)   *I declare that the earth is flat.*
(30)   *The earth is flat.*

Whether or not (29) and (30) share the same truth conditions, and Lewis (1972:210) argues that they do not, it is clear that they have rather different conditions of use. Speakers do not generally fail to delete highest performatives—if they were to, and produced utterances like (31) instead of (32), then they would either not be understood at all, or else they would taken to be implying something more than that carried by the performative complements (cf. R. Lakoff 1977:84–85)

(31)   *I request that you listen to me. I declare that your violin*
        playing is excruciating. I request you to tell me why you don't
        do it elsewhere.
(32)   *Listen to me. Your violin playing is excruciating. Why don't*
        you do it elsewhere?

The difference between (31) and (32) creates a problem for one defending a strictly semantic approach to the PH: putting pragmatic constraints on performative deletion is not really consistent with the goals of one who would eliminate pragmatics by "reducing it to garden variety semantics [G. Lakoff 1972:655]." Nor is it consistent with the requirement that transformations preserve meaning. Indeed G. Lakoff (1975:283–284) himself denies that it makes any sense to talk of meaning-preservation in a grammar which employs transderivational constraints. He may well be right about this; in any event it is clear that the second conjunct of (d) cannot be sensibly maintained. Further discussion as to whether it is false, vacuous or meaningless would be rather beside the point.

(e)   There is only one performative verb in the sentence
    Early in the history of the PH Ross, Postal, G. Lakoff, and McCawley concurred that generalizations were going to be missed if questions were given an underlying structure such as (33):

(33)   (I ASK *you whether* S)

They proposed instead that questions should be represented by something more like (34):

(34)   (I REQUEST *you* (*you* TELL *me whether* S))

If TELL is [-performative] in (34) then it follows that requests and questions are to have EXACTLY the same illocutionary force under this proposal, assuming condition (f) is maintained. The only difference between questions and requests would show up in what Searle (1969) misleadingly calls the propositional content.[11] One way to avoid this slightly counterintuitive consequence would be to mark TELL as [+performative] and allow it to contribute to the illocutionary force of questions. This move entails abandoning (e). Another way to avoid the consequence is to claim that both (33) and (34) exist as underlying sources for interrogative sentences. This position is taken by Sadock (1972, 1974) and it entails regarding many, or most, interrogative sentences as semantically ambiguous.

Fraser (1971:4) gives the following examples of sentences having two performatives where both are employed performatively.

(35)   *I admit that I concede the election.*
(36)   *I announce that I hereby promise to be timely.*

I know of no response to such examples from advocates of the PH and indeed can see no way round their status as counterexamples to condition (e). They are also counterexamples to condition (c).

At least some proponents of the PH have found it necessary to explicitly abandon (e) in their attempts to salvage condition (f). Thus Sadock (1974:134–137) considers the following examples.

(37)   *Isn't Danish beautiful.*
(38)   *Danish is beautiful, isn't it.*

These sentences are wholly or partly interrogative, but, nevertheless, on some occasions of use they will not count as QUESTIONS in some strict sense of the latter term. They are thus counterexamples to (f) if their source is a higher performative of ASKING. Sadock suggests that it might be possible to derive them from an underlying structure like that sketched in (39):

(39)   ((*I* REMIND *you* S) AND (*I* REQUEST *you* (*you*
         CONFIRM S)))

For present purposes we need only note that (39) contains at least two performative verbs and that Sadock can therefore no longer be maintaining condition (e). As for its intrinsic merits as a solution to the problems posed by (37) and (38), comment is best left to Sadock himself who remarks that it "represents a sheer guess with no syntactic backing [Sadock 1974:135]." Other proponents of the PH (e.g., Gordon and Lakoff 1971) abandon (f) and assume (e), but their approach cannot handle (35) and (36).

---

[11] Misleading because the "propositional" content of questions is not a proposition. This very obvious point is exploited to good advantage in the semantics for English interrogatives given in Hamblin (1973).

(f)   The performative verb represents the illocutionary force of the sentence

If, following Gordon and Lakoff (1971), one abandons (f), then it is hard to see how one can maintain a PERFORMATIVE analysis at all, since performative sentences are defined, roughly speaking, as just those sentences which do the act that they say they are doing. Without condition (f), the major semantic motivation for a PH disappears and one might as well revert to the use of merely syntactically motivated IMPERATIVE and INTERROGATIVE morphemes in the deep structures of a transformational grammar. This consequence is clearly recognized by those proponents of the PH who seek to maintain (f), such as Sadock (1974) and Green (1973a).

The following sentences CAN all have the illocutionary force of a request, despite widely differing surface syntactic form:

(40)   *Close the door.*
(41)   *I request you to close the door.*
(42)   *I must ask you to close the door.*
(43)   *I'm asking you to the close the door.*
(44)   *I want you to close the door.*
(45)   *You must close the door.*
(46)   *Why don't you close the door.*
(47)   *Will you close the door.*
(48)   *How about closing the door.*
(49)   *Close the door, will you.*
(50)   *You may close the door.*
(51)   *Can you close the door.*

Since only (40) and (41) can, prima facie, be argued to derive from a simple deep structure containing a single performative of requesting, the advocate of a PH incorporating condition (f) is faced with the problem of explaining how (42)–(51) can have the force of requests. Requests are not a special case, although they are perhaps the speech act whose syntactic manifestations have aroused most interest in the recent linguistic literature.

There seem to be two ways for the proponent of (f) to respond to such examples. These responses are complementary rather than mutually exclusive. The first is to attempt to provide, for a class of examples, a deep structure which can be plausibly claimed to represent the request–type illocutionary force that they can carry. Thus Sadock (1970:235) proposed that something like (52) was the semantic representation for (47):[12]

---

[12] The structure which appears in Sadock (1970:235) contains a typographical error that makes (52) look even more implausible. I have reproduced it along what must have been its intended lines, following that shown in Green (1973:52).

(52)   ((*I ASK you (you will (you close the door)))* and (*I* REQUEST *you (you close the door)))*

Green, in work reported in Green (1973a), proposed the deep structure given in (53) as that underlying (46).

(53)   (*I* REQUEST *you ((you close the door)(or (you tell me (why you do not close the door)))))*

Another possibility she discusses is to derive (47) from (49), which is itself derived from (40) which, of course, derives from (41). According to Green (1973a), who herself wishes to maintain (f), none of these proposals is syntactically workable.[13] I do not intend to discuss how these proposals fail to handle the data because it seems to me that deep structures like (52) and (53) stand as their own reductio ad absurdum. Even if they handled the syntax properly there are enough methodological objections, for example on grounds of simplicity, generality and motivation, to justify their rejection.

The other way of responding to some, or all, of these examples, is to say that they don't in themselves have the illocutionary force of requests but are, in fact, assertions or questions (according as to whether they are declarative or interrogative, respectively). Their "request" force is actually a perlocutionary effect of their utterance. But without an independent criterion to distinguish illocutionary from perlocutionary force, this move is merely terminological. And if one uses surface syntactic mood as one's illocutionary force criterion, then the move is circular. In any event it involves a misuse of Austin's terminology: a perlocution is, by definition, effective, whereas (42)–(51) may be no more effective than the illocutions (40) and (41).

Consider the following pair of examples:

(54)   *I commend that movie.*
(55)   *That is a good movie.*

Both can be acts of commending a movie but they differ in that the former employs an explicit performative verb whereas the latter predicates the adjective *good* of the commended object. How can the fact that they may both have the same illocutionary force be captured in a PH which maintains condition (f)? A traditional move, for the school of grammarians who adhere to the PH, would be to postulate that (55) derives from an underlying structure like (54). In other words, that the adjective *good* derives from a higher verb of commending. For reasons well known to students of recent ethical theory, such a move is not

---

[13] Green (1973a) is discussed at length in Gazdar and Keenan (1975).

possible in this case. It would offer no explanation for the occurrence of *good* in interrogatives, imperatives or those compound sentences which do not entail the clause containing *good*. An alternative move would be to say that, in deep structure, (55) is itself embedded in a clause of commending. Such a deep structure would presumably look something like (56):

(56)   *I commend that good movie.*

Unfortunately for this proposal, sentences like (58) are not acceptable (on the relevant reading). Of course we COULD attempt to salvage it by saying that deletion of either *good* (to get (54)) or of the higher clause—to get (55) via some additional transformations—is obligatory. However, the possibility of such a salvage operation does no more than illustrate the nonempirical status of the performative hypothesis.

(g) Illocutionary force is semantic
The PH postulates deep structures that contain

(i)   a performative verb,
(ii)   a complement sentence,
(iii)   indexical items referring to speaker and addressee.

G. Lakoff (1972) proposes that they should also contain indexical items referring to

(iv)   time of utterance,
(v)   place of utterance.

No syntactic evidence or motivation is advanced for these extras. Item (iv), for example, will not suffice to predict the complex behaviour of English tenses noted in R. Lakoff (1970). G. Lakoff (1975) claims that some variant of standard model-theoretic apparatus, which he barely elucidates, will suffice to give the truth conditions[14] for higher performative sentences having a structure based on (i)–(v). Model-theoretic apparatus is rather different from, though a precondition of, the apparatus

---

[14] Lakoff is actually concerned with what he calls "satisfaction" conditions for performatives. These subsume truth conditions (for embedded sentences) and felicity conditions (for performative sentences). The much-debated issue of whether or not performatives have truth-values is irrelevant to my argument which would go through equally well if Lakoff's notion of SATISFACTION condition is substituted where I have TRUTH condition. I assume throughout that performatives are truth-valued (following Aqvist 1972; K. Bach 1975; Danielsson 1965; Hedenius 1963; Lemmon 1962; and others). It is worth noting that Lakoff's (1975) notion of superordinate satisfaction valuation is a useful innovation for those who would like to see surface performative sentences model–theoretically interpreted, but who can't square TRUTH–valuation of them with their intuitions.

developed, for example, for illocutionary force in Hamblin (1971) or Kasher (1974). Let us call approaches of the latter type FORMAL PRAGMA-TICS. Now the claim (g), made implicitly by Ross (1970) and explicitly by G. Lakoff (1972, 1975) can be formulated more precisely as (g').

(g')   The notion illocutionary force can be wholly captured by model-theoretic apparatus referring to at most (i)–(v). (Ergo it is unnecessary to employ a FORMAL PRAGMATICS to capture illocutionary force.)

In what follows I shall argue that (g') cannot be maintained. Before going on to that argument it should be noted that the claim under consideration is an undefended assertion. No writer on the PH has ever attempted to give more than a representation for illocutionary force.[15] No semantic interpretation in terms of felicity or truth conditions, for even a fragment of these representations has been defined. Nor has any attempt been made to show that an adequate interpretation is possible. This is not a trivial matter as will be shown below. Attacking a claim like (g) or (g') is difficult because one is, in effect, attacking a claim that no one has ever defended. The most one can do is examine what has been said and show that what has been suggested is inadequate to the task defined in (g').

The misconception was once pervasive in the generative semantics literature (G. Lakoff is an honorable exception) that when one had provided a "semantic" representation for some class of sentences, then one had somehow "done" the semantics for that class. This is nowhere more evident than in the writing on the PH. For example, the PH makes very little contribution to the SEMANTICS of interrogative sentences. All that it does is provide a representation which identifies surface structure interrogatives with underlying indirect questions. The basic semantic problem with interrogative sentences is that they do not denote a proposi-tion. This problem is not solved by embedding the sentence under a performative, because, in order to interpret the matrix sentence, we will need to be able to interpret the embedded sentence. That sentence is, of course, still interrogative. One way of semantically interpreting interroga-tives, which, incidentally, makes no reference to a PH, is given by Hamblin (1973). His model theory COULD be applied to the interrogative structures proposed by the PH, but the performatives involved would be semantically gratuitous.

A semantic interpretation of the structures proposed by the PH re-quires that felicity conditions be identified with truth conditions.[16] This is

---

[15] Lewis (1972) might be cited as an exception but Lewis is NOT employing his minimal PH to capture illocutionary force but only to assign truth-conditions to non-declarative sen-tences.

[16] See footnote 14 to this chapter.

recognized by G. Lakoff (1975:268), who adapted some of the ideas of Searle (1969): "In natural logic, satisfaction conditions would be given for each atomic predicate, including all of the performative predicates; the satisfaction conditions are at once both truth conditions and felicity conditions [G. Lakoff (1975:268]." Lakoff suggests that felicity conditions should be given as meaning postulates and offers (57) as an example.

(57) REQUEST (x,y,P)→ATTEMPT (x, CAUSE (y,P))

If we make some charitable assumptions about what this expression is intended to mean, then it follows that (58) entails (59), and, indeed, Lakoff claims that it does:

(58) *Henry requested of Jill that she take her clothes off.*
(59) *Henry attempted to get Jill to take her clothes off.*

However, if (58) entails (59) then (60) should make Henry sound completely irrational and (61) should be contradictory.

(60) *Henry requested of Jill that she take her clothes off because it was the only way he knew of preventing her from doing so.*
(61) *Henry requested of Jill that she take her clothes off but he was only attempting to shock her.*

Since (60) and (61) do not behave in the way predicted, it follows that the relation between (58) and (59) is not one of entailment. Lakoff (1975:269) goes on to suggest that some felicity conditions will not only be entailed by affirmative performative sentences, but that they will also be SEMANTI-CALLY PRESUPPOSED in ANY performative sentence. Unfortunately the notion "semantic presupposition," as standardly defined, appears to have no application in natural language (see Chapter 5 of this volume) and so cannot be used in the semantic interpretation of performative verbs. The examples Lakoff gives only confirm the conclusion: he claims that (62), (63), and (64) ENTAIL (65) in virtue of the semantic presupposition relation involved.

(62) *Sam ordered Harry to get out of the bar.*
(63) *Sam didn't order Harry to get out of the bar.*
(64) *Sam may order Harry to get out of the bar.*
(65) *Sam has authority over Harry.*

If Lakoff were right then (66)–(68) should all be contradictory.

(66) *Sam ordered Harry to get out of the bar but Harry reminded him that he didn't have the authority.*
(67) *Sam didn't order Harry to get out of the bar because he didn't have the authority to do so.*

(68)   *Sam may order Harry to get out of the bar even though he doesn't have the authority to do so.*

If felicity conditions cannot be related to performative verbs by either an entailment relation or a semantic presupposition relation, then it appears that they cannot be related to them SEMANTICALLY at all.

Lakoff (1975:264) does note some apparently genuine entailments that arise if the performative is qualified by *sincerely*. Thus (69) does seem to entail (70):

(69)   *Nixon stated sincerely that he was not involved in Watergate.*
(70)   *Nixon believed that he was not involved in Watergate.*

Lakoff goes on to argue that the meaning postulate given in (71) explains the anomaly that arises in sentences like (72).

(71)   SINCERE (x, STATE (x,y,P))→BELIEVE (x,P)
(72)   *Paul is dead and I do not believe that he is dead.*

Lakoff explains the anomaly by showing that, if (71) holds, then (72) could never be uttered sincerely. However, as Hintikka (1962:78) observes, (73) is anomalous in what appears to be a very similar way.

(73)   *Paul is dead but I do not know whether he is dead.*

This cannot be explained by Lakoff by means of a meaning postulate, because (74) is clearly false.

(74)   (x)(y)(P)[(SINCERE (x, STATE(x,y,P))→KNOW(x,P))]

For a more general solution to Moore's paradox, see Hintikka (1962:64–102). A further objection to Lakoff's introduction of meaning postulates like (71) is that at least one will be required for every performative verb and this effectively removes the possibility of making any generalization about the semantics of *sincerely*.

There has been, to my knowledge, only one model theory defined for a language incorporating performative predicates. That model theory is to be found in Aqvist (1972) and it is instructive to compare it with Lakoff's proposal expressed in (g'). Aqvist argues, in the tradition established by Hedenius (1963), that (75) has roughly the same truth conditions as (76).

(75)   *I hereby promise to pay you £5.*
(76)   *I communicate this sentence to you in this situation and, by doing so, I make a promise to pay you £5.*

Aqvist then sets up a formal language in which to define the truth conditions for analogues of (75) and (76): "We shall now describe a formal language L whose expressive resources we take to be sufficient for the adequate representation of a reasonably large and interesting class of performatives; in other respects, however, its resources are fairly limited, perhaps TO A DEGREE APPROACHING MINIMALITY [Aqvist 1972:6; emphasis added]."

Among the metalinguistic resources employed are indexicals for speaker and addressee [both to be found in (g′)] and an indexical ranging over context of utterance [not to be found in (g′)]. This is not the place to evaluate Aqvist's system, but let us assume, for the purposes of discussion, that he has succeeded in providing the most restricted possible semantics sufficient for at least some performatives.

The conclusion that follows from our assumption is that the semantics for deleted performative sentences will have to be different from those of sentences with undeleted performatives. The essential property of the latter is that utterance in the appropriate circumstances guarantees their truth. Utterance of the "same" sentences, with their performatives deleted, in the same circumstances, fails to guarantee truth for the performative sentences. As Aqvist (1972:20) says: "The EXACT WORDING may be of utmost importance as far as performativeness of sentences is concerned: 'mere' logical equivalence to a performative sentence does not guarantee performativeness."

Searle's (1969:61) formulation of the felicity conditions for promises runs into this problem: He remarks in a footnote that "the use of the biconditional in this condition excludes ambiguous sentences. We have to assume that T (the sentence uttered) is unambiguous." No theory that derives natural language surface sentences via performative deletion can make such an unambiguity assumption.

We are entitled to draw the following conclusions from this discussion of (g).

(i)   The relation between speech act reports and felicity conditions is not SEMANTIC contrary to the predictions of the PH.

(ii) The PH cannot offer a SEMANTIC explanation of the epistemic version of Moore's paradox, despite purporting to offer one for the doxastic version.

(iii) If the PH is to be maintained with its original generality then it must show how the same semantics can be made to work for both DELETED performatives and undeleted ones.

As things stand, (i) is the most damaging objection to (g). Only if a proponent of the PH actually offered a semantics for higher performative sentences could one show conclusively whether (iii) counted against it.

Ironically, the class of data which many see as providing the most convincing[17] case for the PH poses an apparently insuperable problem for the proponent of (g'). Consider (77).

(77)   *Since you're interested, John is a Catholic.*

Böer and Lycan (1978) have shown, in a paper which is much too labyrinthine to be adequately paraphrased here, that sentences like (77) put semantic approaches to deleted performatives in an impossible position. If (77) contains a performative verb in SR which is NOT truth-conditionally interpreted, then (77) is itself uninterpretable. If (77) contains an SR performative which IS semantically interpreted, then the sentence as a whole is assigned the wrong truth conditions.

(h)   All sentences have a higher performative clause in SR
The arguments above have been intended to show that it is rather implausible to think that ANY sentences, except those that show it in surface structure, have a performative verb in SR. Thus I shall only consider (h) briefly.

Lakoff (1975:284–5), in an appendix, himself rejects (h) in favour of a weaker claim given as (h') below:

(h')   All sentences contain a higher performative verb except those which (i) are not used to perform a speech act, and (ii) contain no deictic elements.

He goes on to claim that sentences like (78) and (79) have two possible SRs (this amounts to the claim that they are ambiguous) according to whether or not they are used or considered in the abstract.

(78)   *Two plus two equals four.*
(79)   *Whales are mammals.*

There is no evidence to support the view that these examples are ambiguous. Claim (h') forces us to postulate an undetectable ambiguity. To avoid this, we can only return to (h). But that means committing ourselves to the absurd position that sentences not used to perform a speech act nevertheless have a performative specifying the speech act that they are being used to do.

Let me summarize the findings which emerge from the discussion of the PH. There is no adequate evidence for (a) and (b). The evidence for (c) is methodologically unsound; in addition there are clear counterexamples to show its falsity. Condition (d) is circular in the absence of

---

[17] However, Mittwoch (1977) shows convincingly that the PH fails to provide a general solution to the semantic problem caused by sentence adverbials which do not modify the sentence uttered.

independent criteria for deletability and ambiguity. There are clear counterexamples to (e). Some proponents of the PH have abandoned it; those
who do not are forced to abandon (f). There are many clear counterexamples to (f) and several proponents of the PH have abandoned this
condition. Abandoning condition (f) fundamentally undermines the
whole hypothesis. Condition (g) has yet to be formally defended, however
some of its predictions can be shown to be incorrect. Furthermore it
appears, from the only real work that has been done on the semantics of
performatives, that existing PH proposals for doing the same task are
likely to prove seriously inadequate. Condition must (h) be abandoned
because the PH cannot be extended to cover certain declarative sentences.

In the face of the above, what can we salvage from the performative
hypothesis? One possibility is a weakened version of (8). In the interests of
making a positive contribution to the topic, I suggest the hypothesis
presented in (80). This is the strongest hypothesis possible in the light of
the discussion above.

(80)   Some sentences contain, in their surface structure
        representations, one or more performative verbs.

Claim (80), unlike (8), offers no framework from which to get at the
illocutionary force of utterances or the force-potential of sentences, nor
does it provide a basis on which to write force-dependent rules of
morpheme-placement, mood selection, deletion, intonation or phonolog-
ical reduction. If we want to do these things then we have to begin again.
The clue as to WHERE to begin is to be found, curiously enough, in the
paper which was most influential in initiating the performative
hypothesis:

> The PRAGMATIC ANALYSIS . . . claims that certain elements are present in the context of
> a speech act, and that syntactic processes can refer to such elements . . . . A precise
> theory would have to specify formally what features of the infinite set of possible
> contexts can be of linguistic relevance . . . . The interconnections between syntax and
> pragmatics should be investigated in detail. Possibly when they have been clarified, a
> reason for choosing either a performative analysis or a pragmatic analysis of all sen-
> tence types will emerge [Ross 1970:254–261].

3

IMPLICATURE

Typology and Definitions

This chapter considers the notion of IMPLICATURE and outlines briefly the components of the Gricean program, as presented in Grice (1967).[1] Attention is focused on those implicatures arising from the maxims of quality and quantity. It is argued that the former turn out to be subsumed under the felicity conditions for assertion. Various criticisms of the Gricean program with respect to the maxim of quantity are discussed in the light of their ontological and methodological implications. Finally two functions are developed and defined which assign to each sentence the set of "quantity" implicatures potentially implied by that sentence.

This chapter is in no sense intended as a full exegesis of Grice (1967). I am using his work for my own purposes and these purposes are not exegetical. This fact is reflected in the sloppy use of the term "implicature," which I shall employ both for the phenomenon itself and for referring to the entity implicated (where Grice would use "implicatum"). This particular sloppy use of Grice's terminology seems to be general in the works discussed below that develop his notions and I thought it best to follow common usage rather than stick to etymology. At the end of this

[1] The chapter of Grice (1967) that is most relevant to the present discussion has been published as Grice (1975). Good introductions to his program can be found in Harnish (1976), Kempson (1975), and Sadock (1978).

chapter I shall give definitions of two functions that yield as values sets of im-plicatures, where "im-plicature" is a technical term belonging to the theory presented here. The beginning of Chapter 6 presents a complex system which yields some of these "im-plicatures" as "implicatures." The latter notion is also defined within the theory, but accords more or less closely with Grice's "implicata." By the time the reader has got to the relevant parts of the book, no confusion should arise.

An implicature is a proposition that is implied by the utterance of a sentence in a context even though that proposition is not a part of nor an entailment of what was actually said. Grice claimed that there were two types of implicature: CONVENTIONAL and CONVERSATIONAL. The former arise solely because of conventional features of the words employed in an utterance. Thus, on the not implausible assumption that *but* carries a conventional implicature, examples (1) and (2) would have the same truth conditions and differ only in that (2) conventionally implicates a proposition involving some sort of contrast, unexpectedness, or the like.[2]

(1)   *Mary got pregnant and John was pleased.*
(2)   *Mary got pregnant but John was pleased.*

If conventional, then this implicature arises solely because of the particular (non-truth-conditional) properties of the word *but* and cannot be given some higher-order explanation in terms of conversational rules. For a linguist, this would mean that the dictionary entry for *but* would have to have some pragmatic component that would specify its implicature potential. A formal treatment of conventional implicature within a grammatical theory has been given by Karttunen and Peters (1975), who deal with example (3) by means of some additions to a Montague Grammar:

(3)   *John failed to win.*

Although their formal treatment is very impressive, their particular choice of examples seems to miss Grice's point about the implicatures arising from verbs like *fail*, *try*, and the like. That point is that the implicatures derive from general conversational principles, and not just from the lexical entry of the verb concerned. The discussion of examples (5)–(12) that follows will establish this point.

Grice's second class of implicatures comprises the CONVERSATIONAL ones and this class is itself divided into PARTICULARIZED conversational implicatures and GENERALIZED conversational implicatures. The former are those that arise because of some special factor inherent in the context

---

[2] For a discussion of *but* in the context of Grice's work, see Kempson (1975). For a formally flawed approach to conventional implicature, see Gazdar and Klein (1977).

of utterance and are not normally carried by the sentence used. Thus the second utterance in the following dialogue may well carry a particularized conversational implicature to the effect that the referent is a homosexual.

(4)   A: *What does Julian do when he's not at the hairdresser's?*
       B: *He waits for boys in the restroom of the Y.M.C.A.*

On other occasions of use, say when we already know that the referent is a school truancy officer, this sentence will not carry this particular implicature. A rather similar example is considered in greater detail in Chapter 6, where it is argued that such implicatures can affect the presuppositional content of an utterance. However, their general relevance to linguistic interests appears to be marginal, so I shall not consider them further here.

The second subclass is that of GENERALIZED conversational implicatures and it is with these that this chapter is largely concerned. Generalized conversational implicatures arise when "one can say that the use of a certain form of words in an utterance would normally (in the ABSENCE of special circumstances) carry such-and-such an implicature or type of implicature [Grice 1975:56]." Grice goes on to warn that "it is all too easy to treat a generalized conversational implicature as if it were a conventional implicature [ibid.: 56]." I have already mentioned a case where this warning appears to have gone unheeded. The issue is more important than merely getting the terminology right: In syntax an analogy would lie in the difference between giving each of a set of lexical items a syntactic feature to prevent some transformation applying to them (the conventional case) on the one hand, and on the other specifying a general rule of grammar (like one of Ross's constraints), which makes that transformation inapplicable to them in virtue of some nonarbitrary property which they already have in common (the analogue of generalized conversational implicature). This chapter can be seen as an attempt to provide the formal specification of one type of generalized conversational implicature. It may be that this enterprise is unachievable and all implicatures will have to be regarded as conventional but, methodologically, it seems worth making the attempt.

There is a middle position, that is having a general rule of predictive power but a rule which is otherwise unmotivated, that is, it cannot be plausibly explained in terms of its conversational function. Most syntactic rules are of this type—at least they were before the advent of "functional grammar" (Grossman *et al.* 1975). Such a rule might be said to specify GENERALIZED CONVENTIONAL IMPLICATURES (this is NOT one of Grice's notions). I shall return to the issue intermittently throughout this chapter.

Grice (1975: 57–58) lists five features jointly necessary for an implicature to be considered conversational rather than conventional.

(i) It must not be part of the meaning of the expression to which it attaches. That is it must not be given in the lexicon or specified as the meaning-changing effect of some syntactic operation.

(ii) It must be context-sensitive and cancellable in particular cases, either by the context making it clear that it is inapplicable or by the addition of a clause denying the implicature as in the following example.

(5)   *John failed to win, but then he didn't even try.*

(iii) It must be "nondetachable," that is, it must not be possible to substitute some other expression in the sentence that lacks the implicature in question but which otherwise means much the same thing. Thus examples (6), (7), and (8) should carry the same implicature(s) as (3) if these implicature(s) are conversational rather than conventional.

(6)   *John didn't succeed in winning.*
(7)   *John wasn't able to win.*
(8)   *John didn't manage to win.*

(iv) The implicature must not be a truth condition of the sentence involved. If (9) is false, it does not follow that (3) is false or truth-valueless.

(9)   *John tried to win.*

Note, for contrast, that if (10) is false, then it does follow that (11) is false or truth-valueless, so (10) cannot be an implicature of (11).

(10)   *John won.*
(11)   *John managed to win.*

(v) It must be possible for there to be two or more implicatures such that the choice of which is involved may prove indeterminate. Thus (3) may be seen as having either or both of (9) and (12) as implicatures.

(12)   *John was expected to win.*

Because this last feature is less restrictive than the others (that is, it only has to be POSSIBLE for there to be an indeterminate choice of implicatures) and because indeterminacy is hard to handle formally, I shall mostly ignore it in the discussion that follows. A fuller treatment of implicature would not be guilty of this omission, which is only really defensible on operational grounds. As Karttunen and Peters (1975:278) note, "it is difficult to pin down exactly what the implicature of *fail* is."

Before we move on to consider the maxims that Grice proposes as the conversational principles from which nonconventional implicatures derive, it is worth pausing to examine the issue of definition. Grice himself, very sensibly although rather disappointingly, never gives an explicit definition of conversational implicature, although he does offer the circumspect characterization just sketched. The first general definition that I am aware of is due to Thomason (1973:9) and given in (13).

(13)   A sentence ϕ **conversationally implicates** ψ **relative to** a class C of contexts of utterance, if for all $c \in C$, such that ϕs assertion in c does not violate the maxims of conversation, ψ is presumed in c.

This definition is unsatisfactory for a number of reasons. First, it is not biconditional, so it does not place any restrictions on the class of conversational implicatures. Second, as Thomason himself notes we are forced into a taxonomy of contexts in order to arrive at C for ϕ and ψ. Third, the definition fails to capture the notion "implicature," as the following examples show.

(14)   *Some of the members showed up.*
(15)   *Some of the members didn't show up.*

The relation between (14) and (15) is a paradigm case of implicature and yet, in many contexts in which (14) would be uttered, (15) would not be presumed until (14) had been uttered. Uttering (14) to implicate (15) might be precisely the point of the utterance in such contexts. So if c refers to the context immediately prior to the utterance then the formulation is incorrect. If c refers to the context immediately after utterance then it is also incorrect, since (15) may not be implicated and yet the utterance of (14) can still be perfectly in accord with the maxims of conversation. For example in a proof situation, where (14) has just been derived from (16), (15) will not be implicated.[3]

[3] I am assuming that (16) entails (14). This assumption may appear to clash with a familiar property of predicate calculus, namely that (x) [*member* $(x) \rightarrow$ *turn up* (x)] does not entail $\exists x$[*member* $(x) \wedge$ *turn up* (x)]. The clash is only superficial however. I shall argue in Chapter 5 that Russell was correct in supposing that (i) entails (ii).

(i)   *The members showed up.*
(ii)   *There are members.*

A Russellian translation of (16)—which contains a definite description—WILL entail (14). Note that there does seem to be a meaning difference between (iii) and (iv).

(iii)   *All damaged books must be handed to the librarian.*
(iv)   *All of the damaged books must be handed to the librarian.*

Sentence (iii) could be displayed in any library, but (iv) would be more likely to appear in one which had, say, recently suffered a fire. See also Karttunen (1975:51ff).

(16)   *All of the members showed up.*

If we then restrict C so as to exclude such cases of implicature cancellation, we only succeed in making the whole definition circular. Exactly the
same circularity vitiates Lakoff's (1975) informal suggestion that implicature be treated as context-dependent entailment. The only example
which Lakoff offers in support of his proposal, which implicitly espouses a
definition like Thomason's, is handled quite straightforwardly by the
theory presented in Chapter 6 of this book [see the discussion of example
(77) on p. 145 in that chapter]. Since entailment is not the only definable
logical relation, a failure to identify implicature with entailment does not
have as a consequence, pace Lakoff, an embarkation onto the uncharted
seas of "extralogical (ibid.:253)" and "loose or informal (ibid.:270)" inferences.

A second definition of implicature is due to Walker (1975:157).

> S conversationally implicates ϕ by U iff in uttering U S M-intends to convey ϕ to his
> audience, and intends this intention to be recognised partly because of the audience's
> recognition of the sense of U (together with its expectation that S also knows the sense
> of U); but partly also because the audience expects S to be conforming to the Co-
> operative Principle, and expects S to anticipate this expectation and to act accordingly.

This definition appears to require auxiliary theories of INTENTION, EXPEC-
TATION, and RECOGNITION in order to be useful. In the absence of such
theories, *obscurum per obscurius*.

Katz and Langendoen (1976:13) claim that a hypothetical function,
from utterances into sentences, called PRAG, allows Grice's "special
notion of conversational implicature" to be eliminated. They support this
claim by offering the following "definition": "Someone conversationally
implicates P in saying S in the context C just in case (a) PRAG assigns the
reading R as its output for a structural description of S and appropriate
information about C, and (b) the proposition represented by R semantically entails P." They also tell us that "it is not important or possible to
specify the nature of the rules comprising PRAG (ibid.: 11)." Since PRAG
remains wholly undefined, and since no indication is given as to how
PRAG would acquire "appropriate information about C," I can see no
good reason for taking this proposal seriously. It clearly fails to capture the
notion that Grice discusses. If someone says *Mr. X is hopeless at philosophy*
in a context in which it is clear that he means exactly that, no more and no
less, then, according to Katz and Langendoen's definition, he will have
conversationally implicated that Mr. X is hopeless at philosophy. And, of
course, he has done no such thing. Grice's fundamental distinction between what was SAID and what was IMPLICATED is obliterated by this
definition.

In answer to the question "what is an implicature?" Atlas and Levinson (1973) have offered a version of Kenny's (1966) "practical inference" logic. Although this theory does provide a well-defined account of DEFEASIBILITY, and hence potentially of implicature cancellation, it appears to be of limited relevance to the question being asked, since it only handles imperative or optative sentences. Thus it cannot handle, for example, paradigm implicatures such as (15), given earlier. Furthermore, it legitimates some counter–intuitive inferences but fails to legitimate some intuitively obvious inferences. For example, (17) is a valid inference in their logic but (18) is not.[4]

(17)   *I wish John was here.*
        therefore
        I wish John was here and I wish John was dead.
(18)   *Kill all the conspirators.*
        Brutus is a conspirator.
        therefore
        Kill Brutus.

Reformulating the Maxims

I shall now discuss Grice's four maxims of conversation, starting with those that have least bearing on the contents of this book.

(19)   MANNER: Be Perspicuous.
        i.   Avoid obscurity of expression.
        ii. Avoid ambiguity.
        iii. Be brief (avoid unnecessary prolixity).[5]
        iv. Be orderly.

It is no part of the present enterprise to formalize this maxim but, in view of the discussion in Chapter 1, it may be worth indicating briefly how it might be done.[6] Part (i) can be rephrased as instructing speakers and

---

[4] I am grateful to Stephen Levinson for bring these examples to my attention.
[5] Compare this maxim with the following comment of Suppes (1973:393).

It is an obvious point that the apparatus of model–theoretic semantics is not sufficient to predict the choice of a particular description of an object from among many semantically suitable ones. Suppose John and Mary are walking and John notices a spider close to Mary's shoulder. He says "Watch out for that spider." He does not say, "Watch out for the black, half-inch long spider that has a green dot in its centre and is about six inches from your left shoulder at a vertical angle of about sixty degrees."

[6] Those unfamiliar with Grice's maxims may be daunted by the fact that they are all expressed as imperatives. This is the least of the problems of formalizing however, since the usual equations of "Rewrite X as Y" and "X is rewritten as Y" or "Interpret X as Y" and "X is interpreted as Y" apply.

addressees to use, and interpret each other as using, the same language (where LANGUAGE will be defined by reference to the lexicon, set of syntactic rules, rules of semantic interpretation, and so forth) or to use the intersection of their respective languages or idiolects. Part (ii) instructs conversationalists (a) not to use ambiguous expressions, and (b) if they hear or use an ambiguous expression, then to assign to it one and only one reading and not treat it as simultaneously having several readings (where the notion AMBIGUOUS EXPRESSION is well-defined within some linguistic theory).[7] In the case of speech act categorisation (see Weiser 1974; Sadock 1974: 157–158), this submaxim seems wholly inapplicable and Grice offers us little reason to assume it operational in other areas of language use [but cf. Hankamer (1973) and Langendoen (1975)]. Submaxim (iii) can be rather brutally formalized by quantifying over the length of expressions at some level of representation. Then it can be read as instructing speakers to choose α, given two potentially synonymous expressions α and β such that β is longer than α. It also instructs hearers on hearing β (α and β being as above) to assign it a reading distinct from α, if that is possible (because if it means the same as α, then α would have been used instead). Something along these lines would provide part of the explanation for R. Lakoff's (1972:239) observation regarding English modal verbs and their respective periphrastics: "when the speaker agrees with, or takes upon himself, the atomic meaning of the modal, he can use the simple modal form. Otherwise, he must use the periphrastic variant."[8] Sub-maxim (iv) might be susceptible to something along the following lines: If a sentence ϕ contains the expressions α and β in that order (i.e., ϕ is of the form $X^\frown\alpha^\frown Y^\frown\beta^\frown Z$, where X, Y, and Z are any expressions, possibly null), and where α and β have distinct extensions and are members of some set Σ such that for any two members α and β of Σ the expression $\alpha^\frown before^\frown\beta$ is well-formed, then hear ϕ as implying, or use ϕ to imply, that the event denoted by α occurred before the event denoted by β.[9] This formulation requires tightening up, generalizing to

---

[7] See also in this connection: "*Ceteris paribus*, prefer readings that do not involve operations of movement or deletion in the derivation over those that do [Pullum 1974:2]."

[8] Gazdar and Keenan (1975) make use of this observation in their critique of Green (1973a).

[9] Herb Clark (personal communication, 1976) has drawn my attention to the following putative counterexample to the spirit of Grice's "Be orderly!" maxim.

(i)   *John broke his leg. He tripped and fell.*

It seems that the normal ϕ *precedes–causes* ψ implicature found in sentence pairs of the $\phi^\frown\psi$ form do not arise when ψ explains how ϕ came about. Note that in these cases $\phi^\frown\psi$ cannot be replaced by $\phi^\frown and^\frown\psi$:

(ii)   *John broke his leg and he tripped and fell.*

We cannot interpret (ii) as implying that John's fall caused his leg to break.

cover more than two expressions and generalizing to cover spatial precedence as well as temporal precedence. It would also need to allow for the
possibility of cancellation, although, as will be shown in Chapter 6 of this
book, this is relatively simple to achieve. For discussion and some relevant examples see (19)–(25) in Chapter 4 of this book, Schmerling (1975),
and Linde (1976). Other work by Linde (e.g., Linde and Labov 1975)
indicates the considerable role played by the "Be orderly" submaxim in
the description of the spatial domain. In the temporal domain, it offers a
very straightforward account of the meaning difference exhibited by the
following pair of sentences.

(20)   *John stole the money and went to the bank*
(21)   *John went to the bank and stole the money*

(22)   RELEVANCE: Be relevant

That relevance is relevant to linguistic descriptions is painfully apparent (see, for example, the following condition on the acceptability of
headless relative clauses in Japanese): "THE RELEVANCY CONDI-
TION: For a headless relative clause to be acceptable, it is necessary that it
be interpreted pragmatically in such a way as to be directly relevant to the
pragmatic content of its matrix clause [Kuroda 1976:27]." See also Green
(1968, 1973b), Gunter (1972), and Loetscher (1973). Equally apparent is
the almost complete absence of any kind of formal linguistic treatment of
the notion (but see Sperber and Wilson 1977). Grice himself admits that
the issue involves difficult problems and points out that his terse formulation offers no guide either to what an expression is required to be relevant
to, or to how what is relevant can change during a conversation [but on
this latter point see Adato (1971)]. Thomason (1973:12), after brieffly considering the logical literature on relevance, concludes that "no attempt to
apply formal semantic theory to this notion has been successful enough
to provide a model that would be usable in pragmatics." The present work
has no contribution to make to the topic.

(23)   QUALITY: Try to make your contribution one that is **true**.
        (i)   Do not say what you **believe** to be false.[10]
        (ii) Do not say that for which you lack **adequate evidence**
           [emphasis added]

Any attempt to formalise this maxim as it stands runs into three sets of
problems: Those connected with the notion "truth," those connected

---

[10] Cf. "Thou shalt not make a straightforward assertion that you do not believe [Fogelin
1967:20]."

with the logic of belief, and those involved in the nature of "adequate evidence." Note, however, that these three sets of problems are just those that crop up in the philosophical debate over the status of knowledge and the possibility of equating knowledge with justified true belief. Without engaging in this debate I propose to sidestep the problems connected with the components of (23) and, as a first step, simply replace (23) by (24) (the reader is requested to suspend judgment on these maneuvers for several paragraphs).

(24)   QUALITY': Say only that which you know.

We may then take "know" as primitive and employ an epistemic logic to describe its operation. The most widely accepted version of epistemic logic is that of Hintikka (1962) and I shall employ it in what follows without further comment.[11] We are now in a position to give a simple formulation of quality implicatures:

(25)   Utterance of ϕ by a speaker s implicates Kϕ (where for Kϕ read s^knows that^ϕ).

This type of implicature differs from those arising from the other maxims because it cannot be intelligibly cancelled.

(26)   *Pithium is radioactive $\begin{Bmatrix} and \\ but \end{Bmatrix}$ I don't know that Pithium is radioactive.

This is even more clear if one attempts to cancel the components of Grice's own formulation.

(27)   *Pithium is radioactive but that isn't true, nor do I believe it, nor do I have adequate evidence for claiming that it is.

Grice is aware that there is something different about his maxim of quality because he says (1975:46) that "it might be felt that the importance of at least the first maxim of quality is such that it should not be included in a scheme of the kind I am constructing." Hintikka (1962) noted the

---

[11] For brief details of this logic see the list of symbols and typographical conventions on formalism. That KNOWING and not, say, believing, assuming, or something else is what is involved is evidenced in the following:

We have in the data, "Oh she knows you're crazy hehh!" where that might be different from "She thinks you're crazy", where the problem, I suppose, is that whatever is correct to say about what she figures, then if I say "She knows you're crazy", it's hard for you to be in a position to say "No, she THINKS I'm crazy. She happens to be right." That is to say, if some facts are assertably so, then, that somebody thinks that they're so can apparently be used in such a fashion as to say that they KNOW that it's so; whether or not their thoughts turn out to have a correct basis for that result [Sacks 1968:3].

anomaly of utterances like (26) in his discussion of, and solution to, Moore's paradox [cf. Harnish (1976:370–371) on Moore's paradox]. The problem, which is an exact analogue of Moore's problem (for a comprehensive bibliography on the topic see Hintikka 1962:64), is that the sentence $p \land \neg Kp$, which may be taken to represent (26), is not a contradiction in epistemic logic and so we have no reason to suppose (26) anomalous if we restrict ourselves to consideration of that formulation alone. Hintikka's solution proposes that the utterance of a sentence ϕ commits a speaker to knowledge of that sentence, that is, to $K\phi$, and that the anomaly arises because, if this principle is applied to (26), then inconsistency arises. The sentence $K(\phi \land \neg K\phi)$ is necessarily false in epistemic logic. It can now be seen that my version of the quality maxim given in (25) amounts to no more and no less than Hintikka's treatment of sentences like (26). The relation between ϕ and $K\phi$ which Hintikka (1962:79) defines generally is called EPISTEMIC IMPLICATION and its definition is given in (28).

(28)   The utterance of ϕ **epistemically implies** ψ iff $K(\phi \land \neg \psi)$ is inconsistent.

Under this definition, it may be readily proved that ϕ epistemically implies $K\phi$.[12]

Two possible objections are relevant at this juncture. The first objection is that persons often do not know that which they say: They may only believe it; they may be lying; they may have no evidence. This objection misses the point, which is that implicatures only concern what people commit themselves to in uttering sentences and do not concern what is actually the case. Thus the claim that my treatment of the quality maxim makes is that speakers uttering ϕ commit themselves not only to ϕ, but also to knowing that ϕ. They cannot produce intelligible utterances such as (26) or (27), nor can they admit to disbelief in what they say, nor can they blithely dismiss requests for justification of what they have said. These are empirically verifiable predictions of the maxim, because infringements inevitably lead to conversational consequences. As far as truth is concerned, it is worth noting that at least one philosopher has

---

[12] The proof is as follows:

(1)	$K(p \land \neg Kp) \in \mu$	counterassumption
(2)	$p \land \neg Kp \in \mu$	from (1) by C.K
(3)	$\neg Kp \in \mu$	from(2) by C.&
(4)	$P\neg p \in \mu$	from (3) by C.-K
(5)	$\neg p \in \mu^*$	from (4) by C.P*
(6)	$p \land \neg Kp \in \mu^*$	from (1) by C.K*
(7)	$p \in \mu^*$	from (6) by C.&

advanced the view that a convention of truth is a necessary condition for a language's use. Lewis (1969:174) after giving a formal definition of CONVENTION and applying it in a discussion of possible languages, postulates the following definition of an ACTUAL LANGUAGE.

(29) L is an **actual language** of [a population] P iff there prevails in P a convention of truthfulness in L.

The word *prevail* is important: Lying is an effective enterprise only in a population in which a convention of truth PREVAILS.

   The second objection is that people may, of course, say things which they do not know to be the case and not even be heard to claim that they know them to be the case. Nonassertoric speech acts regularly allow this.

(30)   *You will go to Tibet on Tuesday?*

Where interrogative or imperative sentences are used, no confusion can arise but the utterance of a sentence like (30) CAN be heard as an assertion. If it is so heard, then its epistemic implication is as predicted by (28). Notice the following perfectly plausible dialogue.

(31)   A: *You will go to Tibet on Tuesday.*
         B: *How did you know?*
         A: *I wasn't **telling** you, I was **asking** you.*

   So it appears that the quality maxim may only apply to assertoric utterances. This restriction is hardly surprising (see Harman 1974:10). Indeed, we may cease to accord the notion any status as a maxim whatsoever and instead simply treat KNOWLEDGE THAT ϕ as one of the felicity conditions for asserting that ϕ. Let us represent this claim as follows:

(32)   For any declarative sentence ϕ, **assertion** of ϕ commits the speaker to Kϕ. [See definition XV in Chapter 6 of this volume for a precise expression of this.]

   This formulation, which now stands as our definitive version of the quality maxim, makes no special allowance for utterances involving irony, jokes, or metaphor. Consideration of any of these is beyond the scope of this book. No problem arises, of course, if such utterances are considered to be nonassertoric.

(33)   QUANTITY:
         (i)   Make your contribution as informative as is required (for the current purposes of the exchange).[13]

---

[13] Cf. "Make the strongest possible claim that you can legitimately defend [Fogelin 1967:20]."

(ii)   Do not make your contribution more informative than
        is required.

To formalize this maxim as it stands, that is in its full generality, we
would have to (*a*) be able to quantify over informativeness, and (*b*) have
some function which when applied to a conversation and a point within it
would yield as its value the level of informativeness required. With regard
to (*a*), Thomason (1973:11) comments as follows:

> Model theoretic notions can be used to construct an account of semantic informative-
> ness, as was pointed out by Carnap and Bar Hillel (1952). But this account has failed to
> provide satisfactory explanations of phenomena in inductive and epistemic logic, and at
> the present time there is no agreement on the proper way of overcoming these
> difficulties.

A recent treatment of the notion, due to Hintikka (1973), is not applicable
in any obvious way to expressions of natural language or to their counterparts in semantic representation. And without (*a*), we are in no position to
begin on (*b*).

The tactic adopted here is to examine some of the data that would, or
should be, covered by Grice's quantity maxim and then propose a relatively simple formal solution to the problem of describing the behavior of
that data. This solution may be seen as a special case of Grice's quantity
maxim, or as an alternative to it, or as merely a conventional rule for
assigning one class of conversational meanings to one class of utterance.
Data similar to that found below is discussed in very great detail in Horn
(1972). However, his and my treatment of it differ somewhat, especially
where implicature suspension is concerned.

It is possible, in fact necessary, to give rather a lot of examples in order
to demonstrate that what is going on is a fairly general phenomenon and
not one restricted to a few lexical items.

(34)   a.   *Some of the boys were at the party.*
       b.   *Not all of the boys were at the party.*
       c.   *Some, in fact all, of the boys were at the party.*
       d.   *All of the boys were at the party.*
(35)   a.   *It is compatible with all that I know that he was at the
            party.*
       b.   *It is compatible with all that I know that he was not at
            the party.*
       c.   *It is (not only) compatible with all that I know that he
            was at the party, in fact I do know that he was at the
            party.*
       d.   *I know that he was at the party.*

(36)   a.   *It is possible that porosity leads to osmosis.*
         b.   *It is possible that porosity does not lead to osmosis.*
         c.   *It is possible, and in fact necessary, that porosity leads to osmosis.*
         d.   *It is necessarily the case that porosity leads to osmosis.*

(37)   a.   *Osmosis may involve porosity.*
         b.   *Osmosis may not involve porosity.*
         c.   *Osmosis may, and in fact must, involve porosity.*
         d.   *Osmosis must involve porosity.*

(38)   a.   *Mary tried to cash a check.*
         b.   *Mary did not succeed in cashing a check.*
         c.   *Mary tried, and in fact succeeded, in cashing a check.*
         d.   *Mary succeeded in cashing a check.*

(39)   a.   *I believe he's ill.*
         b.   *I don't know that he's ill.*
         c.   *I believe, in fact I know, that he is ill.*
         d.   *I know that he is ill.*

(40)   a.   *If John sees me then he will tell Margaret.*
         b.   *I don't know that John will see me.*
         c.   *If John sees me, and I know he will, then he will tell Margaret.*
         d.   *Since John will see me, he will tell Margaret.*

(41)   a.   *My sister is either in the bathroom or in the kitchen.*
         b.   *I don't know that my sister is in the bathroom and I don't know that she's in the kitchen.*
         c.   *My sister is either in the kitchen or in the bathroom, and I know which.*
         d.   *I know that my sister is in the bathroom.*
         d'. *I know that my sister is in the kitchen.*

In the examples just given, the b-sentence is an implicature of the a-sentence, the c-sentence contains a clause which explicitly cancels the implicature, and the d-sentence is a sentence which entails the a-sentence but which is inconsistent with the implicature. Now the relation between the a-sentence and the b-sentence cannot be that of entailment, because entailments cannot be cancelled, as we discover if we try to formulate the analogue of a c-sentence with one.

(42)   a.   *I managed to get to the party.*
         b.   *I got to the party.*
         c.   **I managed to, and in fact didn't, get to the party.*

If one considers the suspension clause to be a simple conjunct—and there is no reason not to—then one would not expect to be able to conjoin the negation of an entailment of one of the other conjuncts and still maintain consistency. Another reason why the relation cannot be entailment is that in each case the d-sentence entails the a-sentence. If the a-sentence entails the b-sentence, then transitivity forces us to the conclusion that the d-sentence entails the b-sentence. But in each case b and d are mutually inconsistent, which amounts to a reductio [see Fogelin (1967:18), Horn (1972:76–77), and Horn (1973) for further discussion].

One might be inclined to treat the relation between the a-sentence and the b-sentence as that of presupposition, especially if one notes that the expressions that typically occur in the cancellation clauses, expressions such as *in fact, actually* and *indeed*, also occur when presuppositions are explicitly suspended (cf. Allwood 1972:27). However, unlike presuppositions, implicatures do not usually survive if the a-sentence is embedded in a sentence that does not entail it.

(43)   *Mary managed to tell John when she thought that some of the boys were at the party.* (which does NOT implicate that some of the boys were not at the party)

An informal Gricean account of how these implicatures are derived from the maxim of quantity would go as follows: anyone uttering an a-sentence who was in a position to utter a d-sentence would be being less informative than he could be since the d-sentence makes a stronger claim about the world than the a-sentence. Thus if the speaker is being cooperative and observing the maxim of quantity, it follows that in uttering a he is implicating the negation of d. The negation of d is simply b, so b is an implicature of the utterance of a [note that this argument requires slight elaboration to cope with examples (40) and (41)].

For the reader who doubts the ontological status of quantity implicatures, I provide below a couple of examples drawn from a tape transcript of a naturally occurring conversation which illustrate their operation.

(44)   A: *Is your mother well and back?*
         B: *Well she's back, yes.*
         A: *She's not well then.*

B's reply to A is less informative than it could be since it only confirms one conjunct and A deduces from this that the other conjunct is disconfirmed. It is of interest to note that B's utterance-initial *well* behaves exactly as predicted in R. Lakoff (1973:458), which is to say that it signals an incomplete answer. The second example, drawn from the same transcript, is even more clear-cut.

(45)   A: *What are you doing this evening?*

B: *I'll either go to Fran's or not.*
A: *You're not on call then.*

Here B produces a disjunctive tautology in response to A's question and, by analogy with example (40), this should implicate that it is compatible with all that B knows that she go to Fran's. This it does since A is able to deduce from B's utterance that B is not on call. B is a social worker and if she is on call then she has to stay in unless called out to a client. Fran is a friend and not a client, so it follows that if B could go to see Fran then B cannot be on call. An analysis in terms of implicature shows how tautologies can be informative. I shall return to this point in Chapter 6. Notice that in both (44) and (45) A's second utterance contains a final *then:* It would be nice to think that this is the *then* of *if . . . then . . .* and that its semantic role is to indicate the final consequent of a process of conversational reasoning.[14]

In the c-sentences, we have observed that implicatures can be intrasententially cancelled. One might wonder why this should be permissible, since if one wanted to make the stronger claim in the first place, then a d-sentence would surely do the job better than the longer and potentially confusing c-sentence. However there are cases where a c-sentence allows one to say things not readily sayable with a d-sentence. Thus, (41c) could be used by one participant to another during a game of hide and seek. Somewhat less esoteric is the following example taken from a newspaper report (*Observer*, 20 October 1974).

(46)　　*The roots of these attempts, indeed successes, by Congress to reassert itself . . . are well known to Mr. Ford.*

Obviously the roots of an ATTEMPT to do x may be very different from the roots of one's SUCCESS in achieving x. Thus the roots of the attempt may have lain in the consequences of the Tonkin Gulf resolution, whereas the roots of the success probably lay in the immediately preceding congressional elections.

Some Residual Issues

Having completed our relatively informal discussion of Grice's four maxims of conversation, we are in a position to consider some of the problems and objections that have been, or can be, raised in connection with the Gricean program, before going on to propose a formal treatment for quantity implicatures. One of the motivations of Grice's suggestions is

---

[14] I owe this suggestion to Hans Kamp.

to allow the semantic identification of certain expressions of natural language (*some, all, or, not, if–then* . . ., etc.) with the operators and connectives of first-order predicate calculus. The discrepancies between the operation of these expressions and that of their natural language counterparts would then be accounted for pragmatically by reference to the conversational maxims.

The only detailed attack on the Gricean hypothesis with respect to the semantics and pragmatics of the logical functors of natural language has come from Cohen (1971). In Chapter 4 of this volume, I address myself to the question of whether Cohen's objections can be sustained.

The only other attack in the literature on the use of Gricean explanation is that of Kroch (1972).[15] Kroch considers the sentence given in (47).

(47)   *John ate the apple.*

He argues that the implication that all the apple was eaten can be explained by reference to Gricean maxims. He then considers what would happen if the implication was that only part of the apple was eaten and provides an equally plausible Gricean explanation for this counterfactual case. He concludes that "a theory that accounts for what exists and for what does not exist with equal ease can provide no explanations." The point is a serious one, but Kroch's choice of example is unfortunate. As Wilson (1975:104–106) shows, there is no generalization about this implication when other verbs and nouns are considered and so the sentence is a bad candidate for a Gricean analysis in the first place. Assume for the sake of argument that we could come up with a clear case of a phenomenon to which a Gricean explanation was applicable and to whose counterfactual contrary a different Gricean explanation was equally applicable. One example might be the attempt to build a pragmatic theory of presupposition on Gricean lines, for which see Stalnaker (1974a), and the discussion in Chapter 5 of this volume. What would be the result of this hypothetical case taken together with Kroch's example? The answer, as argued more generally in the first chapter of this book, is a well–defined formal theory. Such a theory will explicitly state its domain of applicability, and thus exclude Kroch's example. Furthermore, it will not generate any pair of predictions p and $\neg p$, since to do so would render it inconsistent and thus not well-defined. This answer has its disadvantages, not least of which is that the sheer difficulty of formalizing some of Grice's notions (for example, "relevance") probably makes parts of his enterprise unusable for linguists at the present time. Furthermore, those parts that are usable have to be so restrictively defined—as in this book—

---

[15] I have not been able to get hold of Kroch (1972) and so it is reported here, secondhand, from my reading of Wilson (1975) and Kempson (1975).

that much of the power and generality of Grice's discussion is lost. But not to stick to formalist methodology in an area like this can only lead out of linguistics and into literary criticism. Consider, by way of example, Kempson's (1975:196) elaboration of Grice's maxim of relevance.

(48)   Make the form of your utterance relevant to its content.

Now any notion of relevance that treated it as some relation between sentences, utterances, propositions, contexts or topics is going to prove inadequate to (48), which requires a relation between one entity that is, by definition, wholly devoid of semantics and another entity which is, by definition, exclusively semantic. Whatever such a relation might be, and it is not clear to me that it could be anything, it certainly is not the relation mentioned in (49), which I take to be the kind of relation Grice's own maxim is dealing with.

(49)   *My esteemed colleague's remarks are hardly relevant to my main point.*

Compare this to (50), which is an instantiation of (48).

(50)   *Make the distribution of vowels in your sentence relevant to its truth conditions.*

Informal explanations, not based on formal theory, particularly those that trade on words like "relevant," are always liable to the fallacy of equivocation.

The reason Grice calls his generalized conversational implicatures CONVERSATIONAL rather than CONVENTIONAL is because he sees the maxims which generate them as more than mere matters of convention.

> My avowed aim is to see talking as a special case or variety of purposive, indeed rational, behaviour. . . . I would like to be able to think of the standard type of conversational practice not merely as something which all or most do IN FACT follow, but as something which it is REASONABLE for us to follow [1975:47–48].

If one could show that there are language communities which do not obey some or all of the maxims, but are nevertheless reasonable and rational, then Grice's strong claim about the nature of the maxims could not be sustained. One such community is discussed in Keenan (1976), where she shows that Malagasy speakers make their conversational contributions as uninformative as possible. For example, if asked where somebody is they may typically reply with a disjunction even though they know, and are known to know, which disjunct is true. Likewise they normally use syntactic constructions which delete the agent in order to conceal the identity of the person responsible for the action described.

Also they use indefinites or common nouns (*someone, a girl*, etc.) even to refer to close relatives. This last mentioned practice is in direct contravention of a special case of Grice's quantity maxim discussed in Sacks and Schegloff (1977), where one of the rules given for reference is: "Use a recognitional where possible." Keenan's findings imply that Grice's maxims are only "reasonable," and "rational" relative to a given culture, community, or state of affairs. They cannot be defended as universal principles of conversation. This does not make them any less interesting to the linguist studying the conversational meanings of a given language community, but it must reduce their philosophical or psychological import (but cf. Harnish 1976:340, fn. 29). The implicatures that the maxims provoke may be better regarded as generalized CONVENTIONAL ones rather than generalized CONVERSATIONAL ones.[16] Since the treatment of presupposition suspension developed in Chapter 6 of this volume trades on implicatures deriving from the maxim of quantity, one must predict that, if Keenan is correct, then certain kinds of presupposition suspension, for example that in disjunctions, will not take place in Malagasy.

Potential Quantity Implicatures

In this section two functions are defined which, taken together, yield for any SENTENCE the set of potential quantity implicatures that the sentence could have. That is, they give all the implicatures which the sentence could possibly have prior to contextual cancellation, I shall call these potential implicatures "im-plicatures." In Chapter 6 another function will be defined which, given a sentence context pair, will yield as value the appropriate postcancellation subset of these im-plicatures, which subset will be referred to as the "implicatures" of the sentence in the context. The im-plicature functions are defined as relations between SENTENCES and SETS OF SENTENCES.

The only previous attempt I know of to formalize such a function for the quantity maxim is due to Horn (1972). I shall incorporate something rather similar, since Horn seems basically correct. It is worth noting that the explanatory purpose of Horn's definition is somewhat different from my own: His aim is largely to explain the distributional facts about the lexical incorporation of negative elements, whereas mine is largely to explain the facts of presupposition cancellation. One independently motivated generalization (Grice's maxim of quantity) serves to explain two additional distinct classes of phenomena.

---

[16] See also Cole (1975:286–288).

Horn's (1972:112) definition is given below:

(51)   Given a quantitative scale of n elements $p_1, p_2, \ldots, p_n$ and a
        speaker uttering a statement S which contains an element
        p_i on this scale, then
        (i)   the listener can infer $\neg S^{p_i}_{p_j}$ for all p_j, p_i ($j \neq n$)
        (ii) the listener must infer $\neg S^{p_i}_{p_n}$
        (iii) if $p_k > p_j > p_i$, then $\neg S^{p_i}_{p_j} \rightarrow \neg S^{p_i}_{p_k}$, where S^a_b denotes
              the result of substituting b for all occurrences of a in S.

Some examples of the quantitative scales that Horn means his definition
to apply to are given in (52):

(52)   ⟨ all, most, many, some, few, . . . ⟩
        ⟨ necessarily, probably, possibly, . . . ⟩
        ⟨ . . . ten, nine, eight, . . . ⟩
        ⟨ must, should, may, . . . ⟩

Horn's definition will not do as it stands, for the trivial reason that he
does not stipulate that $p_j > p_i$, and for the more serious reason that it
makes no allowance for the scope of other logical expressions found in
the sentence, nor for compound sentences. Thus, according to (51), (53)
implicates (54) and (55) implicates (56).

(53)   It is not the case that Paul ate some of the eggs.
(54)   Paul ate all the eggs.
(55)   Mary ate some of the bacon and Paul ate some of the eggs.
(56)   Either Mary didn't eat all of the bacon or Paul didn't eat all of
        the eggs.

Before I go on to amend and expand Horn's formulation, it is worth
pausing to consider at what level of linguistic description such scales as
Horn's should be consulted. It is both in the spirit of Grice's program and
in the interests of economy to read these nonconventional inferences
from the semantic representation. Presumably, at such a level a set of
expressions such as { perhaps, maybe, possibly} will be represented by just
one item for the reading they have in common. To read off conversational im-plicatures from the actual LEXICAL ITEMS given in the surface
structure would be tantamount to treating them as conventional implicatures, besides which the scales would require redundant listing of
synonymous items. To read off im-plicatures from the semantic interpretation of the sentence (i.e., the proposition it expresses) would be impossible, since many different sentences can express a given proposition and
many of these will not contain the scalar item and thus not carry the
im-plicature. An example is given in Chapter 6 of this volume, where it is

shown that two disjunctive sentences having the same truth-conditions (i.e., expressing the same proposition) carry different im-plicatures.[17] In what follows I shall assume that im-plicatures derive from the sentences of a semantic representation, although the exemplification will be entirely by reference to sentences of English. It should be noted that the notion of semantic representation necessary (e.g., to cope with the disjunctive examples just mentioned) is a bit more "surfacey,"[18] or less abstract, than that hypothesized by generative semanticists. Logically equivalent sentences are not required to have the same semantic representation, but only the same semantic interpretation.

To assist in the discussion which follows, I provide two abbreviatory definitions.[19]

(I) A sentence ϕ is **simple with respect to an occurrence of a component expression** α iff ϕ contains no logical functors having wider scope than α.[20]

The set of logical functors includes (but is, perhaps, not exhausted by) negation, quantifiers, connectives, and modal operators.

(II) Sentences ϕ_α and ϕ_β are **expression alternatives with respect to α and β** iff ϕ_α is identical to ϕ_β except that in ONE place where ϕ_α has α, ϕ_β has β.

Horn does not define the notion "quantitative scale," although it is easy to gather ostensively from (52) the kind of thing he has in mind. Definition is difficult for two reasons. The items in the scale must be

---

[17] See examples (18)–(20) in Chapter 6 of this book.

[18] But not too "surfacey". Consider the following examples.

(i)   *Sam went or Mary went.*
(ii) *Sam or Mary went.*
(iii) *Mary believes Sam to have gone.*
(iv) *Mary believes Sam to have gone.*

Clearly we do not want the pragmatics to have to run the syntax in reverse which is what it would have to do if it applied to surface structure in these examples (which generate CLAUSAL IM–PLICATURES, see (V)).

[19] A SENTENCE is to be understood here as any member of the set of proposition-denoting wffs defined by the formation rules of the language employed for semantic representation. An EXPRESSION is any subpart of such a wff. One cannot really be more precise than this without specifying the grammar of semantic representation, a task which is outside our present brief. I am assuming that a precise formulation would avoid problems of the sort discussed by Geach (1965). COMPOUND and COMPLEX will be used interchangeably of any sentences having as a constituent at least one occurrence of any logical functor other than a quantifier or at least two occurrences of members of the set of verbs and sentence adverbs.

[20] I am grateful to Lauri Karttunen for providing me with an example that showed an earlier formulation of this definition to be defective.

qualitatively similar: for example, we want $\langle$ . . ., *know, believe,*. . . $\rangle$ to be a scale, but not $\langle$ . . ., *regret, know,* . . . $\rangle$, and no obvious or available similarity criterion exists. Attempts to use "identity of selectional restrictions" or "identity of item-induced presuppositions" as the similarity criterion, as suggested in Gazdar (1977:72, 181), do not work for reasons which can be deduced from the examples given in the preceding sentence. The other difficulty arises because of the nature of the ordering relation imposed on such scales. It is easy enough to provide a semantic informativeness ordering, but the work of Fauconnier (e.g., 1975a, 1975b) has shown that the ordering relation is pragmatic.[21] The definition of QUANTITATIVE SCALE given in Gazdar (1977:72) runs foul of both these types of difficulty. I shall consequently content myself with a (semantically stated) necessary condition on the class of scales that figure in the examples discussed. For the purposes of definition (IV) I shall simply assume, like Horn, that the scales are, in some sense, "given to us." Caton (1966) provides detailed discussion of, and criteria for setting up, one such quantitative scale.

(III)   Let Q be an n-tuple[22] of expressions such that $Q = <\alpha_0, \alpha_1,$
          . . . $\alpha_{n-1} >$ where $n > 1$. Then if Q is a quantitative scale:
          $[\phi_{\alpha_i}]\subset[\phi_{\alpha_{i+1}}]$[23] where ϕ_{α_i} and $\phi_{\alpha_{i+1}}$ are any pair of simple
          expression alternatives with respect to $\alpha_i, \alpha_{i+1} \in Q$.

This says that any quantitative scale is such that, if one expression precedes another on that scale, then some sentence containing the first expression will always entail but not be entailed by an otherwise identical sentence containing the second expression, subject to the constraint that the expressions are not within the scope of any logical functors in the sentences. If β follows α in a scale, then β is "weaker" than α.

We may define a function f_s which, given a sentence ψ as argument, will return a set of scalar quantity im-plicatures (an "im-plicature" is a POTENTIAL implicature) as its value:

(IV) $f_s (\psi) = \{\chi : \chi = K\neg\phi_{\alpha_i}\}$
          for all $\phi\alpha_i$ such that for some quantitative scale Q, α_i,
          $\alpha_{i+1} \in Q$
          (i) $\psi = X^\frown\phi_{\alpha_{i+1}}{}^\frown Y$ where X and Y are any expressions,
                possibly null

---

[21] See also, in this connection, Harnish (1976:362–363, fn. 46) and the works cited therein.

[22] Note that treating scales as n-tuple obscures the fact that, in general, we are dealing with partial rather than total orderings.

[23] For details of the notational conventions see the list of symbols and typographical conventions on formalism.

(ii) $[\psi]\subseteq[\phi_{\alpha_{i+1}}]$
where ϕ_{α_i} and $\phi_{\alpha_{i+1}}$ are simple expression
alternatives with respect to α_i and α_{i+1}.

This says that ϕ scalar–quantity–im-plicates that the speaker knows that it is not the case that ψ if and only if there is some sentence ψ', just like ψ except that it contains a "weaker" scalar expression, and which is entailed by ϕ and is either identical to ϕ or forms a part of it (e.g., it is one conjunct), subject to the constraint that the scalar expressions are not within the scope of any logical functors in ψ or ψ'.

This definition generates epistemically qualified versions of all the im-plicatures listed as b-sentences in examples (34) to (39) as the reader may verify.

Surprisingly, perhaps, (IV) not only gives us im-plicatures from sentence components like those listed in (52), but also from logical connectives, since the couple $\langle \wedge, \vee \rangle$ will be a quantitative scale. Thus $\phi\vee\omega$ potentially implicates $K\neg(\phi\wedge\psi)$, which explains why disjunctions are commonly heard as exclusive (cf. the discussion in Chapters 4 and 6 of this volume). The deduction for this point is shown in (57).

(57)   1. $\phi\vee\psi$
        2. $K\neg(\phi\wedge\psi)$ im-plicature of 1.
        3. $\neg(\phi\wedge\psi)$ entailed by 2.
        4. $\phi\underline{\vee}\psi$ entailed by 1. and 3.

Scalar im-plicatures are not, however, the only quantity im-plicatures that arise in compound sentences. Thus, (IV) does not generate the im-plicatures noted in (40) and (41). Let us, therefore, define a function f_c which, given a compound sentence ϕ as argument, will return a set of CLAUSAL QUANTITY IM-PLICATURES as its value.

(V) $f_c(\phi) = \{\chi : \chi\in\{P\psi, P\neg\psi\}\}$
       for all sentences ψ such that
       (i) $\phi = X^{\frown}\psi^{\frown}Y$ where X and Y are any expressions, possibly
             null
       (ii) $[\phi]\not\subseteq[\psi]$
       (iii) $[\phi]\not\subseteq[\neg\psi]$
       (iv) ϕ has some expression alternative ϕ_α with respect to ψ
             and α where α is an arbitrary sentence such that
             (a) $\alpha \neq \psi$
             (b) $K\alpha \notin f_p(\phi_\alpha)$[24]
             (c) $K\neg\alpha \notin f_p(\phi_\alpha)$

[24] For the definition of f_p see (VI) in Chapter 5 of this book.

Ignoring condition (iv) for the moment, this says that ϕ clausal quantity im-plicates that, for all the speaker knows, ψ, and, for all the speaker knows, *not* ψ, if and only if ψ is a part of ϕ, but neither ψ nor its negation is entailed by ϕ.

Any set f_c (ϕ) is consistent if every constituent sentence ψ in ϕ is itself consistent. This definition gives us, among others, those im-plicatures first found in examples (40) and (41) and repeated here for convenience.

(58)   *If John sees me then he will tell Margaret.*
(59)   *I don't know that John will see me.*
(60)   *My sister is either in the bathroom or in the kitchen.*
(61)   *I don't know that my sister is in the bathroom.*

More formally, it follows that the set of this class of im-plicatures for otherwise simple disjunctions and conditionals (of whatever type) whose constituents meet (V)'s conditions is as given below:

(62) $f_c (\phi ^\frown or ^\frown \psi) = f_c (if ^\frown \phi ^\frown then ^\frown \psi) = \{P\phi, P\psi, P\neg\phi, P\neg\psi\}$

Condition (iv) of (V) deserves some explanation. What this does is ensure that the im-plicatures are not read from clauses which are already pre-supposed (a "pre-supposition" is a POTENTIAL presupposition) under the definition of f_p given in Chapter 5, page 126. If this condition were not present, then every pre-supposition which was not also an entailment would automatically get cancelled by the system defined in Chapter 6. When a sentence has the same clause in TWO places, one in a pre-suppositional environment and the other not in such an environment, then, assuming the other three conditions apply, this condition generates the relevant im-plicatures despite the presence of the pre-suppositional context. Thus, (63) im-plicates (59), but (64) does not im-plicate (59).

(63)   *If John sees me he will regret seeing me.*
(64)   *If John tells Margaret he will regret seeing me.*

The Gricean argument for the im-plicatures generated by this definition goes as follows. IF one utters a compound or complex sentence having a constituent which is not itself entailed or pre-supposed by the matrix sentence and whose negation is likewise neither entailed nor pre-supposed, THEN one would be in breach of the maxim of quantity if one knew that sentence to be true or false, but was not known to so know, since one could have been more informative by producing a complex sentence having the constituent concerned, or its negation, as an entailment or a presupposition. It follows that, ceteris paribus, the utterance of such a complex sentence implicates that both the constituent sentence and its negation are compatible with what the speaker knows.

This Gricean argument relies on the fact that natural languages provide their users with pairs of sentences of ROUGHLY EQUIVALENT BREVITY which differ only in that in one, one or more constituent clauses are not entailed. This means that strict adherence to the maxim of quantity does not involve violation of the maxim of manner ("Be brief"). If one is in a position to, then one can always utter the stronger and more informative sentence without increasing the length of one's utterance. Here are some examples:

(65) *Since John was there, we can assume that Mary was too.*
(66) *If John was there, we can assume that Mary was too.*
(67) *We know that John was there.*
(68) *We think that John was there.*
(69) *John was there and Mary was absent.*
(70) *John was there or Mary was absent.*

Functions f_c and f_s typically give us several im-plicatures, even from quite simple sentences. Thus (71) im-plicates (72) in virtue of (IV) and implicates (73) and (74) by virtue of (V).

(71) *John believes Margaret to be unfaithful.*
(72) $K\neg$(*John knows Margaret to be unfaithful*).
(73) P(*Margaret is unfaithful*).
(74) $P\neg$(*Margaret is unfaithful*).

The class of verbs that give rise to im-plicatures like (73) and (74) approximates to those called "plugs" in Karttunen (1973a). It includes many verbs of propositional attitude (*believe, think, hope, dream,* etc.) and verbs of saying (*ask, say, tell,* etc.), which have in common that they neither entail nor pre-suppose their complements. This "coincidence" will be shown in Chapter 6 to have some explanatory consequences for Karttunen's own examples. This type of im-plicature was first noted by Sacks (1968), who gives the following example (which I have abbreviated) from a newspaper report (*New York Times* 11 February 1967).

(75) *David Searles returned to the street with his girl and found the car was missing. At first he thought it had been stolen. Then he realized it had been towed away by the police.*

Sacks comments that " 'he realized' stands in opposition to 'he thought', by reference to the fact that 'thought' would be used were it the case that it turned out he was wrong."[25]

[25] Biggs (1976:51) makes the mistake of treating this kind of clausal quantity im-plicature as an entailment. Thus, on his analysis, (i) entails (ii) on both "readings" of (i).

(i)   *Fred still thinks he's married to Oldham's answer to Sophia Loren.*
(ii)   *The speaker of (i) believes that Fred is not married to Oldham's answer to Sophia Loren.*

But this is clearly incorrect in the light of the acceptability of sentences like (iii) and (iv).

(iii) *Fred and me still think he's married to Oldham's answer to Sophia Loren.*

(iv)   *Fred still thinks he's married to Oldham's answer to Sophia Loren and I think so too.*

Under (V) we have that (i) merely im-plicates that it is compatible with all the speaker knows that Fred is not married to Oldham's answer to Sophia Loren. This im-plicature gets cancelled in (iii) and (iv)—see Chapter 6 for an explanation.

4

LOGICAL FUNCTORS

What is the logical form of English sentences containing words like
not, and, or, and *if*? Are such words truth-functionally definable? How?
Which truth-functions are found in natural language? Why? What are the
pragmatic properties of the words that correspond to such functions? The
purpose of this chapter is to provide answers, albeit partial ones, to these
questions. The focus will be on those functors that have most bearing on
the theories of implicature and presupposition espoused in this book.
Accordingly we discuss in turn below NEGATION, TRUTH-FUNCTIONAL
CONNECTIVES, and CONDITIONALS.[1]

Negation

Is Natural Language Negation a Logical Operator?

Cohen (1971) argues, against Grice (1967), that natural language
negation cannot be identified with the truth-functional ⌐. He notes
dialects of English where double negation occurs merely as an emphatic
variant of single negation, thus in such a dialect (1) would have the same
truth conditions as (2).

---

[1] Polish notation is used extensively throughout this chapter because it is the only logical
notation which provides names for all the truth-functional operators and two-place connectives.

(1)   *You won't get no beer here.*
(2)   *You'll get no beer here.*

Similar examples can be drawn from other languages and Cohen lists some. Cohen then puts forward a number of highly implausible straw men in defence of equating natural language negation with ⌐. Not surprisingly, he finds them all unsatisfactory. Two strategies, not considered by Cohen, serve to counter this objection. One is to treat such dialects as having two truth-functionally identical but emphatically different forms of negation: One a single morpheme and the other a pair of morphemes that need not be adjacent.[2] The other strategy, which in effect subsumes the preceding one, is not to identify ⌐ with any surface structure morpheme, but rather with an element of deep structure or of semantic representation. It is no particular syntactic problem to map just one such element into either (1) or (2) using a meaning–preserving rule. As we have noted, "nondetachability" is a feature of Grice's conversational implicatures and so his hypothesis does not concern particular lexical items, but rather any set of lexical items that manifest some one semantic property (e.g., truth-functional negation).[3]

In the absence of any other arguments against identifying natural language negation with some form of logical negation we will assume such an identity.

What are the semantics of natural language negation?

Consider the following familiar sentence:

(3)   *The King of France is not bald.*

Russell (1905) claimed that (3) was ambiguous and could be paraphrased either by (4) or by (5).

(4) $\exists x[King(x)\wedge\neg\exists y[y \neq x\wedge King(y)]\wedge\neg bald(x)]$
(5) $\neg\exists x[King(x)\wedge\neg\exists y[y \neq x\wedge King(y)]\wedge bald(x)]$

Russell's analysis implies that natural language negation is to be identified with a bivalent logical operator, but that the surface manifestation of that operator in such sentences as (3) may obscure its scope.

---

[2] Compare Jespersen (1917:71): "Logically one negative suffices, but two or three in the same sentence cannot be termed illogical; they are simply a redundancy, that may be superfluous from a stylistic point of view, just as any repetition in a positive sentence (*every and any, always and on all occasions,* etc.), but is otherwise unobjectionable." See also the discussion in Palmer (1971:70–71).

[3] Walker (1975:151) makes a similar point.

Strawson (1950) argued against Russell's claim and maintained instead that (3) was unambiguous, and had a paraphrase something like (6). Moreover, he maintained that (3) is neither true nor false when (7) is false.

(6)   *The King of France is un-bald.*
(7)   *There is a King of France.*

Neo-Strawsonians such as Keenan (1972) and Van Fraassen (1969) have formalized the second part of Strawson's position in terms of a trivalent (Keenan) or truth–value gap (Van Fraassen) semantics. Such semantics allow three types of negation operator to be defined:

(8) $N_1\phi$ is true if and only if ϕ is false, and false otherwise.
(9) $N_2\phi$ is true if and only if ϕ is false, and false if and only if ϕ is true.
(10) $N_3\phi$ is true if and only if ϕ is not true, and false otherwise.

Armed with two or more of these definitions the neo-Strawsonian can, if he so wishes, claim that (11) is ambiguous and point to (12) and (13) as "disambiguations" of it.[4]

(11)   *John doesn't regret having failed.*
(12)   *John doesn't regret having failed, because it means he won't have to go into the civil service.*
(13)   *John doesn't regret having failed, because, in fact, he passed.*
(14)   *John sat on the board at the bank.*
(15)   *John failed.*

However, there is even less justification for regarding (11) as ambiguous than there is for regarding (3) as ambiguous. The Russellian ambiguity is merely one of scope, but the neo-Strawsonian ambiguity involves at least two distinct logical operators. We have no independent reasons for believing that all or any of the surface negative morphemes in English are homonymous. Furthermore, since the "ambiguity" claimed for (11) is found in many languages, we would expect some languages to have complementary sets of morphemes manifesting the distinct underlying negation operators. Thus (14) is multiply ambiguous in English because *board* and *bank* are homonyms. But it cannot be translated into French or German, say, and retain this ambiguity. This is unsurprising. But no language, to the best of my knowledge, has two or more different types of

---

[4] Remember that the neo-Strawsonian is committed to the view that (i) is neither true nor false when (15) is false:
(i)   *John regrets having failed.*

negation such that the appropriate translation of (11) could be automatically "disambiguated" by the choice of one rather than the other.

The proponent of a nonbivalent semantics is faced with a dilemma. If he chooses a negation operator which predicts the presupposition in (11), then he loses the ability to account for the possible TRUTH of (13). But if he chooses a negation operator which allows for the TRUTH of (13), then he loses the ability to predict the presupposition of (11), which is what his nonbivalent semantics was introduced to do in the first place.[5] At least one neo-Strawsonian has attempted to escape the dilemma by appearing to deny that (13) could be true: Hausser (1976:253) notes that sentences like (13) are acceptable "under a certain ironic intonation." This observation is beside the point, since (13) is acceptable with other intonations, and since almost any sentence in this book can be pronounced with a certain ironic intonation if one so chooses. However one pronounces it, (13) is a counterexample to any theory—such as Strawson's or Hausser's—which identifies natural language negation univocally with the N_2 operator just defined in (9).

Allwood (1972), Atlas (1975), and Kempson (1975:95–100) have produced a series of arguments which show that natural language negation is unambiguous, and consequently that the Russellian and ambiguity-invoking neo-Strawsonian accounts of sentences like (3) and (11) are equally inadequate. I will not rehearse their arguments here. None of them have, to my knowledge, been challenged in the literature, so we are entitled to assume their validity.

Neither (3) nor (11) is ambiguous: The logical form of each involves a bivalent sentential negation operator having wide scope, thus the logical form of (3) is something like that of (5) (at least with respect to the scope of the negation operator). That (3) presupposes (6) and that (11) presupposes (15) are not semantic facts at all, they are pragmatic facts to be accounted for by the kind of theory provided in the next two chapters. The simplest possible answer to the question "What are the semantic properties of natural language negation?" is also the correct one: The natural language negation operator is that sentential negation operator definable on a standard bivalent semantics.[6]

---

[5] See the discussion in the next chapter.

[6] This discussion is not intended to cover antonym-forming morphemes such as *un-*, or *in-* Clearly (i) and (ii) are not synonymous since (i) entails (ii) but (ii) does not entail (i).

(i)   *The King of France is immoral.*
(ii) *The King of France is not moral.*

McCawley (1972) argues that *not* performs sentence negation and, in the absence of any arguments to the contrary, I have assumed his conclusion throughout the foregoing.

What Are the Pragmatics of
Natural Language Negation?

Although negation in natural language is semantically identical to the of the propositional calculus, it has in addition a pragmatic property that gives negative sentences a status distinct from that of their affirmative counterparts.[7] This makes natural language distinct from languages such as the propositional calculus, where negative and affirmative sentences have exactly the same status.[8] Givón (1975) reports extensive investigation into natural language negation. His work demonstrates, on the basis of data drawn from a number of unrelated languages, that negatives are both restricted in the environments in which they can occur and are quantitatively restricted in their occurrence in permitted environments. He develops a pragmatic explanation for these restrictions based on the following widely shared insight.

> Negative assertions are used in language in contexts where the corresponding affirmative has been mentioned, deemed likely, or where the speaker assumes that the hearer—erroneously—holds to a belief in the truth of that affirmative [Givón 1975:B11].
>
> A negative will not occur unless there is felt to be a possibility of its affirmative being true [Mandel 1974:XIX, 1].
>
> A speaker usually makes an assumption about the beliefs (or apparent beliefs) of his listener when he utters a denial. Specifically, he normally supposes that the listener does or could well believe in the truth of what is being denied [Clark 1974:1312].
>
> A negative statement is appropriate when its affirmative complementary is in some way expected [Allwood 1972:10].

This pragmatic asymmetry between negatives and affirmatives becomes apparent when we examine minimal pairs such as those provided below.

(16)   When John comes, I'll leave.
        ?When John doesn't come, I'll leave.

(17)   She wasn't as fast as he was.
        ?She wasn't as fast as he was not.

(18)   A man came into my office yesterday and . . . .
        ?A man didn't come into my office yesterday and . . . .

[7] See Jespersen (1917:4–5).

[8] There is no necessity for affirmative and negative sentences to have the same status in the propositional calculus. Logicians could abide by the following conventions:

(i)   Every proof must contain at least one negative sentence as a premise.

(ii)   Every compound sentence must contain at least one occurrence of the negation operator.

If they did abide by these conventions, say because they made proofs easier to read, then negative and affirmative sentences would not have the same status.

(19) *I entered, looked around—and near the bar I saw John.*
      ?I entered, looked around—and near the bar I didn't see John.
(20) *And then came John and* . . . .
      ?And then didn't come John . . . .
(21) *There stood a man in front of the house.*
      ?There didn't stand a man in front of the house.

These examples are from Givón (1975), who provides a detailed explanation of the pragmatic peculiarities in these and other negative sentences.[9] In most cases a context can be found in which utterance of the negative sentence would not be anomalous. This shift in acceptability with context shows the anomalies to be pragmatic rather than syntactic or semantic.

Why Do Natural Languages Have a Negation Operator?

There are four one-place truth-functions definable for a language having a bivalent semantics. Their definitions are

T	N	P	Q	Argument
1	0	1	0	1
0	1	1	0	0

Why is that the only one which occurs in natural language is N? Grice's maxims provide us with straightforward answers. The maxim of manner motivates exclusion of T. Because $T\phi \leftrightarrow \phi$, but $T\phi$ is a longer expression than ϕ, use of $T\phi$ in preference to ϕ would involve unnecessary prolixity, which violates the maxim. Furthermore, P and Q are both eliminated by the maxim of relevance. Because $P\phi \leftrightarrow P\psi$ and $Q\phi \leftrightarrow Q\psi$ for ANY sentences ϕ and ψ, it follows that the arguments of such functions are quite irrelevant to the truth valuation of sentences in which they appear. If Grice's maxims capture universal principles of language usage, then it is hardly surprising that no languages have truth–functional operators which would violate those maxims whenever they were used. Use of N will not in general violate any of Grice's maxims. Besides this negative advantage, N can be used to define other operators and connectives in a way which T does not permit. Thus N can be used to define T ($T\phi$ = $NN\phi$), but the converse is not possible. Furthermore, if we add T to a language containing just conjunction and inclusive disjunction, then we

---

[9] For example:

> "Yesterday, upon the stair,
> I met a man who wasn't there.
> He wasn't there again today
> I wish that man would go away."

are no better off. But if we add N to such a language, then we can define all the other connectives and thus increase the expressive power of the language. This fact makes N invaluable in such languages. If the arguments to be given later can be maintained, then it may well be that natural languages are of just this type.

Truth-functional Connectives[10]

The two-place truth-functions are

A	B	C	D	E	F	G	H	I	J	K	L	M	O	V	X	Arguments	
1	1	1	0	1	0	0	1	1	0	1	0	0	0	1	0	1	1
1	1	0	1	0	0	1	0	1	1	0	1	0	0	1	0	1	0
1	0	1	1	0	1	0	1	0	1	0	0	1	0	1	0	0	1
0	1	1	1	1	1	1	0	0	0	0	0	0	0	1	1	0	0

Which English Connectives Are Truth-Functional?

The prime candidates for truth-functional connective status in English are *and* and *or* but Cohen (1971) has argued that meaning differences between them and their logical counterparts cannot be handled by a Gricean pragmatics, but must be treated as semantic properties of the words. These putative semantic properties would render them non-truth-functional. Cohen's argument depends on the use of conditional sentences as counterexamples. This fact wholly undermines it, as I shall demonstrate shortly.[11] Like Cohen, I shall concentrate on the case of *and*.

Cohen argues that (22) could be true but (23) false.

(22) *If the old king has died of a heart attack and a republic has been declared, then Tom will be quite content.*

(23) *If a republic has been declared and the old king has died of a heart attack, then Tom will be quite content.*

On a Gricean account, the temporal order or causality of the events described in the antecedents is only pragmatically implied, and so cannot

[10] This section draws on Gazdar and Pullum (1976), but that paper and this section are, in many respects, complementary.

[11] Walker (1975) also provides counterarguments to Cohen: they differ from mine in that they assume that the Gricean position with respect to indicative conditionals can be maintained. Walker's version of the Gricean position countenances much wider gaps between conveyed and "literal" meaning, and between everyday and technical attributions or truth, than seems methodologically desirable.

affect truth conditions. But, Cohen argues, the sentences differ in their truth conditions, so these implications must be a matter of semantics rather than pragmatics. Consequently the temporal ordering/causality feature of *and* usages has to be built into its dictionary entry.

However, what is going on in these examples has nothing to do with the semantics of *and*, but instead involves the context-sensitive semantics of conditional sentences (see Stalnaker 1968, 1975).[12] Roughly speaking, conditionals like (22) and (23) have their truth conditions assigned relative to a context in the following way: First the antecedent is added to the context and only those changes made to the latter that are necessary for maintaining consistency. Then, if the consequent is entailed by this augmented and modified context, the conditional is true. If it is not entailed, the conditional is false. This account of conditionals explains why they are always "defeasible," that is, one can always add another clause to the antecedent and change the truth value of the resultant. Thus (22) could be changed to (24). It would then appear to have truth conditions more similar to (23) than to (22) despite the difference in conjunct order.

(24)   *If the old king has died of a heart attack and a republic has been declared and the latter event caused the former event, then Tom will be quite content.*

The difference, noted by Cohen, between (22) and (23) can be explained in Gricean[13] terms simply by saying that, GIVEN THE RESPECTIVE IMPLICA-TURES OF THE TWO SENTENCES, one would evaluate (22) in a context in which the king's death preceded the founding of a republic, and (23) in a context in which the king's death followed the founding of a republic. Because (22) and (23) have different implicatures, they will typically be uttered in different contexts. Since the context of an utterance affects the truth-conditions of the English conditional, it is hardly surprising that they appear to have different truth conditions.

Unlike Grice's account, which is not just about the lexical item *and*, Cohen's approach would force him to postulate two completely separate explanations for the following pairs (due to Kempson 1975:56).

(25)   *The Lone Ranger$_i$ jumped onto his$_i$ horse and rode into the sunset.*

(26)   *?The Lone Ranger$_i$ rode into the sunset and jumped onto his$_i$ horse.*

---

[12] See also the discussion of conditionals, below.

[13] Of course, in a strict Gricean account, in which the English conditional was identified with material implication, this response to Cohen would not be available.

(27)   The Lone Ranger$_i$ jumped onto his$_i$ horse. He$_i$ rode into the sunset.

(28)   ?The Lone Ranger$_i$ rode into the sunset. He$_i$ jumped onto his$_i$ horse.

Cohen's argument for the non-truth-functional nature of *or* involves the claim that (29) and (30) have different truth-conditions.

(29)   *If the prize is either in the garden or in the attic, and in fact it is in the attic, the gardener will be glad.*

(30)   *If the prize is in the attic the gardener will be glad.*

It is by no means obvious to my intuitions that these sentences do have different truth conditions. Even if they appear to do so, an alternative explanation to Cohen's—one, along the lines of that just given for (22) and (23), which preserves the truth-functionality of *or*—is available. As Cohen and Grice realize, the equation of all English conditionals with material implication is the weakest part of the general Gricean position although, as Grice demonstrates, some *if . . . then . . .* sentences do have the properties of material implication. If, unlike Grice, we are not tied to a classical view of natural language semantics, then there is no good reason to try and treat all or any conditionals as cases of material implication. At the same time, just because we allow a more complex semantics for *if . . . then . . .* sentences on the basis of rather strong evidence (see the discussion below), this does not entitle us to elaborate the semantics of all the other logical operators on the basis of the arguments presented by Cohen. This is especially so when the apparent deviations of *and* from $\land$ and *or* from $\lor$ are so well accounted for by the Gricean hypothesis.

Apart from *if . . . then . . .*, which is discussed separately later, there are a number of other English words which might appear, at first sight, to have the properties of truth-functional connectives (TFC's hereafter). Closer inspection shows this appearance to be misleading. One such word is *without*.[14]

(31)   *The dike was repaired without the fields being flooded.*

(32)   *The dike was repaired and the fields were not flooded.*

These two sentences seem to have the same truth conditions, so we might suppose that *without* is the TFC L (defined earlier on page 69). However, the syntactic properties of *without* show it to be nothing like a coordinating word linking sentences of equal rank.[15] It is very clearly a

---

[14] The suggestion that *without* might be a TFC is due to Deirdre Wilson (personal communication, 1975).

[15] I owe the syntactic arguments which follow to Geoff Pullum. The syntactic and semantic properties of *without* are complex: my purpose here is only to establish that it is

subordinating expression, making one sentence part of the predicate of another. Consider the following examples:

(33)   *The bomb was tested without the earth was destroyed.
(34)   The bomb exploded without [ ] destroying the earth.
(35)   *The bomb was tested and the earth not being destroyed.
(36)   *The bomb exploded and not destroying the earth.
(37)   The bomb wasn't tested, and the earth wasn't destroyed.
(38)   ?*The bomb wasn't tested, without the earth being destroyed.

Example (33) shows that *without* cannot permit tense in the clause it introduces; (34) shows that *without* defines a context in which Equi-NP Deletion may apply, giving evidence that it introduces a subordinate clause; (35) and (36) show that *and not* has the contrary property of not permitting tenseless second clauses, whether Equi applies or not; (37) and (38) show that in, a true coordinate structure the constituents can take negation independently, but the negation in a *without*-clause is within the scope of negation (or any other operator) on the main clause; the complexity of the negation in (38) seems to render it virtually unintelligible [cf. (40) and the motivation for the principle of confessionality, which follow]. As we would expect there are cases where sentences containing *without . . . not . . .* and *and* have different truth conditions. Consider (39) and (40).

(39)   He is capable of jumping over tall buildings, and she is
         capable of kicking locomotives off the tracks.
(40)   ?He is capable of jumping over tall buildings, without her not
         being capable of kicking locomotives off the tracks.

The semantic difference here is that (39) claims that she can derail trains with her feet, but (40) only claims that it is not necessary for her to be UNABLE to do this trick in order for him to perform his high jump feats. Thus (41) falsifies (39), but not (40).

(41)   She is not capable of kicking locomotives off the tracks.

However $K\phi\psi$ and $L\phi N\psi$ are BOTH falsified by the truth of $N\psi$, so *without* cannot be straightforwardly identified with L.

Can we identify *neither . . . nor . . .* with an underlying X (as in Figure 2) in the structure of English? The answer is no. It is worth noting, first of all, that, contrary to the apparent assumptions of some recent

---

not a coordinating connective. This discussion assumes that the clear syntactic subordination that *without* requires is reflected in semantic representation. Note that where Ross (1967:240) claims that a clearly subordinate structure, namely appositive relatives, have a coordinate remote structure source, he offers syntactic arguments for this claim.

philosophical discussion (Borowski 1976; Halbasch 1975), *neither . . . nor . . .* cannot be used to conjoin sentences in English surface structures:[16]

(42) *Neither Mary will dance nor Tom will sing.*
(43) *Neither will Mary dance nor will Tom sing.*

That negative polarity items are allowed to occur in the clauses of *neither . . . nor . . .* constructions indicates that the negation operator is present in underlying structure.

(44) *Neither Mary nor Tom will budge.*
(45) *Tom would neither lift a finger to help nor contribute a red cent to party funds.*
(46) *Tom neither phoned nor wrote in weeks.*

Examples (44), (45), and (46) give us reason to suppose that the underlying structure of *neither . . . nor . . .* sentences is of the form $NA\phi\psi$, rather than the form $X\phi\psi$. This claim is not controversial: Stockwell *et al*. (1973) provide the necessary motivation and machinery and Klima (1964:265–266) showed that we need a N + *either* incorporation rule anyway in order to relate sentences like (47) and (48).

(47) *Mary won't dance and John won't either.*
(48) *Mary won't dance and neither will John.*

Geis (1973) shows that *unless* is not truth-functional. Apart from conditionals,[17] which are considered elsewhere, there are no other plausible candidates for underlying coordinate TFC's in English. I conclude

---

[16] Huddleston (1976:101) observes that the same restriction applies to *both*:
(i) *Both Mary will dance and Tom will sing.*
(ii) *Both Mary and Tom will dance.*
(iii) *Mary will both dance and sing.*
[17] It is sometimes suggested that *unless = if not*. But this cannot be correct in view of the arguments given by Geis (1973). Note that *unless* does not allow negative polarity items in the clause it precedes
(i) *I'll leave unless you drink a drop.*
(ii) *I'll leave if you don't drink a drop.*
(iii) *Tom was happy unless he had a red cent.*
(iv) *Tom was happy if he didn't have a red cent.*
It has also been suggested by Quine (1941: 16–7) that *unless* corresponds to either inclusive or exclusive disjunction. This is also incorrect in view of the fact that the truth of (v) does not suffice to guarantee the truth of (vi).
(v) *Tom will get drunk and Mary will not be present.*
(vi) *Tom will get drunk unless Mary is present.*
We need to know what would happen if Mary was present in order to be sure that (vi) is true. For a (non-truth-functional) account of *unless* which allows for this, see Geis (1973).

that *and* and *or* are the only ones to be found. In the next section, I consider whether this is an accidental fact about English or whether it follows from more general principles.

Why Do Languages Have the TFC's That They Do Have?

Consider first the implications of some recent work in syntax for the question of what connectives it would be reasonable to expect in the underlying structure of a natural language. A number of linguists have argued (see Pullum 1976b for discussion and references) that underlying structures in syntax are linearly unordered. Evidence that has been cited includes properties of free-word-order languages (Staal 1967), indeterminacy of arguments for verb position in underlying structure (Hudson 1972), mirror-image rules (Peterson 1971; Radford 1975), generalizations about surface order (Sanders 1970) and problems with stating *tough-movement* (Pullum 1976a:203–204). Arguments FOR ordered base structures due to Chomsky (1965) and Bach (1975) are shown to be untenable by Pullum (1976a:199–203).

In the theory of relational grammar[18] developed by Perlmutter and Postal, as in work deriving from it such as Johnson (1974), Cole and Sadock (1976), and Morgan *et al.* (1976), and recent work by George Lakoff and Henry Thompson on cognitive grammars, the nonexistence of linear order in deep syntax is now quite generally assumed.[19] It is also assumed in more semantically-oriented theories, such as natural genera-

---

[18] Matthews (1967), in his critique of Chomsky (1965), presages the two defining characteristics of relational grammar.

> Is it not wiser to treat both hierarchical and SEQUENTIAL "ORDERING" as purely surface concepts? This view of deep syntax would, presumably, lay a much greater stress on . . . collocational RELATIONS. Thus the deep structure of *John came* would be expressed in terms of the Subject-Verb RELATION rather than (and not just in addition to) a relation between "Subject" Noun-phrase and Verb-phrase [p. 149; emphasis added].

[19] The absence of linear order in semantic representation has an important consequence in connection with the derivation of im-plicatures. Consider those that arise from Grice's "Be orderly!" maxim:
(i)   *The old king died and a republic was declared.*
(ii)   *A republic was declared and the old king died.*
If the order of conjuncts is not given in underlying structure, then (i) and (ii) have the SAME semantic representation. The im-plicatures which distinguish them cannot, therefore, be derived from that level of representation, they must instead be read off at a level at which linearization has taken place. Alternatively they can be viewed as constraints on the "process" of linearization itself [Pullum (1976a:207–210) argues that linearization takes place at the end of each cycle]. Compare Chapter 5, footnote 15.

tive grammar (see, e.g., Bartsch and Venneman 1972) and operational grammar (see, e.g., Dahl 1974). Given such an assumption, the most obvious way to handle TFC's is to treat them semantically as functions which take a SET (rather than an n-tuple) of truth-values as their sole argument. McCawley (1972:515)[20] comes very close, informally, to adopting this analysis. He proposes that connectives (which he calls "conjunctions") be "predicated of sets of propositions."

The set of possible arguments $\mathcal{S}$ for set-taking connectives is the set of nonempty subsets of the truth-value set $\mathcal{T}$ ($\mathcal{T} = \{0, 1\}$). This set $\mathcal{S}$ has only three members, as is shown in (49).

(49) $\mathcal{S} = \{\{0\}, \{1\}, \{1, 0\}\}$

The set of definable set-taking truth-functional connectives $\mathcal{C}$ is the set of functions from $\mathcal{S}$ into $\mathcal{T}$:

(50) $\mathcal{C} = \mathcal{T}^{\mathcal{S}}$

$\mathcal{C}$ has only eight members. These are defined as:

A*	D*	E*	J*	K*	O*	V*	X*	Argument
1	0	1	0	1	0	1	0	{1}
1	1	0	1	0	0	1	0	{0, 1}
0	1	1	0	0	0	1	1	{0}

Why do all these not occur in natural language? The answer is to be found among the pragmatic properties of negation in natural languages. Note that a negation operator is an operator which forms a true sentence when its only argument is false.[21] By analogy, we can say that a negative connective is one which will form a true sentence when all its arguments are false. Now there are both linguistic and psychological grounds for predicting that such connectives will not occur in natural language. Givon (1975) documents, at length, the many distributional restrictions on the occurrence of negation operators, these being evidenced in very diverse languages. His pragmatic explanation for these restrictions would lead one to expect that the occurrence, if any, of negative connectives would be even more severely restricted.[22] The work of Garcia (1975:5) points to a similar conclusion:

[20] Gazdar and Pullum (1976) explore in detail an alternative approach to connectives which allows their semantics to be sensitive to the NUMBER of sentences connected although not to their linear order. There is, at present, no motivation for this alternative approach and so it is not considered here.

[21] This specification of negation operators fits, for example, those defined in (8)–(10).

[22] Witness the familiar acceptability paradigm displayed by English tag questions.

(i)   *Your car's outside, isn't it?*

> From an "objective", "grammatical" point of view there is no fundamental differ-
> ence between an affirmative and a negative sentence: a negative sentence merely denies
> what is affirmed in the positive sentence. But in terms of actual communication, for
> *practical* purposes, a negative sentence is, a priori, worth far less than an affirmative
> one.

Working within a psycholinguistic paradigm, Hoosain (1973) and Clark
(1971) have shown that sentences containing negation operators take
much longer to interpret than the corresponding affirmatives.[23] We might
therefore expect the occurrence of negative connectives to pose processing problems. All languages have a negation operator and the effect of
any negative connective can be achieved by using a nonnegative connective within the scope of that operator. Thus it is by no means unnatural to
require a connective to confess to the falsehood of its constituents when
determining the truth value of the whole sentence. I propose to exclude
all connectives which do not, by mean of a principle of CONFESSIONALITY,
which forbids natural languages to have any connective which yields the
value true when all its conjuncts are false. In other words, the principle of
CONFESSIONALITY prohibits negative connectives.

(51)   A connective $c \in \mathscr{C}$ is **confessional** iff $c(\{0\}) = 0$.

Connectives D^*, E^*, V^*, and X^* are not confessional, so our principle
predicts that they will not be found in the logical form of natural language
sentences. Furthermore, Grice's maxim of relevance gives us grounds for
predicting the nonoccurrence of O^*. The argument is exactly analogous
to that given in the case of P and Q earlier.[24] Since $O^*(\{\Box\phi_1\Box, \ldots,$
$\Box\phi_n\Box\}) = O^*(\{\Box\psi_1\Box, \ldots, \Box\psi_m\Box\})$ for ANY $\Box\phi_1\Box, \ldots, \Box\phi_n\Box,$
$\Box\psi_1\Box, \ldots, \Box\psi_m\Box$ whatsoever, it follows that the arguments of this
function are quite irrelevant to the truth valuation of the compound
sentence in which they appear.

If natural language TFC's are set-taking functions and if the principle
of confessionality can be maintained, then only three definable TFC's are
admissible items in the logical form of natural language sentences.[25] One,

---

(ii)   *Your car isn't outside, is it?*
(iii)   *Your car's outside, is it?*
(iv)   **Your car isn't outside, isn't it?*
Only the sentence which negates both clauses is unacceptable—for reasons which almost
certainly have more to do with human psychology than they do with English syntax.
   [23] There is a lot of other psycholinguistic work which bears on this issue, see, for
example, H. Clark (1969, 1974b), Clark and Lucy (1975), E. Clark (1973), Klima and Bellugi
(1973), Wason (1959, 1961), and Wason and Johnson Laird (1972).
   [24] $\Box\phi\Box$ denotes the truth value of ϕ.
   [25] Let us be clear about what is to qualify as a counterexample to this claim. It would
have to be shown that there is some item α in some language such that

K^*, is extremely widespread and corresponds to the most basic use of English *and*. It may be a substantive universal of language if it is taken into account that zero realization is always possible for very basic notions (such as active voice, indicative mood, nonpast tense, singular, third person, and others). Even languages with no overt morpheme for sentential conjunction seem always to have conjunction by straightforward syntactic connection subject to the K^* truth table. Another connective, A^*, corresponding in general to English *or*, is similar widespread, though perhaps not every language possesses a device for directly indicating it. Beja, a language of the Sudan, has no item corresponding to *or*,[26] nor, in general, do Australian languages (see Dixon 1972:361). Whether or not anything corresponding to J^* occurs in natural languages is more problematic—the issue is addressed separately later.

The analysis provided here offers solutions to a number of problems concerning natural language TFC's. Zwicky's (1973) puzzle about why no language has a connective corresponding to the Sheffer stroke (D = *not both . . . and . . .*) is answered: The Sheffer stroke is nonconfessional. The same can be said of the logician's familiar material equivalence E. The analysis eliminates occurrence of McCawley's (1972:540) connective *schmor*, "which yields a true sentence if and only if at least two of its conjuncts are true," because *schmor* cannot be represented as a set-taking function. The difficulty of equating the natural language conditional with material implication is also explained: C is a prohibited TFC for the same reason that *schmor* is. Various testable claims about the internal structures of particular languages arise too. For instance, by claiming that X^* is impossible, the principle of confessionality predicts that English *neither . . . nor . . .* does not appear in logical form and so must be syntactically derived by the incorporation of the negation operator into *either . . . or . . . .* Klima (1964) provided ample syntactic evidence for this source, evidence which has never, to my knowledge, been seriously questioned.[27] It should be noted, in this connection, that Halbasch (1975) gives a formal demonstration that surface structures of the form *neither . . . nor . . .*

(a) α is truth-functional (this excludes *if* and *unless*).
(b) α coordinates (this excludes *without*).
(c) α is present in underlying structure (this excludes *neither . . . nor . . .*)
(d) α does not correspond to A^*, K^*, or J^*

[26] Dick Hudson (personal communication, 1975).

[27] We need morphological rules for negative "agreement" in any case: for example, for dialects that allow multiple negation.
(i)   *He don't never know nothing about nothing*
See also footnote 2 of this chapter.

nor . . . [etc.] CANNOT be handled semantically by associating occurrences of the BINARY connective X. However, both the syntax AND the
semantics of these indefinitely extensible iterated *neither . . . nor . . .*
constructions can be simply and naturally captured by an underlying
representation involving GENERALIZED INCLUSIVE DISJUNCTION inside the
scope of the negation operator. This analysis thus provides a straightforward solution to the problem posed in Halbasch's paper.[28]

Is Exclusive Disjunction Manifested in Natural Languages?

The question of whether morphemes corresponding to EXCLUSIVE
DISJUNCTION occur in natural language is not easily answered because the
pragmatics of INCLUSIVE DISJUNCTION can often make it seem very exclusive, as is predicted by the theory of implicature presented in the last
chapter. The work of Horn (1972) has shown that there is a real pressure
in language against independent lexicalization of notions made redun-
dant by implicature. That is, if uttering $X^\frown\alpha^\frown Y$ regularly conveys in most
contexts the implicature that $X^\frown\beta^\frown Y$, there will tend not to be a lexicalization of β.[29] Horn's results would therefore suggest that exclusive disjunction is unlikely to be lexicalized in a natural language. And, indeed, there
is no clear evidence to the effect that exclusive disjunction has ever been
lexicalized in any language. Latin *aut* is traditionally taken to correspond
to J, but the entry for *aut* in the *Oxford Latin Dictionary* seems not to
back up this claim. Some uses of *aut* that are exemplified there give clear
evidence that the possibility of both disjuncts being true together is not
semantically excluded, and the compilers of the dictionary explicitly note
this. There is no question that pragmatically *aut* was often used to
highlight the stark contrast between alternatives, but this is not the point.
It seems unlikely that a Roman could have been found guilty of perjury
for stating $\phi^\frown aut^\frown\psi$ when he knew that $\phi^\frown et^\frown\psi$ was true (in a situation
where $\phi^\frown vel^\frown\psi$ would not have been counted as a lie). Even with living
languages, informant work on the topic is extremely difficult, because of
the potent pragmatic factors which interact with the semantics of the
connectives: Informants' reports cannot be trusted as reports of the
semantic facts. Eid (1973) attempts to show that Cairene has exclusive

---

[28] This solution has been proposed independently by Borowski (1976).

[29] Horn's principle explains why we don't have a derived lexical item *nand* in natural
languages corresponding to the derived item *neither . . . nor . . .* : $\phi^\frown or^\frown\psi$ im-plicates
$\phi^\frown nand^\frown\psi$. See Horn (1972:261).

disjunction, but his arguments are unconvincing, since he does not recognize the pragmatic factors involved. It has been suggested (Collinson 1948:317) that Finnish *vai* is exclusive disjunction, but according to Karttunen (personal communication) *vai* merely serves to disambiguate alternative questions, and is only found in that context.[30]

Hurford (1974:410–411) has an interesting argument to the effect that there are two *ors* in English, one inclusive and the other exclusive. However, his argument does not succeed, because it rests on the peculiar logical properties of permission–giving utterances and not on there being two truth-functional definitions of *or*. I shall reproduce the relevant part of Hurford's argument and then go on to show where it goes astray.

(52)   The joining of two sentences by *or* is unacceptable if one sentence entails the other; otherwise the use of *or* is acceptable.

(53)   *Inmates may smoke or' drink or" both.*

If the general pattern of *or* characterized in (52) is followed here by *or"*, then we must consider both of the propositions in (54) and (55) are true.

(54)   *Inmates may both smoke and drink* does not entail *inmates may smoke or' drink.*

(55)   *Inmates may smoke or' drink* does not entail *inmates may both smoke and drink.*

If *or'* is taken to be inclusive, then (54) is false, and sentence (53) is incorrectly predicted by (52) to be unacceptable. But if *or'* is taken to be exclusive, then both (54) and (55) are true and (53) is correctly predicted to be acceptable. We therefore conclude that *or'* is exclusive. The semantic effect of the expression *or both* here is to modify an exclusive *or* in order to express inclusive disjunction.

Note first that it is very curious that, if we really have two *ors*, we should need an expression to convert one into the other. But that is a functional argument and incidental to my main points, which are that Hurford is relying on a too-simple view of the logical structure of permission giving utterances, and on an overly strong acceptability constraint on disjunction.

There are two logical complications to the analysis of sentences (53)–(55). First, they contain a modal expression, modal both in the sense of being an English modal verb and modal also in the logical sense of being

<hr />

[30] Gazdar and Pullum (1976) show that the exact nature of exclusive disjunction, if it occurs, is criterial between a set–taking approach to connectives and one which treats their arguments as "occurrence sets (in the terminology of Humberstone 1975)." See footnote 20 of this chapter. See also Borowski (1976), who is only able to reach his nihilistic "language is awfully complicated" conclusion by failing to notice that there might be a pragmatic explanation for the intuitions that he fails to account for semantically.

an intensional operator, and, second, they are nonassertoric. Let me begin by ignoring the second point. For the first point, let μ be an operator such that it combines with a sentence ϕ to form the sentence $\mu\phi$, to be read as *it is permitted that$^\frown\phi$*. Further, let p_0 be the sentence *inmates smoke* and p_1 the sentence *inmates drink*. Then (53) may be represented as (56) or (57), if we assume that both *or'* and *or"* are inclusive.[31]

(56) $(\mu p_0 \vee \mu p_1) \vee \mu(p_0 \wedge p_1)$
(57) $\mu(p_0 \vee p_1) \vee \mu(p_0 \wedge p_1)$

But on any plausible interpretation[32] of the μ operator, none of the entailments given in (58) to (61) can be maintained.[33]

(58) $(\mu p_0 \vee \mu p_1) \Vdash \mu(p_0 \wedge p_1)$
(59) $\mu(p_0 \wedge p_1) \Vdash (\mu p_0 \vee \mu p_1)$
(60) $\mu(p_0 \vee p_1) \Vdash \mu(p_0 \wedge p_1)$
(61) $\mu(p_0 \wedge p_1) \Vdash \mu(p_0 \vee p_1)$

And, in (58)–(61), $\vee$ has its usual inclusive sense. So, pace Hurford, it does not follow that, if *or'* is taken to be inclusive, then (55) is false. Perhaps what is happening here is due to the special properties of permission giving, or to the modal *may*. To test for this, let us replace (53) with an analogous sentence which is clearly both assertoric and nonintensional.

(62)   *John smokes or' drinks or" both.*

Now the analogue of (54), namely (63), is false.

(63)   *John both smokes and drinks* does not entail *John smokes or' drinks*.

If there is any doubt about this, consider (64), which would be contradictory if *or'* was interpreted exclusively.

---

[31] Another possible representation is $\mu(p_0 \vee p_1 \vee (p_0 \wedge p_1))$ but this is not relevant. It is only necessary to show that there is a least one inclusive representation to which Hurford's remarks are inapplicable for his argument to be rebutted.

[32] Although "plausible" interpretations for μ are available in the deontic logic literature, none of them are adequate because a logic of permission cannot be coherently formulated assertorically (see Kamp 1973, 1976 for discussion). Those interested in the "paradox of free choice permission" should consult Von Wright (1969) and Kamp (ibid.).

[33] I take the invalidity of (58) and (59) to be self-evident. In case readers do not immediately see the invalidity of (60) and (61), they should reinterpret p_0 as *inmates attend classes* and p_1 as *inmates have books in their cells* and see whether the putative entailments can be maintained then.

(64)   *John smokes or' drinks all the time, usually concurrently.*

It follows from the falsity of (63) that (52) incorrectly predicts (62) to be unacceptable. Thus (52) must itself be incorrectly formulated. Example (65) provides conclusive evidence that (52) is too strong.

(65)   *Some or all of them were there.*

We can modify (52) to (66).

(66)   The joining of two sentences by *or* is unacceptable if one entails the other but the entailed sentence does not potentially implicate the negation of the entailing sentence; otherwise the use of *or* is acceptable

This modified constraint correctly accounts for the acceptability of (53), (62), and (65) if we assume that any occurrence of *or* potentially implicates the negation of the corresponding conjunction and that *some* potentially implicates *not all* (for defense of these assumptions see the discussion in the previous chapter). It also continues to account, as Hurford's constraint did, for the unacceptability of (67) and (68), since there is no potential implicature in these examples.

(67)   *John is an American or a Californian.*
(68)   *That painting is of a man or a bachelor.*

Hurford's observations, far from constituting counterexamples to a Gricean account of disjunction, actually provide further evidence of its explanatory potential. We are left with no reason to believe, and good methodological reasons for not believing, that English has two homophones *or*, one inclusive and the other exclusive [see Barrett & Stenner (1971) and Pelletier (1977) for further argumentation against an exclusive reading of English *or*].

We have seen that there are two well articulated theories concerning the meaning of the English expression *(either) . . or . .* and its counterparts in other languages. One theory claims that it is ambiguous between inclusive and exclusive disjunction. I shall refer to this theory as the A (ambiguity) theory. The other theory maintains that the expression is unambiguous, having only the inclusive reading: The exclusive "reading" which it appears to have in certain cases is explained by reference to implicature. Is there any data that would allow us to decide between these two theories? It turns out that there is:[34] one theory makes a bizarrely false

---

[34] See also: "Only modus tollendo ponens exists in conventional modus brevis, a fact that suggests that the logic of such expressions, if not that of the whole language, is like classical logic in having inclusive *or* [Sadock 1977:550]."

prediction with respect to cases where the expression occurs within the scope of negation.

Consider (69).

(69)   *John isn't either patriotic or quixotic.*

Note that, for some speakers, negative incorporation applies obligatorily to yield (70).

(70)   *John is neither patriotic nor quixotic.*

This fact has no bearing on the present argument. If we assume the A theory, then there are two possible semantic representations for (69). These are shown in (71) and (72) (where p = *John is patriotic* and q = *John is quixotic*).

(71) $\neg(p \lor q)$
(72) $\neg(p \veebar q)$

Note that two other representations (73) and (74), which appear at first sight to be possibilities, are blocked by the derivational constraint (or its interpretivist inverse) discussed by G. Lakoff (1971a).

(73) $(\neg p) \lor (\neg q)$
(74) $(\neg p) \veebar (\neg q)$

Now (71) is equivalent to (75), and (72) is equivalent to (76).

(75) $(\neg p) \land (\neg q)$
(76) $((\neg p) \land (\neg q)) \lor (p \land q)$

But (76), and hence (72), is true when $p \land q$ is true. Thus the A theory predicts that there is a reading of (69) whose truth is ensured by (77).

(77)   *John is both patriotic and quixotic.*

But (69) has no such reading and the A theory is thereby falsified.[35]

We now have a test for exclusive disjunction. Clearly it should be applied to the relevant morphemes in those languages, such as Cairene, which have been claimed to possess exclusive disjunction. If these languages turn out not to have it, then we will have good grounds for taking (78) to be a linguistic universal.

(78)   No language has an exclusive disjunction morpheme.

More generally, the "negation test" employed above provides a novel way

---

[35] This argument appeared first as Gazdar (1977b). Essentially the same argument has been propounded independently by Pelletier (1977:67).

of deciding between competing AMBIGUITY and UNIVOCALITY PLUS IMPLI-
CATURE accounts of the meaning of particular words or constructions (cf.
Sadock 1978).

The Conditional

We come now to the sticky issues surrounding natural language conditionals. *If . . . then . . .* is another case of an item that fails to meet our
criteria for being a TFC. Fairly clear syntactic arguments could be given
to show that *if* demands subordination.[36] In addition, it seems to fail to
meet the criteria on semantic grounds. The truth table that comes closest
to representing the meaning of *if* is that of C the table on page 69. This
connective is the logician's MATERIAL IMPLICATION. $C\phi\psi$ is equivalent to
$A\psi N\phi$, i.e., $\psi \hat{} or not \hat{} \phi$. However, it is the intuitive reaction of most
speakers that (79) does not have the same meaning as (80), and it appears
that this intuition accurately reflects a semantic distinction.

(79)   *If you have your ankle removed your foot will drop off.*
(80)   *Either your foot will drop off or you will not have your ankle
        removed.*

The question of whether the natural language conditional can be
equated semantically with material implication has been a bone of con-
tention among philosophers for many years. The consensus inclines, at
present, against such an equation, and thus against such defenders of it as
Grice (1967) and Clark (1971). Strawson (1967), Cooper (1968), Stalnaker
(1968, 1975), Young (1972, replying to Clark 1971), Mackie (1973), Lewis
(1973), Harman (1975), Adams (1975), and Downing (1975) are among
those arguing against this equation. Three arguments that seem especially compelling are as follows. First, material implication has certain
properties which make for gross contraventions of our intuitions about
how to reason with *if*. One of the worst contraventions is that the
negation of $C\phi\psi$ entails ϕ. Consider Cooper's examples, given in (81)–
(84).

[36] Bartsch (forthcoming) provides the following pronominal evidence that conditionals
are subordinating rather than coordinating.
(i)   *If he$_i$ wins a car every man$_i$ is happy.*
(ii)   **If every man$_i$ wins a car he$_i$ is happy.*
(iii)   *Every man$_i$ is happy if he$_i$ wins a car.*
(iv)   **He$_i$ is happy if every man$_i$ wins a car.*
(v)   *That he$_i$ wins a car makes every man$_i$ happy.*
(vi)   **That every man$_i$ wins a car makes him$_i$ happy.*
See also Tedeschi (1977:634–636) and citations therein.

(81)   *It is not the case that if the peace treaty is signed, war will be
        avoided. Therefore the peace treaty will be signed.*

This is an impeccable argument if C correctly represents *if*, but speakers
of English would not regard it as such, which casts grave doubts on the C
= *if* thesis.

(82)   *If both the main switch and the auxiliary switch are on, then
        the motor is on. Therefore, if the main switch is on the motor
        is on or if the auxiliary switch is on the motor is on.*

Like (81), (82) would be a perfectly valid argument if we identify *if* . . .
then . . . with C.

(83)   *The function will be held in the main hall, or, if the weather
        is warm enough, it will be held on the green. Therefore either
        the function will be held in the main hall or it will be held on
        the green.*
(84)   *If the new manager is successful, he will be promoted, or, if he
        is not successful, he will be transferred. Therefore the new
        manager will either be promoted or transferred.*

Both (83) and (84) would be examples of fallacious reasoning if we identify
C with *if* . . . *then* . . . . Cooper (1968; see also the references therein)
has many other examples of both types.

   Grice (1967) is aware of examples like (79)–(81) and be attempts to
show that his account of implicature will handle them. However, this
attempt involves the introduction of much unmotivated machinery, such
as a reinterpretation of the notions "true" and "false," a "pointering
principle," and a bracketing device to shift the scope of sentence
operators. This last device allows, though hardly entitles, Grice to treat
(85) semantically as (86), but pragmatically as (87).

(85)   N(*if*⌐φ⌐*then*⌐ψ)
(86)   NCφψ
(87)   ANφNψ

   Even with all this extra machinery, it is not obvious that the account
could be generalized to handle (82)–(84). Grice does not examine examples of this kind. Grice (1967:Lecture V, 10–11) himself notes two powerful counterarguments to his own proposals, of which at least one cannot
be handled by recourse to his special machinery. Given that an adequate
semantic analysis, albeit non-truth-functional, of the conditional is available (and is presented later), and given that Grice's pragmatic treatment is
not demonstrably adequate, it seems methodologically sensible to adopt

the semantic analysis and not encumber one's pragmatic theory with "pointering principles" and bracketing devices.[37]

Notice that the examples given so far are NOT counterfactuals, so they are not subject to the not-so-strict Gricean claim that all conditionals EXCEPT counterfactuals are translatable with C. If we bring counterfactuals into the picture, then the discrepancy becomes even sharper. Consider the following piece of valid C reasoning, due to Stalnaker (1968:106).

(88)   *If J. Edgar Hover had been born a Russian, he would have been a communist.*
        If he had been a communist, he would have been a traitor.
        therefore
        If he had been born a Russian, he would have been a traitor.

Thus transivity fails in counterfactuals, and material implication cannot allow for this. On the other hand it is not plausible to claim that the *if* of counterfactuals is learned as a totally distinct item from the *if* of indicative conditionals. Yet, because of the impossibility of providing an account of counterfactual *if* as C, the proponent of the *if* = C thesis would have to claim that (89) and (90) contain homophonous morphemes *if* with distinct meanings.[38]

(89)   *If yesterday was a Saturday, it was the milkman who rang the bell.*
(90)   *If yesterday had been a Saturday, it would have been the milkman who rang the bell.*

Finally, as McCawley (1974) has pointed out, equating C with *if* gives no basis for explaining why the words *only if* would be used for its converse. If, as seems to be the case, one merely has to know the meaning of *only* and the meaning of *if* to be able to use and interpret sentences like $\phi^\frown only\ if^\frown \psi$, and if analysing *if* as C offers no way of explaining this, then that analysis must be wrong. *If* would appear to have (as argued by Geis

---

[37] This discussion of Grice's views on the conditional may appear rather cursory in the light of the fact that his account of the issue fills two chapters of Grice (1967). However it is noteworthy that these chapters are practically the only part of that manuscript which has not been published and it seems that Grice himself may not be happy with them, especially in the light of the counterarguments to his thesis which he notes there. It would clearly be most unfair to mount a detailed critique of an unpublished manuscript that the author himself was dissatisfied with. Furthermore, the manuscript has numerous typographical errors (e.g., missing negation signs) that make some of the formal arguments opaque or ambiguous. The only other recent defence of the *if* = C hypothesis that I am aware of is Clark (1971) and his arguments are more than than adequately dealt with in Young (1972).

[38] Note that if *if* is homophonous then *if and only if* is four ways ambiguous.

1973) a meaning approximately like the phrase *in the event that* or *in cases in which*. This kind of approach shows a chance of accounting for both the uses that are approximately equivalent in truth-conditional terms to material implication AND the uses, such as the counterfactual use, for which material implication cannot even provide a coherent basis for an analysis.

It is no task of this book to provide a unitary semantic theory of natural language conditionals, but it is worth indicating where such might be found. Unlike the theory propounded in Cooper (1968), which deals only with noncounterfactuals, Stalnaker (1968, developed in Stalnaker and Thomason 1970 and Thomason 1970) provides a uniform treatment of conditionals that subsumes the counterfactuals. Apart from an example of Lewis's (1973:80), whose status as a counterexample is in dispute, I know of no counterexamples to Stalnaker's theory which appears to exactly capture the semantic properties of the English conditional.[39]

In the light of this discussion and the works cited above, we can see that any attempt to identify all occurrences of English *if . . . then . . .* with material implication, with or without implicatures, is doomed to failure. The question then becomes, not "is *if . . . then . . .* equivalent to C?," but "given that we need something more complex than C for *if . . . then . . .* , do we still need to read implicatures off conditionals?." Stalnaker's connective does NOT capture the implicatures of conditionals as he himself (1968:110) recognizes: "There are further rules beyond those set down in the semantics, governing the use of conditional sentences. Such rules are the subject matter of a *pragmatics* of conditionals. Very little can be said, at this point, about pragmatic rules for the use of conditionals."

Lewis (1973:3), whose theory of counterfactuals is closely related to Stalnaker's theory, also notes the residual role of pragmatic factors: "Some or all sorts of presupposition, and in particular the presupposition that the antecedent of a counterfactual is false, may be mere matters of conversational implicature, without any effect on truth conditions." Stal-

---

[39] Stalnaker's system treats $(\phi > \psi) \lor (\phi > \neg\psi)$, where $>$ is Stalnaker's conditional connective, as a tautology. So sentences like (i) come out as necessary truths:

(i)   *If I had a child it would be a son or if I had a child it would not be a son.*

My own intuitions offer no conclusive comment on this example, but some find it counterintuitive to treat (i) as a tautology. However, Stalnaker's system can be modified in the direction of that of Lewis (1973) to eliminate this consequence, but without introducing Lewis's distinction between indicative and counterfactual conditionals. (I owe the substance of these remarks to Hans Kamp.) Stalnaker's system also has the property that if $\Box\phi\Box = \Box\psi\Box = 1$ then $\Box\phi > \psi\Box = \Box\psi > \phi\Box = 1$. This feature of $>$ is, of course, shared by material implication.

naker (1975) offers an account of the pragmatic properties of indicative conditionals in terms of a notion of REASONABLE INFERENCE.

A part of the pragmatics of conditionals is predicted by the apparatus defined at the end of the previous chapter. Since neither the antecedent nor the consequent is entailed by the conditional as a whole, they become subject to definition (V). Thus a conditional of the form $if^\frown\phi^\frown then^\frown\psi$ potentially implicates $\{P\phi, P\neg\phi, P\psi, P\neg\psi\}$. In the case of counterfactuals, the implied falsity of both antecedent and consequent appears much stronger than in indicative conditionals. But this may well not be due to a distinction in the type of conditional, but rather to negative presuppositions set up by the use of the subjunctive in both antecedant and consequent. As will be shown in the next two chapters, presupposition, like implicature, is a wholly pragmatic phenomenon.

There is a sense in which natural language conditionals behave pragmatically rather as we would expect material implication to behave if it occurred. It is this fact, as Strawson (1967) notes, which lends what force there is to Grice's argument for the identity of *if* with C. Imagine that C and M occurred in a natural language. Then the definitions given in a previous chapter predict that utterance of $C\phi\psi$ would, more often than not, implicate that the speaker knows that $NM\phi\psi$, since C and M would lie on a quantitative scale. $NM\phi\psi$ entails $C\psi\phi$ which, taken together with the proposition denoted by the original utterance, entails $E\phi\psi$. Thus (91) below would be expected to imply (92).

(91)   C(*You mow the lawn, I'll give you five dollars*)

(92)   E(*I'll give you five dollars, you mow the lawn*)

But this is exactly the phenomenon (discussed by Geis and Zwicky 1971) know as CONDITIONAL PERFECTION, which occurs with natural language conditionals. Thus (93) strongly implies (94) on most occasions of use.

(93)   *If you mow the lawn I'll give you five dollars.*

(94)   *I'll give you five dollars if and only if you mow the lawn.*

However, given that M does NOT occur in natural language, and given that *if* cannot be identified with C, conditional perfection remains as puzzling as when Geis and Zwicky first drew attention to it.[40] It is worth noting in this connection that Stalnaker's connective collapses into material implication under certain circumstances. This may offer an explanation for at least some of the C-like properties of *if* (see also Stalnaker 1975).

---

[40] But see Böer and Lycan (1973) for an informal Gricean approach to the phenomenon.

5

PRESUPPOSITION

This chapter deals with presupposition. First recent semantic definitions of presupposition are considered and arguments noted or given for their irremediable inadequacy.[1] A number of definitions of pragmatic presupposition which have appeared in the recent literature are listed and it is shown that none are satisfactory, given the nature of the phenomenon they are attempting to describe. Next, the only well-defined pragmatic account of presupposition, apart from the one found in this book, is criticized on methodological grounds and by reference to numerous counterexamples. Arguments and evidence are given in favor of a view which regards simple affirmative sentences as ENTAILING most of their presuppositions. Finally, a function f_p is defined which assigns to each sentence the set of sentences potentially presupposed by that sentence. I shall refer to these potential presuppositions as "pre-suppositions".

So much has been written on presupposition by linguists since the late 1960s that I shall be more cursory in my treatment of the background than in the chapter on implicature. In the course of this debate, there have been two main issues that turn out to be heavily interdependent: One has been whether the notion should be semantically or pragmatically defined, and the other has been the thorny issue of "projection," the problem of how one predicts the presuppositions of complex sentences

[1] Much fuller arguments to the same effect are to be found in Böer and Lycan (1976) and Wilson (1975).

from knowledge of their components. The solution adopted at the end of this chapter involves a trivial "projection" method which, instead of projecting presuppositions only projects POTENTIAL presuppositions. These are then subject to intrasentential and contextual cancellation by the system defined in the next chapter. It will be shown in the course of this chapter that the only potentially viable alternative to this system—the "plugs, holes, and filters" approach of Karttunen—is not, in fact, viable.

Semantic Theories

I shall take the relation between (1) or (2) and (3), and (4) or (5) and (6) as my paradigm cases of presupposition.

(1) *The king of Buganda is asthmatic.*
(2) *The king of Buganda is not asthmatic.*
(3) *There is a king of Buganda.*
(4) *John regrets that he failed.*
(5) *John doesn't regret that he failed.*
(6) *John failed.*

The first three are instances of the type of presupposition discussed by Russell (1905) and Strawson (1950). I have not changed the example gratuitously, but because I do not know if (3) is true, and I assume that most of my readers will be equally ignorant. The second three sentences involve the presupposition of a factive verb, as discussed in Kiparsky and Kiparsky (1970). I do not propose to get involved in fruitless pretheoretical debates as to whether (1), (2), (4), and (5) are true, false, truth-valueless or meaningless when (3) and (6) are false.

The first candidate for a semantic account of presupposition uses entailment (under an assumed bivalent semantics).

(7) ϕ **presupposes** ψ iff
   (i) ϕ entails ψ
   (ii) $\neg\phi$ entails ψ

But, as everyone who has discussed the subject is well aware, this definition will not do because of the reductio proof given informally in (8).

(8) 1. Assume $\neg\psi$
    2. $\neg\phi$ from 1. and (7i) by modus tollens
    3. $\neg\neg\phi$ from 1. and (7ii) by modus tollens
    4. ϕ from 3. by negative elimination
    5. $\phi\wedge\neg\phi$ from 2. and 4.

6. ψ since to assume the contrary leads to
   contradiction
7. Presuppositions are always true given definition (7)

This definition makes it impossible to presuppose anything but tautologies. Clearly, examples (3)˙and (6) are not tautologies, so this definition fails to capture the paradigm cases.

The only way out of this impasse for the proponent of semantic presupposition is to turn to a logic in which modus tollens need not hold. Here the most obvious choice is a three-valued logic. The definition of presupposition remains that of (7), only ENTAILMENT is now a relation for which modus tollens does not obtain: If ϕ entails ψ and ψ is false, then ϕ can either be false or have the third truth value. Horn (1972) adopts this solution in a fairly informal manner and Keenan (1969, 1972) gives a full well-defined presupposition logic, including quantification, based on a trivalent semantics. His definition of logical presupposition is given in (9).

(9) ϕ **logically presupposes** ψ iff ϕ has the third value whenever ψ
         is not true

A somewhat less obvious solution, but one which retains a kind of bivalent semantics, is that of Van Fraassen (1968, 1969, 1971), who introduces the notion of supervaluations, and, concomitantly, truth-value gaps. His definition is given below as (10).

(10)   If ϕ and ψ are sentences of L, then ϕ **presupposes** ψ in L iff,
         for every admissible valuation v of L, if $v(\phi) = T$, then $v(\psi) = T$ and if $v(\phi) = F$, then $v(\psi) = T$

If one admits nonclassical valuations of L, as Van Fraassen does, then this definition provides a nontrivial account of presupposition. I do not propose to go into the technical details of Van Fraassen's system, which are, in any case, well set out in the works referred to, because it can be regarded as a species of three-valued definition and can be shown to be inadequate for the same reasons as the latter. I shall not differentiate between Van Fraassen's account and the three-valued account below except where the distinction is important. The differences between the two accounts would only be of interest if both accounted for all the data and it was a question of choosing between them. In such an event logicians, at least, would choose Van Fraassen's system because it preserves two-valuedness (of a sort).

Proponents of semantic presupposition are forced to postulate an ambiguity in natural language negation in order to simultaneously capture the presuppositions in (2) and (5) and the absence of the relevant presupposition in (11).

(11)   *John doesn't regret having failed, because, in fact, he passed.*

But, as we saw in Chapter 4, there is no independent motivation for treating natural language negation as ambiguous, and there are no grounds for thinking that natural language negation is semantically distinct from the bivalent operator found in the propositional calculus. If negation is univocal, then (11) stands as a counterexample to semantic theories of presupposition.

Even if one grants the semantic account an ambiguity of negation, enabling it to cease treating (11) as a counterexample, it is still inadequate. Detailed and complex argument to this effect is given in Wilson (1975) and I do not propose to paraphrase her work here. Instead I give the summary of her findings.

> Presuppositions of positive simple sentences do not carry over intact to related negatives, or to conjunctions one clause of which is a related negative, or to disjunctions or conditionals in which either the positive simple sentence or its related negative occurs as a main constituent, or to certain types of sentence in which the positive simple sentence or its related negative occurs embedded. It is quite clear that in many cases the predicted presuppositions either do not occur at all or else can be cancelled, suspended, or removed [Wilson 1975:28].

Many examples of the types she mentions will be found in the next chapter, as will a formal explanation of why they behave the way they do.

One major problem with the semantic notion of presupposition is its behavior when modal operators are introduced. Intuitively, (12) and (5) bear the same relation to (6).

(12)   *It is possible that John regrets that he failed.*

But if the relation is supposed to be one of semantic presupposition, it only holds of (5) and (6). Proof that (12) cannot semantically presuppose (6) if the POSSIBILITY operator is taken to be that of S5 can be found in Thomason (1973). The strongest semantic presupposition deducible from (12) is (13).

(13)   *It is possible that John failed.*

This fact is noted by Karttunen (1971), who suggests that semantic presupposition should be redefined along the lines of (14).

(14) ϕ **presupposes** ψ iff $\Diamond\phi$ entails ψ and $\Diamond\neg\phi$ entails ψ

However, this definition cannot be given coherent semantic formulation when we maintain the standard principles which govern the logic of modal operators (the proof is due to Herzberger 1971). This finding is recognised by Karttunen in subsequent work (e.g., Karttunen 1973a:171).

Martin (1975) has shown that a coherent semantic formulation can be given if we employ a four-valued two-dimensional model theory. In the absence of any external motivation for such a nonstandard semantics, it seems to me that this approach collapses under its own weight. As Karttunen (1973a:171) notes, this is a general problem for semantic accounts of presupposition and not just associated with the word *possibly*. Thus both (15) and (16) intuitively presuppose (6), but this will only be predicted of (15) by a semantic account, since (16) neither entails nor presupposes the factive clause.

(15)   *I know John regrets failing.*
(16)   *I hope John regrets failing.*

In the face of this evidence, how might one set about salvaging the semantic account of presupposition? And why would one want to? Let me answer the second question first: Semantic accounts have usually involved well-defined formal systems. The alternative to a semantic account is a pragmatic account and some of those that have been proposed (e.g., Kempson 1975; Stalnaker 1974a) have not been well-defined, nor, consequently, have they been testable in any obvious way. Given the choice between attempting to repair a rigorous system or changing to a less rigorous one, many writers have, not unreasonably, chosen the former. This choice is no longer a real one because there are now two, more or less rigorous, alternative pragmatic accounts, namely that developed by Karttunen and Peters and that developed in this book.

One writer who has retained a semantic account of presupposition is Hausser (1973), who gives the following definition, which assumes a Van Fraassen semantics.

(17) ϕ **presupposes** ψ iff
(i) ϕ is an elementary formula
(ii) ϕ entails ψ
(iii) $not^\frown\phi$ entails ψ

This definition has the effect of simply ruling out all the known counterexamples by fiat, since every counterexample to the semantic hypothesis involves nonelementary formulae. Anyone interested in why such formulae behave the way they do will not find Hausser's definition of the slightest use to them. In a subsequent paper (1976), Hausser addresses himself specifically to the projection problem in the framework of Kleene's "strong type" trivalent logic.[2] Curiously, Hausser appears less

---

[2] The discussion of Hausser that follows is heavily indebted to points made by Lauri Karttunen (personal communication, 1977).

than conversant with the formal properties of this logic and his putative semantic solution to the projection problem suffers as a result. He defines presupposition as follows:

(18) ϕ **presupposes** ψ iff
    (i)   if ϕ is true, then ψ is true
    (ii)   if $not^\frown\phi$ is true, then ψ is true

He then claims that this definition is equivalent to (19).

(19) ϕ **presupposes** ψ iff ϕ has the third value unless ψ is true

This claim is correct: (18) and (19) are provably equivalent if we assume a trivalent semantics and the definition of negation given by Hausser. Given this provable equivalence, it is somewhat surprising to find a footnote later in the paper in which Hausser remarks that "it seems that (18) and (19) are in fact not equivalent [Hausser 1976:269]," as if the question of their equivalence was somehow a matter to be resolved empirically.

Given the Kleene truth tables employed by Hausser, logically compounded sentences NEVER presuppose any of the nontautological presuppositions of their components. Hausser omits to mention this important and nonobvious fact about his theory, although he appears to be aware of it since he implicitly adopts an additional definition of presupposition in order to explain our intuitions about the presuppositions of logically compounded sentences. The nearest he comes to defining this second type of presupposition is the following passage:

> The intuitive phenomenon of filtering is explained over POSSIBLE influence of a component presupposition on the truthvalue of the whole: if a component presupposition has no possible influence on the truthvalue of the whole, then the component presupposition seems intuitively to be filtered; on the other hand, if a component presupposition does have a possible influence on the truthvalue of the whole, then it APPEARS not to be filtered [ibid.:265].

This is regrettably vague, but we may reasonably conclude that if something "appears not to be filtered" then it must "appear to be presupposed" and we can define "appear to presuppose" (a-presuppose) in the light of the previous quotation and other remarks made by Hausser (e.g., "the presupposition seems filtered, BECAUSE ITS FAILURE NEVER RESULTS IN TRUTHVALUELESSNESS [ibid.:264]") as follows:

(20)   A logically compound sentence ϕ **a-presupposes** ψ iff there exist some pair of assignments of truth-values to ψ and the component sentences of ϕ such that this pair differ only in

their assignment to ψ: under one assignment ψ is true and ϕ is not third-valued, and in the other ψ is false and ϕ is third-valued.

Let us see how Hausser uses (18) and (20) to explain the presuppositional properties of compound sentences. Under (18), neither (21) nor (22) presupposes (23).

(21)   *If Jack has children, then all of Jack's children are bald.*
(22)   *If baldness is hereditary, then all of Jack's children are bald.*
(23)   *Jack has children.*

However (22), but not (21), does a-presuppose (23) under (20). This accords with intuition and so, it seems, (20) is the notion of presupposition relevant to natural language (note that anything presupposed under (18) is a-presupposed, a fortiori). But now consider (24), an example which Hausser discusses at length (ibid.:268–269) and which he appears to think provides crucial evidence for his own theory.

(24)   *The liquid in this tank has either stopped fermenting or it has not yet begun to ferment.*
(25)   *In the past, the liquid was fermenting.*
(26)   *In the past, the liquid was not fermenting.*

Under (18), (24) does not presuppose either (25) or (26) but under (20), (24) DOES a-presuppose both (25) and (26) because, as Hausser notes, "both (25) and (26) are component presuppositions with an influence on the truth-value of the compound sentence [ibid.:269]." Hausser has demonstrably failed to provide a solution to the projection problem: definition (18) predicts the absence of an intuitively present presupposition in (22), and definition (20) predicts the presence of intuitively absent presuppositions in (24).

Hausser remarks that it is "interesting question" whether compound sentences in natural language ever have presuppositions which are not presupposed by any of their components. But he does not seem to be aware that his use of Kleene's logic, together with definition (18), predicts that this will GENERALLY be the case. If ϕ presupposes ψ then $\chi \wedge \phi$ presupposes $\chi \rightarrow \psi$, $\chi \rightarrow \phi$ presupposes $\chi \rightarrow \psi$, $\chi \vee \phi$ presupposes $\neg\chi \rightarrow \psi$, etc. If Hausser had realized this then he would have been able to see that the solution to the projection problem induced by Kleene's logic and (18) is very little different to the one he devotes so much space to attacking (namely, Karttunen's "filters"). The two approaches differ only in respect of the predictions they make about presuppositions due to the antecedent of conditionals and the first conjunct of conjunctions. Consider (27)–(29):

(27)   *If all of Jack's children are bald, baldness is hereditary.*
(28)   *Jack has children.*
(29)   *If baldness is not hereditary, then Jack has children.*

Hausser's theory, under (18), predicts that (27) presupposes (29) but not (28). Karttunen's theory predicts that (27) presupposes (28). Clearly Karttunen's approach is to be preferred.

Katz and Langendoen (1976) have claimed that semantic presupposition is not just relevant to natural language, but is, in fact, the only notion of presupposition that is relevant to natural language.[3] Karttunen (1973a) offered two putative solutions to the projection problem for presuppositions. The first putative solution (the Semantic) solution, hereafter) involves: (*a*) categorizing complement-taking verbs as "plugs" or "holes," depending on whether they do or do not block the presuppositions of their complement clauses, and (*b*) treating sentential connectives as "filters" which may or may not block the presuppositions of their component clauses depending on various semantically stated conditions. The second putative solution (the P(ragmatic) solution, hereafter) is the same as the first except that the filter conditions make reference to "sets of assumed facts," that is, they are pragmatic conditions.

Although Katz and Langendoen's paper is presented as if it were a full-blown rebuttal of Karttunen's views, they are, in fact, largely concerned with rejecting the pragmatic aspect of P. They unreservedly adopt a version of S in a manner which might suggest, were the reader not already familiar with Karttunen (1973a), that they had thought of it themselves.[4] Their "formal explication [p. 9]" of Karttunen's "metaphorical notions [p. 3]" amounts to little more than the provision of an alternative notation (heavy parentheses and wipe-out rules) for expressing aspects of Karttunen's S theory. This is nowhere more blatant than in their treatment of "filters," about which they comment: "another explanation is possible . . . we must provide a rule of semantic interpretation that converts holes into plugs [p. 6]." Karttunen, of course, provided rules of exactly this kind—only he called them "filtering conditions."

The notation and terminology used by Katz and Langendoen gives rise to a number of problems.[5] We are told that: "The presuppositions

---

[3] See Rodman *et al.* (1977) for a complementary critique of Katz and Langendoen's paper.

[4] Katz (1977 92 fn. 60) refers to Karttunen's (1973) paper in the following dismissive footnote: "For all the formalism this paper uses, its account of presupposition remains at the descriptive level, using metaphorical notions like "hole," "plug," and "filter" to refer to the phenomena that should be formally reconstructed."

[5] Stanley Peters (personal communication, 1977) has pointed out to me that there are a

associated with an expression in a sentence are not, in general, associated with the complex sentences in which such a sentence appears as a verbal complement, because referentially opaque verbs remove such presuppositions. [p. 2]."

It would be reasonable to infer from this that all verbs that give rise to referential opacity are "plugs." But *regret* gives rise to referential opacity, as is shown by (30) and (31).

(30)   *John regrets that the author of the Waverly novels is Scott.*
(31)   *John regrets that the author of Ivanhoe is Scott.*

(30) and (31) do not have the same truth-conditions. *Regret* is uncontroversially a "hole" (Karttunen 1973a:175; Katz and Langendoen 1976:4). It emerges subsequently that "the sense of 'referential'. . . is different from the standard one in terms of substitutivity of identicals [Katz and Langendoen 1976:3]." There is thus no generalization to be made about "plugs" and verbs which occasion failures of Leibniz's law, contrary to the impression created by the quotation with which this paragraph begins.

More serious is Katz and Langendoen's (1976) generalization about "holes" and factives. They define (p. 4) "holes" as those verbs whose sentential argument is enclosed in heavy parentheses, and they tell us that sentential arguments "will be enclosed in heavy parentheses just in case they are associated with factive predicates [p. 4 n]." From these two stipulations it follows immediately that that the class of factive verbs is identical with the class of "holes." But this conclusion is clearly unacceptable, since there are many "holes" (e.g., *possible, manage*) that are not factive. This problem arises because Katz and Langendoen are using their heavy-parentheses notation to do two distinct jobs. First, it differentiates "holes" from "plugs," and second, it marks predicate arguments which give rise to existential or factive presuppositions. As things stand, (32) and (33) are straightforward counterexamples to their analysis.

(32)   *It is possible that Jack regrets having children.*
(33)   *Jack managed to get the king of France into the cupboard.*

What happens when the parentheses requirements of matrix and

couple of serious technical problems with the heavy parentheses notation. (i) Referentially transparent verbs (in Katz and Langendoen's sense) have somehow to provide heavy parentheses for the object(s) of the verb in the complement when that verb is transitive, but not otherwise. (ii) There appears to be no way to capture counterfactive presuppositions (e.g., those due to subjunctive mood) since there is nothing in the sentence around which heavy parentheses can be put which is such that it corresponds to the presupposition. For the same reason there is no way of representing the presuppositions due to words like *even*.

subordinate sentences conflict? Katz and Langendoen discuss this case, an example of which is given below as (34):

(34)   *Bob believes that Santa Claus came last night.*

The unembedded complement sentence requires heavy parentheses around the argument that stands in subject position, whereas the matrix verb requires that there be no heavy parentheses around the argument that is subject of the complement. The principle that Katz and Langendoen implicitly espouse (ibid.:5) to resolve this dilemma is "matrix wins." So the requirements of *believe* in (34) overrule those of *came* and the existence of Santa Claus is not presupposed by the sentence. But now consider example (35).

(35)   *Bob regrets that Santa Claus does not exist.*

Here *exist* does not provide heavy parentheses round its subject argument, but *regret* requires that they be provided for the subject of its complement clause (ibid.:5). If we apply the "matrix wins" principle to this example, then Katz and Langendoen's apparatus predicts that (35) presupposes the existence of Santa Claus. But it plainly does not. Katz (1977:117) seems to have become aware of problems of this sort and suggests an extension of his wipe-out rule to handle cases of generic complements. In these cases, he proposes a feature [+generic] on the complement that overrules the "matrix wins" principle and wipes out the heavy parentheses provided by the superordinate verb.[6] This delightfully ad hoc innovation will not, unfortunately, rescue (35), since the complement there is not generic.

The main problem that Katz and Langendoen face is that the S theory, as Karttunen demonstrated, is unambiguously refuted by a formidable list of straightforward counterexamples. Why would anyone wish to salvage such a theory? The answer lies in the incompatibility of any available alternative theory (i.e., Karttunen's P theory) with Katz's metatheory of language. Katz and Langendoen (ibid.:9) write as follows:

> Karttunen's argument . . . implies either that grammars can make no predictions about what the presupposition of a sentence is, or that generative grammar must be abandoned in favor of grammars that determine the assignment of properties like presupposition non-formally . . . the issue here between a contextual and a semantic theory of presupposition is part of the larger issue of whether an adequate grammar of a natural language is a formal system.

---

[6] See Nunberg and Pan (1975:415–416) on the inadequacy of Katz's treatment of the presuppositions of generic sentences.

This passage seems to imply that anyone who embraces Karttunen's P theory will be committing themselves to an analysis which either makes no predictions or else is nonformal. There is a sense in which both disjuncts are true but it is not a sense which need worry anyone who does not accept Katzian metatheory. The P theory makes no predictions about the presuppositions of sentences: It is a category mistake to even talk about "the presupposition of a sentence" in this framework. But the P theory DOES make predictions about the presuppositions of utterances (i.e., sentence–context pairs) and these predictions are falsifiable (as will be demonstrated later in this chapter). The P theory is non-formal in Katz and Langendoen's sense, but they are employing "non-formal" to indicate that "something other than the form and arrangement of symbols in strings determines the theory's treatment of its subject [ibid.:15]." In this sense even the most rigorous and mathematically precise model-theoretic semantics is correctly described as "non-formal." As Katz and Langendoen point out in an appendix, Karttunen's version of the S theory is not formal in their sense, since it crucially relies on a semantic entailment relation. They give two examples [given here as (36) and (37)] that show that the two versions of the S theory make different predictions.

(36)   *If it is true that Jack has children, then all of Jack's children are bald.*
(37)   *If Jack has grandchildren, then all of Jack's children are bald.*
(38)   *Jack has children.*
(39)   *Jack has grandchildren.*

Katz and Langendoen's S theory incorrectly predicts that (36) presupposes (38), and correctly predicts that (37) presupposes (38). Karttunen's S theory correctly predicts that (36) does not presuppose (38) but its prediction with respect to (37) is unclear. If (39) is taken to presuppose (38), then Karttunen's S theory correctly predicts that (37) presupposes (38). But if (39) is not taken to presuppose (38), then Karttunen's filters will incorrectly predict that (37) does not presuppose (38).

Unlike Karttunen, Katz and Langendoen do not regard *and* and *or* as filters. They say that "the claim that *and* and *or* result in filtering rests ultimately only on the intuitions of the investigator [ibid.:16]." This is silly. In a theory like Karttunen's, the filters apply to each other's outputs recursively to make predictions about the presuppositions of an infinite set of compound sentences. The defensibility of treating *and* and *or* as filters does not rest on Karttunen's personal intuitions about (40).

(40)   *Jack has children, and all of Jack's children are bald.*

Rather, it rests on the intuitions of readers of Karttunen's papers who can be bothered to invent and evaluate members of the infinite set of sentences to which his conditions apply. One such sentence is (41).

(41)   *If Jack has children and all his children are bald, then either his wife drank hair restorer or his children are monks.*

This rather elementary methodological point should not need to be made.

Katz and Langendoen's only argument against Karttunen's treatment of *and* and *or* runs as follows.

(42)   *Jack has children, and all of Jack's children have children.*
(43)   *Jack and all of Jack's children have children.*

Given these examples, Katz and Langendoen (ibid.:16) present the following argument.

> Suppose that Jack does not have children. On Karttunen's analysis (42) is false and (43) is truth-valueless (fails to make a statement). On our analysis, both (42) and (43) are truth-valueless. Thus (42) and (43), on Karttunen's analysis, cannot have the same logical form; this will force him to give up the generalization that conjoined sentences and their counterparts with conjoined NPs always have the same logical form.

But Katz and Langendoen assume incorrectly that Karttunen's analysis will make (42) false and (43) truth-valueless. Since (43) is usually derived from the same underlying representation as that of (42), via conjunction reduction, and since Karttunen's filters apply to underlying representations, (42) and (43) will both be assigned the value false under his analysis if Jack has no children. Far from conflicting with the generalization they mention, a conjunction reduction analysis actually assumes and exploits it.

"For simplicity [ibid.:16]," Katz and Langendoen only consider examples with *and* in their appendix but, unsurprisingly, clear-cut counterexamples to their approach emerge when we consider *or*.

(44)   *If Jack has children then all of his children are bald.*
(45)   *Either Jack doesn't have children or else all of his children are bald.*

Karttunen's filters correctly predict that neither (44) nor (45) presuppose (38), Katz and Langendoen get (44) right, but incorrectly predict that (45) presupposes (38). Let us be clear what this means: According to Katz and Langendoen's theory, but pace the intuitions of all native speakers of English, (45) has no truth-value when Jack has no children. Note that it is not possible for Katz and Langendoen to hand over counterexamples like (32), (33), (35), (36), and (45) to the pragmatic component of their approach (on which topic, more later). To do so would mean violating Katz's own "anonymous letter criterion" (see Katz 1977:14) for distinguishing semantic and pragmatic facts. Under this criterion, the counterexemplary facts about the presuppositions of (35), (36), and (45) are clearly semantic in character. The presuppositions that Katz and Langendoen's theory predicts that they have are absent EVEN IN THE NULL CONTEXT (e.g., if each sentence was to occur as the whole text of an anonymous letter). In the case of (32) and (33) the presuppositions, whose absence Katz and Langendoen's theory predicts, are present in the null context.

The sympathetic reader of Katz and Langendoen might conceivably think that the issues we have been discussing are minor technical difficulties with the Katz and Langendoen S approach that are resolved in the much fuller treatment which purports to be found in Katz (MS). We are often referred to this work by Katz and Langendoen:

> This is done by Katz (1972, MS) . . . [ibid.:3].
> See further Katz, MS [ibid.:5].
> The definition . . . is spelled out in greater detail by Katz (MS) [ibid.:5].
> Such a rule is proposed by Katz (MS) [ibid.:6].
> Katz (MS) uses HPWR to explain . . . [ibid.:6].
> The details of how we represent this plugging do not concern us here (cf. Katz, MS) [ibid.:7].

Unfortunately for the plausibility of Katz and Langendoen's paper, Katz (MS) has now appeared as Katz (1977). Consider, for example, the "heavy parentheses wipe-out rule," the details of which are crucial to Katz and Langendoen's position. Katz and Langendoen direct their readers to Katz (MS), but the only reference to this rule in the index of Katz (1977) directs the reader to a footnote on page 117. This footnote merely refers the reader. back to Katz and Langendoen's paper.

The reader who is familiar with Morgan (1969), or Karttunen (1973a), but not with Katz and Langendoen's paper, must, by now, be wondering what Katz and Langendoen do about examples such as (46) below, which have justifiably been taken to show that no S-type theory can be maintained.

(46)   *If LBJ appoints J. Edgar Hoover to the cabinet, he will regret having appointed a homosexual.*

To handle this example Katz and Langendoen invoke something called PRAG. PRAG, we are told, is a function from utterances (sentence–context pairs) into sentences, and it is capable of truly amazing things.

Thus it can map utterances such as (47a) and (48a) into (47b) and (48b) respectively.

(47a)   *We have a genius in the White House now.*
(47b)   *We have a moron in the White House now.*
(48a)   *John is here.*
(48b)   *The person named "John Jacob Jingleheimer Smith," who is employed by the Smith and Wesson Company, who is seven feet tall, etc., etc., etc., is at 11:59 a.m., December 31, 1974, at the very center of Times Square in New York City.*

More to the point, it will, we are assured, transform utterances of (46) into (49).

(49)   *If LBJ appoints J. Edgar Hoover—who, as we all know, is a homosexual—to the cabinet, he will regret having appointed a homosexual.*

This is just what is needed, because the additional relative clause in (49) now allows the "heavy parentheses wipe-out rule" to get rid of the presupposition associated with the factive verb in the consequent (we need not worry, anymore than Katz and Langendoen do, about the exact details of how this happens).[7] PRAG, it is claimed, will handle all possible contextual counterexamples to an S theory: "Whenever a Karttunen-type argument for a contextual presupposition C is made . . . then we may recast C in terms of a constituent of the sentence . . . whose reading is the output of PRAG for the appropriate arguments [ibid.:12]." Miraculous. It does not matter, of course, that PRAG is left completely undefined, since "it is not important or possible to specify the nature of the rules comprising PRAG [ibid.:11]."

It's tricky to work out the implications of a theory which does not exist, but let us try. Consider the utterance of (46) in a context in which it is assumed that J. Edgar Hoover is homosexual. If it turns out that LBJ never appoints J. Edgar Hoover or any homosexual to his cabinet, then Katz and Langendoen are committed to maintaining that the sentence actually uttered was truth-valueless and hence not a statement. And yet this truth-valueless nonstatement somehow gets converted into a sen-

---

[7] Actually, we ought to worry, and so should Katz and Langendoen, since, as Stanley Peters (personal communication, 1977) notes, it seems that even (49) will not do the job required of it. The relative clause is nonrestrictive, entailed by the sentence as a whole, and hence out of reach of the hypotheticality induced by the antecedent of the conditional. But without this hypotheticality, no "heavy parentheses wipe-out" can take place.

tence which has a determinate truth-value. Consider also the case of the disjunction whose presuppositional behavior exactly parallels (46).

(50)   *Either LBJ won't appoint J. Edgar Hoover to the cabinet,*
        or else he will regret having appointed a homosexual.

Presumably, in those contexts in which PRAG turns (46) into (49), PRAG will convert (50) into (51).

(51)   *Either LBJ won't appoint J. Edgar Hoover—who, as we*
        all know, is a homosexual—to the cabinet, or else he will
        regret having appointed a homosexual.

But the "heavy parentheses wipe-out rule" will not be triggered in (51), so the unwanted factive presupposition will be retained. Of course, it is open to Katz and Langendoen to claim that PRAG will, in fact, treat (50) in the appropriate way [by converting it into (49) rather than (51)]. And it is equally open to them to claim that PRAG will wash dishes, cure cancer, and solve the riddle of the sphinx.

Apart from the papers by Hausser and Katz and Langendoen considered above, the only other attempt that I am aware of to get a semantic definition of presupposition to cope with the projection problem is Peters (1977). Since Peters' apparatus makes the same predictions as Karttunen's (1974) theory, which is shown to be inadequate later in this chapter, I shall not discuss it separately here except to note that his noncommutative semantics for conjunction and disjunction is incompatible with unordered semantic representation (cf. Chapter 4 of this book).

Pragmatic Definitions

We have considered several semantic accounts of presupposition and shown them to be incapable of handling the projection problem in a satisfactory way. Let us now turn to the various pragmatic accounts that have been proposed. In what follows I shall list all of the recent pragmatic definitions of presupposition that I am aware of and make some critical remarks respecting their potential utility. The earliest approach to definition is due to Stalnaker (1972:387) and Keenan (1971:49). The version of it given in (52) below is largely due to Karttunen (1973a:169–170):[8]

---

[8] The notational conventions respecting variables are suspended for the ensuing discussion of pragmatic definitions. This is partly to increase comparability and partly because I am not sure whether certain of the variables are intended to denote sentences, propositions or statements.

(52)   Sentence A **pragmatically presupposes** a proposition B iff,
        whenever A is uttered sincerely, the speaker of A assumes B
        and assumes that his audience assumes B also.

Stalnaker (1973:448) offers a speaker-based definition of the notion that
would require extension to include the sentence uttered, if it were to be
strictly comparable with (52).

(53)   A speaker **pragmatically presuppposes** that B **at** a given
        moment in a conversation just in case he is disposed to act,
        in his linguistic behaviour, as if he takes the truth of B for
        granted, and as if he assumes that his audience recognizes
        that he is doing so.

Stalnaker (1974:200) develops (53) still further.

(54)   A proposition B is a **pragmatic presupposition** of a speaker
        in a given context just in case the speaker assumes or
        believes that B, assumes or believes that his audience
        assumes or believes that B, and assumes or believes that his
        audience recognizes that he is making these assumptions or
        has these beliefs.

He then goes on to define (in Stalnaker 1974:200) three alternative
relations between sentences or statements and their pragmatic presuppositions.

(55)   Sentence A **pragmatically presupposes** that B just in case
        the use of A to make a statement is appropriate (or perhaps
        normal) only in contexts where B is presupposed by the
        speaker [in the sense of (54)].
(56)   The statement that A (made in a given context)
        pragmatically presupposes that B just in case one can
        reasonably infer that the speaker is presupposing that B [in
        the sense of (54)] from the fact that the statement was made.
(57)   The statement that A (made in a given context)
        pragmatically presupposes that B just in case it is necessary
        to assume that the speaker is presupposing that B [in the
        sense of (54)] in order to understand or correctly interpret
        the statement.

Thomason (1973:6) defines pragmatic presupposition in terms of his
definition of conversational implicature, which I gave as (13) in Chapter
3.

(58)   Sentence A **pragmatically presupposes** a proposition B

relative to a context C if A conversationally implicates B relative to C and ¬A conversationally implicates B relative to C.

Karttunen (1973c:11) defines pragmatic presupposition as follows.

(59)   A **pragmatically presupposes** B **relative to** a set of assumed facts C iff it is not acceptable to utter A in the context of C unless C entails B.

This definition reappears in a slightly different guise in Karttunen (1974:149).

(60   Surface sentence A **pragmatically presupposes** a logical form B, iff it is the case that A can be felicitously uttered only in contexts which entail B.

This is modified again when it appears in Karttunen and Peters (1975:268).

(61)   Sentence A **pragmatically presupposes** proposition B iff it is felicitous to utter A in order to increment a common ground C only in case B is already entailed by C.

These definitions have much in common, not least of which is a propensity to invoke undefined terms. Thus (52) uses "sincerity" and "assumption," (53) uses "disposition" and "recognition," (55) involves "appropriacy," (56) uses the notion of "reasonable inference," and (58) to (61) involve the notion of "acceptability" or "felicity." Apart from this vagueness, which is admitted, there are two main things wrong with (most of) these definitions. The first is that utterances which have a presupposition that clashes with the context are not INFELICITOUS, UNAC-CEPTABLE, INCOMPREHENSIBLE, INAPPROPRIATE, INSINCERE, etc.; they simply lose the presupposition. Thus (62) presupposes (63), but in a context in which an argument about the truth of (63) has finally persuaded the speaker of the falsity of (63), it will not be presupposed.

(62)   *So John doesn't regret killing his father.*
(63)   *John killed his father.*

The standard reply to this is to say that (62) is ambiguous because of two sorts or scopes of negation, but this claim simply fails to capture the fact that (62) presupposes (63) UNLESS the context indicates the contrary. Of course, the corresponding affirmative sentence to (62), namely (64), CAN-NOT have its presupposition—also (63)—cancelled in this way, but then this is simply explained by the fact that (64) also ENTAILS (63). Not surprisingly, one cannot cancel entailments.

(64)   *So John regrets killing his father.*

If this negated example is unconvincing to the diehard "two-sorts-of-negation" presuppositionalist, then observe that exactly the same cancellation may occur in unnegated *before* sentences, as in Heinämäki (1972).

(65)   *John got to safety before the boiler blew up.*
(66)   *John got to the safety handle before the boiler blew up.*

If we assume in (66) that John's getting to the safety handle prevented the boiler blowing up, then (66) does not, but (65) does, presuppose that the boiler blew up. If we treat *before* as being "ambiguous," then we are again left with no principle for deciding whether or not the presupposition attaches to a particular sentence. Note also that, if all presupposing constructions are ambiguous, then the notion of "infelicity" or "unacceptability" is inapplicable, since we will always have an alternative reading with respect to which the sentence will be acceptable.

The second major problem with these various definitions is that they require the presupposition to be already a part of (strictly speaking AN ENTAILMENT OF) the existing context. Most of them stipulate that the presupposition be shared by the addressee. If this is taken seriously, then it rules out any possibility of acceptably communicating new information, however trivial, in presuppositional form. Suppose that I am late for a meeting and I know that the persons at this meeting do not know whether I own a car or am coming by public transport. When I arrive I utter (67).

(67)   *I'm sorry I'm late, my car broke down.*

But this is (under these definitions) unacceptable, infelicitous, or inappropriate. What I should have said, if these definitions are correct, is (68), in which I assert the presupposition before presupposing it.

(68)   *I'm sorry I'm late, I own a car and my car broke down.*

Note also the classic use of factive *regret* to introduce previously unshared information in example (69).

(69)   *Madam, I regret that I must inform you that your son,*
        Captain Rupert Brooke, was killed in action. . . .

Now the proponents of these definitions are aware of examples like (67) and (69), and it is of some interest to note what their reaction is to them. Karttunen's strategy (1974:156) is to say that ordinary conversation is LESS THAN IDEAL and that in real life addressees have to figure out what the context actually was, retrospectively. Stalnaker's strategy (1974:202–203) is to say that speakers PRETEND that their addressee already knows about his presuppositions and that parties to a conversation conspire together to behave AS IF everyone already assumes what has been presupposed. Peters' strategy (1975:131–133) is to argue that strict adherence to the contextual entailment requirement would involve violations of conversational rules concerning brevity and politeness, so conversationalists violate the requirement instead. These strategies have a number of methodologically undesirable features: They involve treating the bulk of the data (i.e., ordinary conversation) as something special, they circumvent any possibility of counterexamples and, concomitantly, they render the inclusion of a notion like "appropriacy" in the definition wholly vacuous. These problems can be completely avoided by dropping the requirement that pragmatic presupposition be ENTAILED by the context in favour of the weaker requirement that they be CONSISTENT with the context. For those unfamiliar with the exact nature of the distinction in semantic terms, I give informal definitions in (70).

(70)   A sentence ϕ is **entailed by** a set of sentences Γ just in case ϕ is true in every possible world in which all members of Γ are true.
A sentence ϕ is **consistent with** a set of sentences Γ just in case ϕ is true in some possible world in which all the members of Γ are true.[9]

Consistency is the basis of the definitions of both implicature and presupposition to be given in the next chapter.

There is a third general objection to the definitions given above, although it is not sufficient in itself to count decisively against them. Curiously enough, it has an analog in the definitions of semantic presupposition, most of which have as a consequence that tautologies are presupposed by every sentence. The problem with unrestricted appropriacy definitions is that there are certain propositions that any sentence at all will have to presuppose in the defined sense. For example the proposition expressed by (71) might be a candidate for one such.

(71)   *The addressee can understand what the speaker is saying*

This might not matter if it weren't for the fact that the definitions no longer have any way to distinguish between the relation between (72) and (71) and the relation between (73) and (71).

[9] Logicians usually use the expression "consistent with" to refer to a syntactically defined relation. The corresponding semantic relation is usually referred to as "satisfiable by." The distinction between consistency and satisfaction is not an issue here and so I have chosen to use the more familiar term throughout.

(72)   *You are the most stupid person I've ever had the misfortune of talking to.*

(73)   *I didn't realize that you can understand what I say.*

Before we leave these definitions, it is worth directing a few remarks specifically towards the definition provided by Thomason (1973) given as (58), which is noticeably different from the others. In addition to the objections raised in the previous chapter to the definition of conversational implicature upon which (58) depends, there are a couple of other points concerning its applicability to presupposition. If, as I shall hope to demonstrate in the next chapter, presuppositions can be cancelled by conversational implicatures, then (58) cannot be right, since we would then have conversational implicatures cancelling conversational implicatures without any basis on which to decide which ones get cancelled. Furthermore, if at least some cases of presupposition are CONVENTIONAL—those arising through a syntactic operation such as "clefting" might be good candidates—then they will fall outside the scope of Thomason's definition, which is based on CONVERSATIONAL implicatures. We will require another separate definition to describe their behavior, even though they appear to behave in exactly the same way as other sources of presupposition.[10]

"Plugs, Holes, and Filters"

The only current pragmatic account of presupposition (apart from the one developed in this book) that begins to come to grips with the projection problem is that developed by Karttunen (1974), referred to as PLC

---

[10] There are cases of pseudo-presupposition generated by conversational implicature. Consider the following examples which I owe to Andrea Howard (personal communication, 1976).
(i)   *One of the two articles was published.*
(ii)   *One of the two articles wasn't published.*
It looks as if (i) and (ii) presuppose (iii) and (iv), since both they and their negations (i.e., (ii) and (i) respectively) imply (iii) and (iv).
(iii) *An article was published.*
(iv)   *An article wasn't published.*
However, the negation test gives a misleading result here. Example (i) entails (iii) and im-plicates (v), which entails (iv).
(v)   *Speaker knows that it is not the case that both articles were published.*
Likewise (ii) entails (iv) and im-plicates (vi), which entails (iii)
(vi)   *Speaker knows that it is not the case that both articles were not published.*
Thus the pseudo–presuppositions are exhaustively accounted for by the notions of entailment and conversational implicature.

hereafter, and Karttunen and Peters (1977), referred to as CI hereafter. In this section I shall show that their proposed solution to the projection problem is defective. In discussing this theory of projection I shall treat CI as definitive and only refer back to PLC if CI leaves some matter unspecified. There are two differences between PLC and CI which need to be noted before we begin. PLC refers to presuppositions as "presuppositions," whereas CI refers to them as "conventional implicatures." I shall follow the PLC terminology. The other difference has to do with the empirical interpretation of the presupposition relation: In PLC the presuppositions of a sentence must be entailed by any context (or "common ground") in which that sentence is used. In CI the presuppositions of a sentence are just non-truth-conditional aspects of the sentence's meaning, which are only required to be noncontroversial in the context of use. The CI interpretation is clearly to be preferred in the light of the discussion in the previous section.

Let me begin by drawing attention to an unexplained and ad hoc component of the PLC–CI projection mechanism, namely the categorization of complementizable verbs shown in (74), which comes from Karttunen (1974:154), that is, PLC.

(74) I. Verbs of saying: *say, ask, tell, announce*, etc. (including external negation).

II. Verbs of propositional attitude: *believe, fear, think, want*, etc.

III. All other kinds of complementizable verbs: factives, semi-factives, modals, one- and two-way implicatives, aspectual verbs, internal negation.

Class I verbs ("plugs" hereafter) block presuppositions due to the complement clause. Class II verbs turn the complement presuppositions into presupposed beliefs of the subject of the matrix sentence. Class III verbs ("holes" hereafter) make all of the presuppositions of the complement into presuppositions of the matrix. Why? "These distinctions . . . presumably follow from the semantics of verb complementation in some manner yet to be explained [PLC:154]." In Peters's (1977) semantic account of presupposition, certain distinctions do indeed follow from the semantics of the verbs in question, but that is of no demonstrable relevance to the pragmatic theory espoused in PLC and CI. Why these three classes should have the properties they are claimed to have is a mystery (actually it is doubtful whether they DO have the properties ascribed to them.)

Equally worrying is the fact that classes I, II, and III are not "natural" classes in any apparent sense. That is, there is no obvious way in which we can predict in which class a verb is going to fall without having recourse to the very phenomena that the classification is supposed to explain. It will not do to say that if the verb is a verb of saying then it is in class I, if a verb of propositional attitude then class II, otherwise class III. For example, verbs of saying used performatively belong to class III, as Peters (1975:130) observes. External negation is NOT a verb of saying, but it IS in class I. *Know* and *be aware that* ARE verbs of propositional attitude, but they are NOT in class II. What class would *maintain* or *conjecture* fall into? The only way to discover is to check out their presuppositional properties.

The observant reader will have noticed that negation appears twice in (74). "External negation" is a plug, whereas "internal negation" is a hole. No rationale is given for this in PLC, and the only negation which figures in CI is treated as a hole. Nevertheless, the necessity for these two negations in the system under discussion is obvious. Negation has to be a hole, otherwise we have no explanation for the fact that presuppositions (usually) survive negation (often taken to be a defining characteristic of presupposition). But there are sentences like (75)–(78) below which show that negation can sometimes block the presuppositions (otherwise these sentences would be contradictory or pragmatically anomalous).

(75)   *John doesn't regret failing, because, in fact, he passed.*
(76)   *Since he doesn't exist, it really isn't possible for the king of France to have seduced your mother.*
(77)   *I don't know that Maria is a secretary.*
(78)   *I am not aware that she is allowed to use that area.*

Semantic theories of presupposition, which abandon bivalence, allow one to define (at least) two distinct types of negation. These are often referred to as "internal" and "external" negation. Such semantic theories claim that negative particles like *not* are ambiguous, and that sentences like (75)–(78) are interpreted on the external reading of *not* (since the alternative, internal, reading would be contradictory). But none of this carries over to the PLC–CI theory since a bivalent semantics is assumed, and even if a nonbivalent semantics was invoked, it could not affect the projection of presuppositions in the sort of framework elaborated in CI. So the claim has to be that the two sorts of negation mentioned in (74) are distinguished, not by their semantics (or their phonetics, phonology, morphology, or syntax either for that matter) but only by their presupposition-projection potential. Note the following points: (i) implicit in this analysis is a radical innovation in linguistic ontology: PRAGMATICALLY AMBIGUOUS LEXICAL ITEMS, and (ii) an ambiguity analysis (semantic

OR pragmatic) fails to explain why the presuppositional reading of negative sentences is always preferred.

Thus the PLC–CI projection theory is faced with a problem. There is no independent motivation for the two types of negation and there are good grounds for not having the two types of negation (see Chapter 4 of this book, pages 64–66), but without two negations the PLC–CI theory has no way to account for the normal cases of negative presuppositional sentences AND for sentences like (75)–(78). Setting up special filtering rules for *because* and *since* to handle (75) and (76) will not help with examples (77) and (78). Note finally that if *not* and *no* are both ambiguous (as they have to be in the PLC–CI theory), then the orthographic sentence which immediately precedes this one has at least 16 possible readings.

If the PLC–CI theory made the correct predictions about the presuppositions of compound sentences of arbitrary complexity, then an unmotivated ambiguity of negation and an ad hoc taxonomy of complementizable verbs would be a small price to pay. However, as I shall show, this is not the case. Expressions like *possibly* and *perhaps* are clearly holes as is shown by examples like (79).

(79)   *Possibly Boris regrets insulting the king of France.*

Their hole status is not in dispute. But there are examples where these holes interact with the PLC–CI filters (= projection rules for conjunctions, disjunctions, and conditionals) and get blocked, contrary to the clear predictions of the PLC–CI approach. Consider the following examples:

(80)   *It is possible that John has children and it is possible that his children are away.*

(81)   *Possibly Boris killed Louis and possibly Boris regrets killing Louis.*

Example (80) does not imply that John has children, and (81) does not imply that Boris killed Louis. These examples are of the form *possibly$^\frown\phi^\frown$and possibly$^\frown\psi$*, where ϕ is a presupposition of ψ. What does the PLC–CI theory do with such examples? To answer the question we need to know that the projection or filtering rule for *and* is as follows.

(82) $\mathscr{P}(\phi^\frown and^\frown\psi) = \mathscr{P}(\phi) \cup \{\phi \rightarrow \chi \colon \chi \in \mathscr{P}(\psi)\}$
        where $\mathscr{P}(\xi)$ is that set which contains all and only the presuppositions of ξ.

From (11), and from the fact that *possibly* is a hole, we may deduce that sentences of the form $possibly^\frown\phi^\frown and\ possibly^\frown\psi$, where ψ presupposes ϕ, themselves presuppose $(possibly^\frown\phi)\rightarrow\phi$. Now the antecedent of this conditional is entailed by the original sentence, so it follows, by modus ponens, that such sentences, taken together with their presupposition, entail ϕ. In other words, the theory predicts that (80) implies that John has children and that (81) implies that Boris killed Louis. This prediction is clearly false. It is not really open to Karttunen and Peters to claim that such sentences actually map into a semantic representation in which there is only a single modal operator outside the scope of the conjunction, since they would then be faced with the job of explaining why (83) and (84) are not synonymous.

(83)　　*It is possible that John has children and it is possible that John is childless.*

(84)　　*It is possible that John has children and is childless.*

Neither PLC nor CI provide a projection rule for *but*, but examples like (85)–(87) show that the conditions have to be the same as those for *and* if the PLC–CI approach is to work at all.

(85a)　　*If John has children and his children are away then we can go and play in his garden.*

(85b)　　*If John has children but his children are away then we can go and play in his garden.*

(86a)　　*If John is at home and his children are away then we can go and play in his garden.*

(86b)　　*If John is at home but his children are away then we can go and play in his garden.*

(87a)　　*If John's children are away and he is at home then we can go and play in his garden.*

(87b)　　*If John's children are away but he is at home then we can go and play in his garden.*

The b-examples behave exactly the same way as the a-examples with respect to the presupposition that John has children. This indicates, unsurprisingly, that *but* would require the projection rule shown in (17), which is equivalent to (ii) with *and* replaced by *but*.

(88)　　$\mathcal{P}(\phi^\frown but^\frown\psi) = \mathcal{P}(\phi) \cup \{\phi\rightarrow\chi\colon \chi \in \mathcal{P}(\psi)\}$

Now consider (89), which is adapted from an example originating in Liberman (1973:350).

(89)　　*Possibly John does not have children but possibly his children are away.*

From (88), and the fact that *possibly* is a hole, we may deduce that sentences of the form *possibly not⌢φ⌢but possibly⌢ψ*, where ψ presupposes φ, themselves presuppose (*possibly not⌢φ*)→φ. And the latter entails φ under any plausible semantics for the possibility operator. So the PLC–CI theory predicts that (89) presupposes something which entails that John has children. Again, this prediction is clearly false. And it cannot be maintained that there is one modal operator with wide scope with respect to *but* in (89), for obvious reasons.

Now consider (90) and (91).

(90) *It's possible that Boris regrets killing Louis and it is equally possible that he didn't actually kill him.*

(91) *It's possible that Boris regrets killing Louis but it is equally possible that he didn't actually kill him.*

According to (82) and (88), these sentences should presuppose that Boris killed Louis. But they do not. Note that the *equally* in the second clause ensures that *possible* does not have wide scope over the connective.

For the purposes of the following discussion, I shall adopt the CI assumption that English indicative conditionals can be identified with translations employing material implication. The assumption is counterfactual, but this does not, I think, have any bearing on the matters under discussion. The CI projection rule for conditionals is the same as that for conjunction.

(92) $\mathcal{P}(if⌢φ⌢then⌢ψ) = \mathcal{P}(φ) \cup \{φ{\to}\chi: \in \mathcal{P}(ψ)\}$

Wilson (1975) has drawn attention to examples like (93), (94), and (95).

(93) *If all Bill's friends have encouraged him, he must have friends.*

(94) *If Nixon knows the war is over then the was is over.*

(95) *If Sartre regrets that Chomsky is alive, I'll be supprised, but if Sartre regrets that Chomsky is dead I'll be amazed.*

Rule (92) predicts that (93), (94), and (95) will presuppose that Bill has friends, that the war is over, and that Chomsky is alive, respectively. But (93), (94) and (95) do not have these presuppositions. Karttunen and Peters devote all of a one-and-a-half line footnote to such examples, concluding with "we find them unconvincing." An even shorter footnote tells us that they are also unconvinced by Reis's (1974) arguments against the asymmetry in their conjunction filter. I am not greatly enamoured of (93)–(95) but, nevertheless, in the absence of any accompanying argumentation whatsoever, I find these footnotes unconvincing. It is open to Karttunen and Peters to change (92) so that it shares the symmetry of the projection rule for disjunctions, for which see (114). But that would involve weakening the predictive power of the theory by necessitating that all the unproblematic examples have their presuppositions restored by conversational implicature. The latter strategy is discussed later.

No amount of tinkering with the asymmetry of (92) will salvage the following example, however.

(96)   *If John murdered his father, then he probably regrets killing him, but if he killed him accidentally, then he probably doesn't regret having killed him.*

Intuitively, (96) presupposes (97), but according to (92)—and via (88)—it can only presuppose (98). The latter, however, is analytic, and hence trivial.

(97)   *John killed his father.*
(98)   *If John murdered his father then John killed his father.*

The following example suffers a similar fate at the hands of (92).

(99)   *If all countries are now republics, then it is unlikely that the president of France still feels lonely.*
(100) *There is a president of France.*
(101) *If all countries are now republics, then there is a president of France.*

Example (99) presupposes (100), but this fact is not predicted by the PLC–CI theory, which only allows (99) to presuppose (101). But the latter is trivially true assuming that all republics have presidents.

Now consider (103) in the light of the contextual assumption noted in (102).

(102) *Speaker and addressee both know that John is a policeman who is always getting drunk, picking fights and having to be dragged off by his colleagues.*
(103) *If John came to the party, then the hostess must have been really glad that there was a policeman present.*

There are (at least) two interpretations of (103) possible in the context described by (102). On one interpretation, which would presumably be appropriate if (103) was uttered ironically, *a policeman* "refers" to John. On the other interpretation *a policeman* "refers" to some other policeman (who, we may assume, would have kept John in check). What is interesting is that it is ONLY on the former interpretation that the presupposition that there was a policeman present (due to factive *be glad that*) gets cancelled. The PLC–CI approach, which is insensitive to the identity of the "discourse referents" set up by indefinite NPs (on which, see Karttunen 1976 for an illuminating discussion) cannot capture this presuppositional difference between the two interpretations of (103). According to (92), (103) invariably presupposes (104), which follows from (102) in any case.

(104)   *If John came to the party then there was a policeman present.*

Recall that the projection rule (92) for conditionals generates conditional presuppositions when the presupposition originates in the consequent. This leads to some remarkably zany predictions, even on seemingly straightforward examples.

(105a)   *If I go to bed with her, then Maria's children get jealous.*
(105b)   *If I go to bed with her, then Maria has children.*
(105c)   *Maria has children.*
(106a)   *If I torture him, Boris regrets laughing at me.*
(106b)   *If I torture him, Boris laughs at me.*
(106c)   *Boris laughs at me.*
(107a)   *If I pull this handle, the explosion is inhibited.*
(107b)   *If I pull this handle, then there is an explosion.*
(107c)   *There is an explosion.*

Intuitively, the a-sentences presuppose their respective c-sentences, but according to the PLC–CI theory they ought to presuppose, not the c-sentences, but the b-sentences. In order to rescue the analysis, CI invokes a notion of conversational implicature to get from the b-sentences to the c-sentences. The argument goes as follows: Presuppositions have to be uncontroversially true, but the only way such conditional presuppositions can be uncontroversially true is if their consequents are true, so one is entitled to infer the c-sentence from the b-sentence. This line of argument does not look too implausible when applied to the one example Karttunen and Peters discuss—given as (110)—or when applied to (106) above. But it looks pretty shaky when applied to (105)—especially if we know that *Humanae Vitae* is Maria's favorite reading. And it is hopeless for examples like (108) and (109) below.

(108a)   *If I scold him, Boris regrets sulking.*
(108b)   *If I scold him, Boris sulks.*
(108c)   *Boris sulks.*
(109a)   *If gold is missing from Fort Knox, then the crooked accountants in the U.S. Treasury will be worried.*

(109b)   *If gold is missing from Fort Knox, then there are crooked
           accountants in the U·S. Treasury.*
(109c)   *There are crooked accountants in the U·S. Treasury.*

Sentences (108b) and (109b) could easily be accepted as uncontroversially
true without there being any need to assume the truth of their consequents. So CI has no explanation to offer for why (108a) and (109a)
presuppose (108c) and (109c) respectively. Even if CI's resort to conversational implicature worked, it would still be a rather unsatisfactory way of
salvaging the theory. Intuitively there is no difference between the relation that (110) bears to (112) and the relation that (111) bears to (112).

(110)   *If the bottle is empty then **John** drinks too.*
(111)   *If **John** drinks too then the bottle is empty.*
(112)   *Someone other than John drinks.*

But according to the CI theory, (111) directly presupposes (112), whereas
(110) presupposes a rather strange conditional sentence from which the
addressee is entitled to infer (112).

   The arguments developed above against the projection rule for conditionals apply equally to the projection rule for conjunctions (the examples
have to be more complex however, since simple unembedded conjunctions entail their factive and existential presuppositions). Thus (113a)
intuitively presupposes (113c), but the projection rule for conjunctions
only allows it to presuppose (113b).

(113a)   *If I go to bed with Maria and her children get jealous, then I
           get to feeling maybe we should call the whole thing off.*
(113b)   *If I go to bed with Maria, then she has children.*
(113c)   *Maria has children.*

   The CI projection rule for disjunction is as follows:

(114) $\mathscr{P}(\phi^\frown or^\frown \psi) = \{\psi \lor \chi: \chi \in \mathscr{P}(\phi)\} \cup \{\phi \lor \chi: \chi \in \mathscr{P}(\psi)\}$

This rule is too weak to get the desired results, so CI again invokes
conversational implicature to infer what is really presupposed (namely χ)
from the disjunctive presuppositions that the rule provides. Putting aside
worries about the methodological desirability of this move, a problem
with (114) arises in connection with CI's very plausible requirement that
presuppositions be noncontroversial. Consider a Hausser–Wilson sentence such as (115B). These sentences are to presupposition theories what
Bach–Peters sentences are to pronominalization theories.

(115)   A: *Hilary is married, I tell you!*
          B: *Rubbish! Hilary is either a bachelor or a spinster.*

According to (114), B's utterance has presuppositions which entail (116), which is equivalent to (117), assuming $(x)[(not\ female(x)) \leftrightarrow male(x)]$.

(116)   ((*Hilary is male*) $\lor$ (*Hilary is a spinster*)) $\land$ ((*Hilary is female*) $\lor$ (*Hilary is a bachelor*))

(117)   *If Hilary is male then Hilary is a bachelor and if Hilary is female then Hilary is a spinster.*

But (117) is just as controversial in the context set up by (115A) as (115B), so how can (115B) presuppose (116) if presuppositions are required to be noncontroversial?

One characteristic shared by every member of the class of plugs—with the exception of "external negation" whose ontological status is, in any case, suspect—is leakage. Indeed, leakage is the norm.

(118a)   *Harry claims that even Fred likes your wife.*

(118b)   *Addressee has a wife.*

(118c)   *Fred is the least likely person to like addressee's wife.*

(119a)   *The repairman didn't tell me that my camera was suitable for color too.*

(119b)   *Speaker has a camera.*

(119c)   *Speaker's camera is suitable for something other than color.*

Intuitively, (118a) presupposes (118b) and something like (118c), and (119a) presupposes (119b) and, on one reading, (119c). But this is not predicted by the PLC–CI theory. On the contrary, the PLC–CI theory clearly predicts that (118a) and (119a) do not have those presuppositions since *claim* and *tell* are both plugs and prevent the presuppositions of the complement becoming presuppositions of the matrix. A footnote to CI tells us that the relation that, for example, (118a) bears to (118c) is one of "generalized conversational implicature," but no argument is given to show how such a "generalized conversational implicature" might arise, nor to show why it should turn out to be identical to the presupposition that the sentence would have had if *claim* had not been a plug. The only grounds that Karttunen and Peters offer for calling the relation one of "generalized conversational implicature," rather than one of presupposition, is the fact that the implication can be cancelled. But that simply begs the question as to whether or not presuppositions are cancellable. A theory that allows presuppositions to be cancelled has no need of plugs.

One might attempt to argue (compare the CI discussion of *criticize*) that the "generalized conversational implicatures" arise in the following way. (i) Speakers conventionally utter sentences whose presuppositions are satisfied. (ii) If we report the utterance of some sentence whose presuppositions are not satisfied then, in view of (i), this fact should be noted. (iii) If the report does not note any unsatisfied presuppositions then, in view of (ii), we are entitled to assume that the presuppositions of the reported sentence are satisfied. This sort of argument, if it works at all, only works for simple affirmative sentences like (118a). It has nothing to say about plugs which leak in conditional, interrogative, modal and negative sentences [e.g., (119a)] and cannot, therefore, be taken seriously. Note that it is not open to Karttunen and Peters to simply reclassify all class I verbs as holes, because then sentences like (120) would be counterexamples to the projection rule for conjunction.

(120)   *Boris claims that his car was given to him by the king of France, but Boris doesn't have a car and there is no king of France.*

The PLC–CI theory, as it stands, provides NO EXPLANATION WHATSOEVER for our intuitions about sentences like (118a) and (119a)—it merely offers us a label for them.

Consider the following examples, due to Karttunen (1971).

(121)   *If I realize later that I have not told the truth, then I will confess it to everyone.*
(122)   *If I discover later that I have not told the truth, then I will confess it to everyone.*
(123)   *If I regret later that I have not told the truth, then I will confess it to everyone.*
(124)   *I have not told the truth.*

If *realize* and *discover* are categorised, along with *regret*, as verbs which presuppose their complements, the PLC–CI theory will incorrectly predict that (121) and (122) presuppose (124). If they are not so categorised then the theory loses the ability to capture the presuppositions of such sentences as (125) and (126).

(125)   *Louis didn't realize that Boris was after him.*
(126)   *If Maria discovers that I am the father of her children, then I shall be ruined.*

A theory that allows presuppositions to be cancelled can escape the horns of this dilemma. Such a theory is discussed in connection with examples (150)–(152) in Chapter 6.

The life expectancy of theories in contemporary linguistics is dramatically low. More often than not they are showing signs of senility at the time they are first announced in an established journal. By these standards, the "plugs, holes, and filters" theory of presupposition projection has had a long and distinguished career. First formulated in 1971, published in 1973, modified and reconceptualized in 1974, and formalized and reterminologized in 1975. But the theory as of 1978 is in poor shape, enmeshed in its own epicycles, beset by counterexamples and constantly in need of "conversational implicatures" to unclog the filters and explain the leakage from its plugs. The time for euthanasia has, at last, arrived.

Entailment

It is one of the claims of this book that simple affirmative factive sentences ENTAIL their complements and that definite descriptions used in simple affirmative sentences ENTAIL the existence of their referent. Thus (127) entails (128), and (129) entails (130).[11]

(127)   *John regrets having killed his father.*
(128)   *John killed his father.*
(129)   *The king of Buganda killed his father.*
(130)   *There is (or was) a king of Buganda.*

This claim is not especially controversial. All semantic definitions of presupposition required the entailment in affirmative sentences, a Russellian treatment of definite descriptions gives one the entailment from (129) to (130) and several recent works (Boër & Lycan 1976; Kempson 1975; Wilson 1975) have argued strongly that the relation between (127) and (128) is one of entailment. Note that this claim can be made neutrally with respect to the issue of whether or not one's semantics is a simple bivalent one, hence the integration of the entailment into nonbivalent presupposition theories. If one proposes to employ modus tollens in proofs, however, then one has to settle for a simple bivalently defined entailment relation. Since, as shown above, nonbivalent semantics cannot offer us an adequate definition of presupposition, I shall take the conservative stance of assuming a bivalent semantics for these entailments and allow modus tollens. On this view, if (128) is false, then it follows that (127) is also false.

---

[11] Böer and Lycan (1976:10), make a distinction between "entailment" and "necessitation," but I am using "entailment" here as cover term which subsumes both relations. This usage seems to me to be quite legitimate in the light of the theorems proved by Van Fraassen (1971:156–159). Böer and Lycan correctly point out that semantic presupposition cannot be defined in terms of entailment when the latter is defined so as to support contraposition. They use "necessitation" to denote an implication relation which does not support contraposition. See the remarks about modus tollens later in this chapter.

Some writers, such as Karttunen, who have embraced a pragmatic definition of presupposition, seem implicitly to have abandoned the entailment relation between affirmative sentences and their presuppositions. This means, I take it, that they would regard (127) as merely infelicitous or inappropriate if used in a context in which (128) was known to be false. I cannot find a clear statement to this effect, so it may be that I am misrepresenting these writers.[12] If I am, then what follows should be seen just as additional arguments for entailment, and not as an attempted refutation of someone else's view. Karttunen (1973c) considers example (131).

(131)   *Jack has children and it is strange that all of them are bald.*

and comments as follows:

> As a factive verb, *be strange* is supposed to have a complement which is presupposed by the superordinate sentence. But our intuitions tell us that the second clause in (131) does not necessarily PRESUPPOSE that all of Jack's children are bald; here it conveys new information. For some reason, factive verbs can, and often are used precisely with that intent in straightforward assertions. It is only in questions, disjunctions and conditionals that they must always carry their presuppositional load [p. 21].

If we allow that factive verbs both entail and presuppose their complements, then we have a straightforward explanation for Karttunen's intuitions about simple affirmative assertions. Since entailments do not (usually) survive embedding in questions, disjunctions and conditionals, but presuppositions (usually) do, we also have an explanation for the distinction Karttunen observes.

If affirmative and negative factive sentences presuppose their complements, but only affirmative ones entail their complements, then we would expect an asymmetry to show up in the acceptability of various kinds of conjoined structure. Exactly such asymmetries do show up— Wilson (1975:25–28) lists some not noted below—but they have not been discussed by proponents of pragmatic theories of presupposition, because they have had no way to explain them. The clearest asymmetry emerges with negative sentences.

(132)   John $\begin{Bmatrix} {}^*has \\ hasn't \end{Bmatrix}$ *stopped beating his wife because, in fact, he never*

beat her at all.

---

[12] In fact, Karttunen (personal communication, 1977) thinks that cognitive factives like *know* do entail their complements, but he is agnostic with respect to emotive factives like *regret*.

(133)   Oedipus $\begin{cases} *does \\ doesn't \end{cases}$ regret killing his father

$\begin{cases} and \\ but \\ although \end{cases} \begin{cases} in\ fact \\ actually \end{cases} \begin{cases} he\ didn't\ kill\ him \\ I\ don't\ know\ that\ he\ killed\ him \end{cases}$.

The proponents of semantic presupposition only had to invoke the supposed ambiguity of negation in order to account for these examples, but this response is not really open to the proponent of pragmatic presupposition, who has no special justification for retaining the nonbivalent semantics which permits two negation operators.

(134)   *For all I know, Oedipus regrets killing his father although, in fact, he didn't kill him.

The unacceptability of this example can be readily explained if we allow the factive to entail its complement. The argument goes as follows. The sentence as a whole—assumed to be a conjunction—EPISTEMICALLY IMPLIES (see the discussion of Grice's quality maxim in Chapter 3) that the speaker knows that Oedipus did not kill his father, because of the second clause, but the first clause, and hence the sentence as a whole, ENTAILS that it is compatible with all the speaker knows that Oedipus did kill his father. These two implications are contradictory, hence the anomaly. (This is an informal rendition of what is a simple proof in epistemic logic.[13]) Correspondingly we expect, and indeed get, no inconsistency and consequent anomaly in (135):

(135)   For all I know Oedipus regrets killing his father, although, in fact, I don't know that he killed him.

If one's empiricist inclinations lead one to go beyond mere intuitive acceptability judgments in favor of "hard" psycholinguistic evidence for claimed asymmetries, then there is no shortage of the latter in this case.

---

[13] Let p be the sentence Oedipus regrets killing his father and q be the sentence Oedipus killed his father, then we may represent (75) as $Pp \wedge \neg q$.

(1)	$K(Pp \wedge \neg q) \in \mu$	counterassumption
(2)	$Pp \wedge \neg q \in \mu$	from (1) by C.K
(3)	$Pp \in \mu$	from (2) by C.&
(4)	$p \in \mu^*$	from (3) by C.P*
(5)	$q \in \mu^*$	from (4) and the fact that p entails q
(6)	$Pp \wedge \neg q \in \mu^*$	from (1) by C.K*
(7)	$\neg q \in \mu^*$	from (6) by C.&

Harris (1974) shows that subjects have a 91% success rate in a comprehension test on the "presuppositions" of simple affirmative sentences, but only a 57% success rate with negative sentences. Forty-one percent of responses to negative sentences were indeterminate, as against less than 9% for the affirmative sentences. A psychological model which claimed that the affirmative sentences entailed their complements, but that the negative sentences only presupposed them, and that maintenance of the presupposition in such sentences was heavily context-dependent would go a long way (if not all the way) toward explaining these findings. Further confirmation for such a model is to be found in Just and Clark (1973), who compared presuppositions and entailments in affirmative and negative sentences.

Klein (1975:B12) argues that the hypothesis that emotive factives like *regret* entail their complements "predicts that the following sentences should be anomalous, since entailments can't be cancelled."

(136)   *Falsely believing that he had inflicted a fatal wound,*
          Oedipus regretted killing the stranger on the road to Thebes.
(137)   *Mary, who was under the illusion that it was Sunday, was*
          glad that she could stay in bed.

Klein comments: "Since they are not anomalous, I conclude that emotives do not entail the proposition expressed by their complement."

However, it is by no means obvious that the entailment hypothesis would predict anomaly in the class of sentences to which (136) and (137) belong. What seems to be happening in such sentences is that the verb of propositional attitude in the subordinate clause delimits a restricted set of worlds (not including the actual world), and it is only with respect to this set of worlds that the verb of propositional attitude in the matrix sentence gets evaluated [cf. (142) and (143)]. The evidence for this is twofold. First, cognitive factives which, as Klein acknowledges, DO entail their complements, can occur in exactly analogous sentences without anomaly.

(138)   *Falsely believing that he had inflicted a fatal wound,*
          Oedipus became aware that he was a murderer.
(139)   *Mary, who was under the illusion that it was Sunday,*
          realized that she could stay in bed.

Second, we find similar examples where the matrix sentence allows definite reference, via noun phrase or sentential pronominalisation into the subordinate clause, EVEN THOUGH the individuals referred to do not exist and the events referred to have not occurred.

(140)   *Oedipus, who (mistakenly) thought he had kidnapped the*
          King of France, locked him in a broom cupboard.

(141)   *Oedipus, who (mistakenly) believed that he had killed his father, deeply regretted it.*

The strange thing about these sentences is that material which is syntactically subordinate appears to be semantically superordinate. However, they do not, of themselves, provide sufficient grounds for arguing that some or all factive verbs do not entail their complements, especially in the light of the examples to be considered shortly.

I have concerned myself above almost exclusively with the presupposition of verbs and done no more than mention definite descriptions. The only class of putative counterexamples to the claim that simple affirmative sentences containing definite descriptions entail the existence of the referent, that I am aware of, are like (142).

(142)   *The Yeti has a thick hairy coat, humanoid feet, and is popularly known as the "abominable snowman," only it doesn't exist.* (said by Himalayan explorer to television reporter)

Example (142) seems to me to be a generic statement akin to (143), which, I take it, would be assigned a truth-value independent of whether or not there were any beavers:

(143)   *The beaver builds dams.*

We have good reason to think that generic statements set up an intensional context (see Bacon 1973), within which existence in the actual world would be irrelevant and so such sentences do not constitute true counterexamples.

It must be noted that I have only been defending the claim that simple affirmative sentences entail their presuppositions in the case of factives, verbs like *stop* and *start*, and definite descriptions. However, the same is fairly obviously true of clefts: since (144) entails and presupposes (145); pseudoclefts: since (146) entails and presupposes (147); and temporal subordination: since (148) entails and presupposes (149).

(144)   *It was Oedipus who killed his father.*
(145)   *Someone killed his father.*
(146)   *What Oedipus wants is ice cream.*
(147)   *Oedipus wants something.*
(148)   *Jocasta cried when Oedipus sang.*
(149)   *Oedipus sang.*

I leave the question of entailment open in the case of the existence presupposition of proper names and quantifiers, and the numerous other sources that generate presuppositions.

Potential Presuppositions

I will define the potential presuppositions of sentences in terms of their components and constructions, as if potential presuppositions were something given to us by the lexicon and the syntax. But I do this without prejudice to the possibility of some future general explanation as to why these lexical and syntactic sources of presupposition are such. Let me now introduce a piece of technical terminology, peculiar to the present enterprise, namely "pre-supposition." A pre-supposition is a POTENTIAL presupposition. Sets of them are assigned to sentences in a completely mechanical way. They are what the presuppositions would be if there was no "projection problem," no "ambiguity" in negative sentences, and no context-sensitivity. A compound sentence has all the pre-suppositions of its components (this is the Langendoen and Savin 1971 projection rule) but may not, of course, presuppose all its pre-suppositions. Even if a given sentence can NEVER on any occasion of use actually presuppose one of its pre-suppositions, this fact in no sense makes the assignment of that pre-supposition to the sentence incorrect: Pre-suppositions are entities whose only role is a technical one in the process of assigning actual presuppositions to utterances. No ontological claims are made in respect of them.

I now define a function f_p which takes a SENTENCE as its argument and yields a SET OF SENTENCES as its value, this set being the set of pre-suppositions. The function is assumed to apply to the sentences of the semantic representation, as in the case of the im-plicature function, but this assumption is not critical. More complex rules could be written so that it could apply to surface structure. For example factive verbs and *before* can take gerundial clauses in surface structure:

(150)   *He doesn't regret **going**.*
(151)   *He washed before **going**.*

But I shall assume that the gerundial clause is a sentence in semantic representation, so that only one rule is required rather than two or three per pre-supposition source.[14] This means, however, that one needs to assume that cleft sentences, such as (152), have a different semantic representation from their corresponding simple sentence, namely (153), although, of course, their truth conditions may be exactly the same.[15]

---

[14] Compare Kiparsky and Kiparsky (1970:356), who would derive both (150) and (i) from the same source.
(i)   *He doesn't regret that he went.*

[15] Thus one might postulate that (i), (ii), and (iii) were the semantic representations (in relevant respects) of (iv), (v), and (vi), respectively.   (*Continued on page 125*)

(152)   *It was John who went.*
(153)   *John went.*

This assumption runs contrary to some theoretical inclinations, but is perfectly compatible with Montague grammar, for example. In any event, the issue is peripheral to the matters in hand and anyone sufficiently motivated can rewrite the rules to suit their own theoretical prejudice.

In defining f_p I take the notions "noun phrase" and "sentence" for granted and assume that they are well-defined on whatever formal language is employed for the semantic representation.

Let F be a set of cardinality n, where n is some small finite number and where F is to be regarded as the set of all the subfunctions required to tap the various sources of sentential pre-suppositions. Among the members of F will be f_1, f_2, f_3 defined as follows:[16]

(154) $f_1(\phi) = \{\psi : \psi = K\chi . \phi = X^\vee v^\vee that^\vee \chi^\vee Y\}$[17]
       where v is a factive or semifactive verb, ϕ and χ are
       sentences, and X and Y are any strings, possibly null.

According to (154), (155) pre-supposes (156) (for the use of K in these formulae, see the list of symbols and typographical conventions, pages xiii–xv):

(155)   *Oedipus regrets that Jocasta drinks.*
(156)   *Speaker knows that Jocasta drinks.*

(i)   *wants(Sam,Fido)*
(ii)   λx[*wants(Sam, x)](Fido)*
(iii)   λx[*wants(x,Fido)](Sam)*
(iv)   *Sam wants Fido.*
(v)   *What Sam wants is Fido.*
(vi)   *It is Sam who wants Fido.*
The pre-suppositions of (v) and (vi) could be read off straightforwardly from (ii) and (iii). Note that if it can be shown that clefts and pseudoclefts are NOT distinct in semantic representation, then we would have reason to suppose that pre-suppositions have to be read off at MORE than one point in a derivation. The pre-suppositions due to contrastive stress might also lead one to this conclusion.
(vii)   **Sam** *wants Fido.*
(viii) *Sam wants* **Fido.**
   [16] I am not seriously proposing that sentences of semantic representation contain items like *that*, *there*, and *is*. They appear in the definitions partly to increase perspicuity and partly because it is not obvious to me what should stand in their place. Note also that I am ignoring complications introduced by tense.
   [17] This is insufficient, since most factives also presuppose that the subject of the matrix sentence knows the complement to be true; for some examples see (139)–(149) in Chapter 6.

(157) $f_2(\phi) = \{\psi{:}\psi = K\chi.\phi = X\widehat{}the\widehat{}\alpha\widehat{}Y.\chi = there\ is\ a\widehat{}\alpha\}$
where $the\widehat{}\alpha$ is the longest string, having that occurrence of
the as its initial element, which is of category noun phrase,
ϕ and χ are sentences and X and Y are any strings, possibly
null.

According to (157), (158) pre-supposes (159):

(158)   *The king of Buganda drinks.*
(159)   *Speaker knows that there is a king of Buganda.*
(160) $f_3(\phi) = \{\psi{:}\psi = K\chi.\phi = X\widehat{}before\widehat{}\chi\widehat{}Y\}$
where ϕ and χ are sentences and X and Y are any strings,
possibly null.

According to (160), (161) pre-supposes (162):

(161)   *Oedipus drank before he married his mother.*
(162)   *Speaker knows that Oedipus married his mother.*

Obviously one can go on and define f_4, f_5, f_6, etc. for all the other sources
of pre-suppositions but, as far as I can see, this is a theoretically trivial
task[18] and I do not propose to pursue it here. Given a definition for every
$f \in F$ we may now define f_p as follows:

(VI) $f_p(\phi) = \bigcup\limits_{f \in F} f(\phi)$ for any sentence ϕ

This definition requires no additional projection clause for the
pre-suppositions of compound or embedded sentences, because the individual functions in F operate without respect to the complexity of the
sentence they apply to. Thus, for example, the result of applying f_p to
(163) will be a set which includes, inter alia, the sentences listed under
(164).

(163)   *Before the headwaiter left, I attempted to ensure that the*
         king of Buganda realized that the restaurant was closed.
(164)   *Speaker knows that there is a headwaiter.*
         Speaker knows that there is a king of Buganda.
         Speaker knows that there is a restaurant.
         Speaker knows that the headwaiter left.
         Speaker knows that the restaurant was closed.

Since I have not spelled out the precise membership of F, I list below
some examples of pre-supposition types which I assume to have appro-

---

[18] Except in the case of presuppositions arising from words like *even*. See Karttunen and
Peters (1977) for an elegant formulation of the function required.

priate functions in F. This is not a closed list, since I would expect the formal system defined in (VII) to (XXI) in the next chapter to have a rather wider scope. Conversely it may turn out that certain of the pre-supposition types listed below may not be capable of treatment by it, in which case they should be removed from the scope of F.

(165)   PROPER NAMES
John wasn't at the party.
John exists.

(166)   CLEFT CONSTRUCTIONS
It wasn't John who went.
Someone went.

(167)   ASPECTUAL VERBS
John didn't stop working.
John was working.

(168)   PSEUDO-CLEFT CONSTRUCTIONS
What Oedipus wants is not his mother.
Oedipus wants something.

(169)   ITERATIVES
John didn't go again.
John had been.

(170)   QUANTIFIERS (but cf. Karttunen 1975:51-54)
All dodos can eat grass.
Dodos exist.

These examples will have to suffice, because one could fill a whole chapter with pre-suppositional types—Karttunen (n.d.) lists THIRTY—and their respective exponent expressions. All that is required for f_p to be well-defined is for F to be such that for each $f \in F$ there is some definition along the lines of (154), (157), or (160). One subfunction that might be expected to appear in F, but which does not, is one for the "uniqueness presupposition" of definite descriptions. Any pre-supposition is liable to cancellation, but it appears that the "uniqueness presupposition" cannot be cancelled. Horn (1972:27) has pointed out the unacceptability of sentences such as (171)–(173).

(171)   *The King of France isn't bald, if indeed there is only one.
(172)   *The King of France isn't bald, but there may be several.
(173)   *It is not true that the senator of America is a fascist, there are one hundred of them.

The only apparent exceptions I know of to this claim involve either generic constructions, as in (174),

(174)   *The London M.P. is fat, stupid, and middle–aged, and there*
          are about fifty of them.

or anaphoric reference to a unique entity, where such exists, as in (175).

(175)   *If there is only one of them, then the Emperor of Rome must*
          be very powerful.

The explanation for the peculiar behaviour of the "uniqueness presupposition" is perhaps to be found in Hawkins (1978). He argues that the
definite article specifies a set consisting of every member of some pragmatically given set. When the noun is in the singular, this pragmatically
given set must be a singleton, hence the "uniqueness" effect. Unfortunately, this quick presentation cannot do justice to his arguments. All
that needs to be noted here is that the "uniqueness presupposition" falls
outside the scope of the presuppositional machinery developed in this
chapter and the next.

As remarked above, the formulation of the members of F involves
certain assumptions about the nature of the semantic representation. It
may be that some versions of the latter would permit a more economical
f_p in which certain potentially distinct members of F collapse. One,
hypothetical, example would be that of aspectual verbs like *stop* that, on a
lexical decomposition analysis, might well turn out to have *before* as the
operative constituent component in semantic representation. Other good
candidates for a single collapsed rule are clefts, pseudoclefts and wh-
questions, all of which share a pre-supposition which is arrived at, more
or less, by extracting the wh-clause and substituting the appropriate
existentially quantified phrase for the wh-phrase within it.

6

PROJECTION AND
CONTEXTUAL CHANGE

The Theory Defined

This chapter begins by presenting the formal system that, given an utterance, tells us what that utterance implicates and presupposes. The central sections of the chapter consist of examples, mostly counterexamples to other theories drawn from the literature, together with proofs that the system defined correctly predicts their implicatures and presuppositions. The chapter concludes with a reconstruction, within the theory, of Stalnaker's notion of sentence meaning.

A presupposition and implicature assignment device Π is a 6-tuple:

(VII) $\Pi = \langle f_c, f_s, f_p, D, W, [\ ] \rangle$

f_c, f_s, and f_p are the im-plicature and pre-supposition functions defined in Chapters 3 and 5, respectively. D is the set of all sentences of the semantic representation of English. W is the set of all possible worlds. We define the set J of propositions as the power set of W:

(VIII) $J = \mathscr{P}W$

We could elaborate on the analysis and take sets of propositions as our working unit to allow formal coverage of interrogative sentences and indirect questions (see Hamblin 1973), but although this elaboration is technically simple, it is of interest in the case of only one or two types of example and its main effect would be to make the notation that much less perspicuous. [   ] is a function from D into J and is to be understood as the semantic interpretation function for the language D that assigns to each sentence a proposition, namely the set of possible worlds in which that sentence is true. Such functions are available for the semantic representations of various fragments of English (see, e.g., those in Groenendijk and Stokhof 1976, Montague 1974, Partee 1976, Thomason 1976).

We define a consistency predicate, "con," on sets of propositions as follows.

(IX)   con X iff $\cap X \neq \Lambda$

I will adopt the convention of writing inc X for $\neg$ con X. Next we define a set of M of contexts:

(X) $M = \{X : X \subseteq J \cdot \text{con } X\}$

Thus, contexts are sets of propositions constrained only by consistency. Treating context here as a set of propositions makes no theoretical claim and is intended as no more than a technical convenience: we could have treated context as a single proposition, as a sentence, or as a set of sentences, but any of these alternatives would have complicated the definitions to be given shortly. The consistent sets of propositions that comprise contexts are to be interpreted as the unique speaker's own "commitment slate" in the sense of Hamblin (1971:136). No provision is made in the system as defined for stipulations about interaction (e.g., that one may not presuppose propositions which would render some other participant's commitment slate inconsistent), though these could be incorporated straightforwardly if a Hamblin–style dialogue model was elaborated to include the present treatment of implicatures and presuppositions.

We are now in a position to define a set E of possible utterances as follows:

(XI) $E = N \times D \times M$

where N is the set of nonnegative integers, where for all $e \in E$, $e = <n, d, m>$ whose members will be referred to as e_0, e_1, and e_2 respectively, and which may on occasion, be superscripted with the number of the utterance (i.e., $e_0^n = n$). This notational procedure is due to Hamblin (1971:131). The superscript convention will be used both for the utterance number given by e_0 and also, as a notational convenience, for the example number used in the text to index the sentence. [In the latter case, of course, (XVIII) will not apply.]

Each utterance, then, is a triple consisting of the sentence uttered (e_1), the sequential position (e_0) at which it occurred, and some set of propositions representing the context (e_2). Essentially this is the Bar-Hillel (1954) view of an utterance as the ordered pair of a sentence and a context, only here context has been split into two components: an integer and a set. This specification is sufficient for the purpose at hand and is offered without prejudice to the other indices that might be needed for other purposes (e.g., ones for speaker and adressee, as in Chapter 2). In fact, the specification is more than we need for the purpose of cancelling the im–plicatures and pre–suppositions of a single sentence. For these two phenomena, the integer index for sequential position is irrelevant; it is included here to allow the inductive definition of succeeding conversational contexts, given in (XVIII).

We adopt the following abbreviatory definitions to give us, for each utterance in E, the sets of propositions corresponding to the sets of clausal and scalar im-plicatures and pre-suppositions deriving from the sentence uttered.

(XII) $e_c = \{x : x = [\phi] \cdot \phi \in f_c(e_1)\}$ for all $e \in E$

(XIII) $e_s = \{x : x = [\phi] \cdot \phi \in f_s(e_1)\}$ for all $e \in E$

(XIV) $e_p = \{x : x = [\phi] \cdot \phi \in f_p(e_1)\}$ for all $e \in E$

We saw, in Chapter 3, that when a speaker asserts a sentence ϕ he is, in effect, committed to KNOWING THAT ϕ under Grice's maxim of quality. If we continue to exclude nonassertoric speech acts from our domain of enquiry, we can capture this fact by defining a new context of utterance (e_u), which consists of the union of the old context (e_2) and the speaker's knowledge of the sentence uttered (Ke_1):

(XV) $e_u = e_2 \cup \{[Ke_1]\}$ for all $e \in E$

We move now to the single most important definition in the present theory, which can be usefully glossed as a formal rendition of the slogan "all the news that fits."

(XVI)[1]   The **satisfiable incrementation** of a set of propositions X by a set of propositions Y $(X \cup !Y)$ is defined as follows (for all $X, Y \subseteq J$):
$X \cup !Y = X \cup \{y : y \in Y \cdot (Z \subseteq X \cup Y)[\text{con}(\{y\} \cup Z) \leftrightarrow \text{con } Z]\}$

If the definitions that follow are to be properly understood, the reader will need a good intuitive grasp of what (XVI) does. $X \cup !Y$ is the union of X with a set that consists of all those members of Y that can be added to X

---

[1] Strictly speaking we do not need the biconditional here, since con $(\{y\} \cup Z) \rightarrow$ con Z for all y and Z.

without ANY RISK of an inconsistency arising. Any member of Y which is a necessary component of some inconsistent subset of $X \cup Y$ is excluded from $X \cup !Y$.

Here are some examples of the way $\cup!$ operates:

(1) $\{[\phi], [\psi]\} \cup !\{[\chi]\} = \{[\phi], [\psi], [\chi]\}$
(2) $\{[\phi], [\psi]\} \cup !\{[\neg \phi], [\chi]\} = \{[\phi], [\psi], [\chi]\}$
(3) $\{[\phi], [\psi]\} \cup !\{[\phi \rightarrow \neg \psi], [\chi]\} = \{[\phi], [\psi], [\chi]\}$
(4) $\{[\phi], [\psi]\} \cup !\{[\phi \rightarrow \neg \chi], [\chi]\} = \{[\phi], [\psi]\}$
(5) $\{[\phi], [\psi]\} \cup !\{[\phi \rightarrow \pi], [\chi], [\neg \pi]\} = \{[\phi], [\psi], [\chi]\}$

This notion of SATISFIABLE INCREMENTATION allows us to capture formally the context-sensitivity of both implicature and presupposition. ONLY those im-plicatures and pre-suppositions which are satisfiable in the context of utterance actually emerge as the implicatures and presuppositions of the utterance. The "process" is complicated by the fact that the incrementation is ORDERED: Clausal im-plicatures are added to the context first, then scalar im-plicatures and finally pre-suppositions. This ordering plays a part in the explanation of the data discussed below, but it is not itself explained. We define the new context e_U that results from utterance of a sentence e_1, as follows:

(XVII) $e_U = (\,(e_u \cup !e_c) \cup !e_s) \cup !e_p$ for all $e \in E$

The initial context is, to all intents and purposes, taken as primitive in the apparatus just given, but contexts need not be as unspecified as this makes it appear. If, in the interest of simplicity, we continue to restrict ourselves to a world in which there is a single speaker producing a monologue consisting entirely of assertions, and if we also assume that, once this monologue is under way, no additions are made to the context except through the monologue itself, then we can provide an inductive clause for giving us the context for each successive utterance after the first:

(XVIII) $e_2^{n+1} = e_U^n$

This is, of course, a gross oversimplification allowed by the restrictive assumptions made above. However, it should be possible to see that these assumptions could be removed and the consequences of their removal built into the clause in a plausible manner. Given commitment slates for each participant in a dialogue, we could provide a rule to augment them all in the manner shown in (XVIII) UNLESS the immediately succeeding utterance questioned or contradicted some part of the increment. Such elaborations, though readily definable (see Hamblin 1970:253–282, 1971), are not pertinent to the matters in hand, however.

Formal pragmatic definitions for quantity implicature and presupposition follow straightforwardly from (XVII):

(XIX)   A proposition x is a **quantity implicature** of an utterance e
         iff $x \in e_U \cap (e_c \cup e_s)$

That is, an utterance e QUANTITY IMPLICATES a proposition x if and only if (i) the sentence uttered quantity im-plicates some sentence which denotes x, and (ii) x belongs to the context which results from the utterance.

(XX)   A proposition x is a **presupposition** of an utterance e iff x
         $\in e_U \cap e_P$.

That is, an utterance e presupposes a proposition x if and only if (i) the sentence uttered pre-supposes some sentence which denotes x, and (ii) x belongs to the context which results from the utterance.

I shall refer, indifferently, to a pre-supposition as having been CANCELLED, SUSPENDED or FILTERED OUT when $\phi \in e_P$ but $[\phi] \notin e_U$ for some e. Analogously with im-plicatures. Given the restrictive assumptions noted above, we can also readily define the CONVERSATIONAL CONTRIBUTION of an utterance.

(XXI)   The **conversational contribution** of an utterance e^n is that
         proposition $cc(e^n)$ such that
         $cc(e^n) = W \sim (\cap e_2^n \sim \cap e_2^{n+1})$

That is, the conversational contribution of an utterance e is that proposition which consists of all possible worlds EXCEPT those that have both the following properties, (i) they were included by ALL the propositions in the context of utterance e_2, and (ii) they are each excluded by at least one proposition (not necessarily the same one in each case) in the context that results from the utterance.

Hiz (forthcoming) has independently proposed a rather similar definition to (XXI) which, in my notation, would go as follows

(6) $cc(\phi, \Gamma) = Cn(\{\phi\} \cup \Gamma) \sim Cn(\Gamma)$

where ϕ is the sentence uttered, Γ is a set of background assumptions and Cn is an operator that closes sets under a syntactically defined notion of logical consequence. Carnap and Bar-Hillel (1952:229) proposed a definition of this form for the relative amount of semantic information of a sentence ϕ with respect to a sentence ψ [written $In(\phi/\psi)$].

(7) $In(\phi/\psi) = In(\phi \wedge \psi) \sim In(\psi)$

If the utterance is a tautology (i.e., $[e_1^n] = W$) that has no im-plicatures and no pre-suppositions then clearly $\cap e_2^n = \cap e_2^{n+1}$ and no conversational contribution is made (i.e., $cc(e^n) = W$). However, tautologies can carry implicatures and presuppositions, so they do have a potential conversational contribution to make. Thus, if the context allows it, the sentence given in (8) will have [9] as an implicature (inter alia) and [10] as a presupposition.

(8)   *The Senator for Wisconsin either is or is not a communist.*

(9)   *It is compatible with all the speaker knows that the Senator for Wisconsin be a communist.*

(10)   *The speaker knows that there is a Senator for Wisconsin.*

If the sentence uttered entails, presupposes, and implicates no more than was already present in the context, then again $\cap e_2^n = \cap e_2^{n+1}$ and no conversational contribution is made by the utterance.

Searle (1969:124–125) discusses the conversational contribution made by the utterance of sentences like (8), but does not offer any explanation for the phenomenon apart from attributing it to the introduction of "new and rather weak kinds of illocutionary force," Gordon and Lakoff (1971:70) offer the "conversational postulate" given in (11) as an explanation for Searle's observation.

(11)   SAY(a, b, P OR Q) → (ASSUME (a, POSSIBLE (P)) AND ASSUME (a, POSSIBLE (Q)))

However, in view of the contextual defeasibility [see (28)] to which this implication is liable, the apparent use of material implication in (11) is quite inappropriate. The postulate also suffers both from being essentially an ad hoc condition on one class of compound sentence and from assuming the demonstrably unworkable performative hypothesis (see Chapter 2). The explanation for Searle's observations which is implicit in definitions (I) through (XXI), suffers from none of these defects.

Wilson (1975:137) has attacked a hypothetical cancellation account of presupposition as follows.

> It would be natural for a pragmatic presuppositional analyst to respond that there are cancelling mechanisms of either an implicit or explicit nature, and that when such cancellations take place the presupposition must be regarded not as violated, with resulting infelicity, but simply removed, with no resulting defects at all. My reply to this would be that . . . this places him in a totally unassailable position, since there are no conceivable counterexamples which cannot be handled by such machinery.

At first sight, her remark appears to be a substantive objection to cancellation theories of presupposition in general, and one which must be met by any proponent of such a theory. Since the device defined in this chapter is readily seen to constitute such a theory it requires defense against the charge of vacuity.

First, the ordering built into the cancellation procedure (entailments BEFORE implicatures BEFORE presuppositions) makes a strong empirical claim. Any case where a presupposition could be shown to have cancelled an im-plicature would constitute a counterexample to the theory. Any case where either an im-plicature of a pre-supposition failed to be cancelled by an entailment would constitute a counterexample to the theory. Any case where a pre-supposition failed to be cancelled by an implicature would constitute a counterexample to the theory. Second, the involvement of the notion "context" in the cancellation process does not allow the analyst to use it as he chooses to explain any case. Thus, given an inductive clause for successive contexts along the lines of (XVIII), we get clear-cut and falsifiable predictions concerning im-plicature and pre-supposition cancellation in succeeding utterances.

Thus it can be seen that Wilson's objection, appropriate as it may be to informal remarks about presupposition suspension, does not apply to the cancellation theory presented here.

Implicature Projection

Consider the following examples.

(12)   *Some of the boys were there.*
(13)   *Not all of the boys were there.*
(14)   *Some of the boys, in fact all of them, were there.*

Examples (12) and (14) both im-plicate K(13), but utterance of (14), unlike (12), can never implicate [K(13)]. That (12) and (14) im-plicate K13 follows straightforwardly from the definition of f_s given in (IV). The formal explanation for the behavior of utterances of (14) is marginally more complex, so I present in (15) an abbreviated proof.

(15)   i. $[K(13)] \in e^{14}_s$ by (IV) and (XIII)
        ii.   inc $\{[(13)],[(14)]\}$ by inspection
        iii. inc $\{[K(13)], [K(14)]\}$ from ii.
        iv. $[K(14)] \in e^{14}_u$ by (XV)
        v. $[K(13)] \notin e^{14}_U$ by (XVI) and (XVII)

A similar proof can be given for Grice's (1967:23) example of intrasentential im-plicature cancellation, given here as (16).

(16)   *I saw Mrs. Smith trying to cash a check at the bank at noon*
        today, and I have not the slightest doubt that she succeeded.

Likewise the following example, discussed in Chapter 3 as example (46).

(17)   *The roots of these attempts, indeed successes, by Congress to*
        reassert itself . . . are well known to Mr. Ford.

The fact that clausal im-plicatures get added to the context before
scalar im-plicatures has an interesting consequence for a certain class of
sentences. Consider (18)–(20).

(18)   *John did it or Mary did it.*
(19)   *John did it or Mary did it or both of them did it.*
(20)   *John did it and Mary did it.*

Although (18) and (19) are truth-functionally equivalent, only (18) which
can have the pragmatic exclusive disjunction interpretation induced by
the scalar im-plicature $K\neg(20)$ in the manner discussed in Chapter 3,
example (57). Example (19) never has this interpretation, because the
scalar im-plicature $K\neg(20)$ is inconsistent with the clausal im-plicature
$P(20)$ arising from the final clause under definition (V). Rule (XVII) has
the effect of excluding the scalar im-plicature in favor of the clausal one.
The same intrasentential cancellation is involved in the second of the
following examples.

(21)   *Some of the students were there.*
(22)   *Some, if not all, of the students were there.*
(23)   *All of the students were there.*

Examples (21) and (22) have the same truth conditions, but (22), unlike
(21), will not carry the scalar implicature $[K\neg(23)]$, because this is inconsistent with the clausal implicature $[P\neg\neg(23)]$ induced by the antecedent
of the conditional under (V). Predictably, (24) and (25) behave in a similar
fashion.

(24)   *John or Mary did it, if not both.*
(25)   *Some, or all, of the students were there.*

The preceding paragraph shows, in a rather striking manner, that the
CONVERSATIONAL CONTRIBUTION (under XXI) of two materially equivalent
sentences, uttered in the same context, may be quite different. Of course
we all know this intuitively, but the system defined above explains, for a
restricted range of data, how this comes to be the case. Note that I am
assuming, both here and elsewhere in this book, that sentences like (25)
decompose into something like (26) in semantic representation.

(26)   *Some of the students were there or all of the students were*
        there.

This assumption is not critical, but it makes the formulation of the
definitions a great deal less complicated than if some contrary assumption
were made.

So far we have only considered cases where an im-plicature is prevented from becoming an implicature because it is inconsistent either
with an entailment of the sentence or with an implicature of the utterance. There are also cases where im-plicatures are prevented from being
implicatures by the previously established context. This is most readily
shown using preceding discourse as the context, as in the examples
below.

(27)   1. *All of the cats talk.*   assumption
                  2. *If some of the cats talk,*
                      then dogs are unhappy.   assumption
                  3. *Some of the cats talk.*   from 27.1

therefore,

                  4. *Dogs are unhappy.*   modus ponens from
                                                           27.2, 27.3

Statement (27.3) im-plicates that the speaker knows that not all of the cats
talk (by IV), but this im-plicature is cancelled by its consistency with the
context, which, at (27.3), includes [K(27.1)], which was registered in the
context initially by reference to (XV) and then retained in it by the
inductive clause (XVIII). The following example is analogous.

(28)   1. *Cats talk but dogs don't.*   assumption
                  2. *If either cats or dogs talk,*
                      then I'll eat my hat.   assumption
                  3. *Cats talk.*   from 28.1
                  4. *Cats or dogs talk.*   from 28.3

therefore,

                  5. *I'll eat my hat.*   modus ponens
                                                           from 28.2, 28.4

Here (28.4) im-plicates (inter alia) that it is compatible with all the speaker
knows that dogs talk, but this im-plicature is cancelled by the preceding
context established initially by (28.1). These examples may seem artificial,
but the principles involved are completely general, as is illustrated by (29).

(29)   *Mrs. Smith has three children.*

Now (29) im-plicates that the speaker knows that Mrs. Smith does not have more than three children (any number greater than 3 will precede 3 on the quantitative scale in which 3 appears), but there are plausible situations in which this im-plicature will get contextually cancelled. Imagine that we are discussing the eligibility of each of a group of women for welfare benefits and that we know of each how many children she has (Mrs. Smith, for example, has five). If one of the welfare benefit eligibility criteria is having three children, then one could utter (29) in such a discussion without having been heard as implicating that Mrs. Smith did not have more than three children. Lakoff (1975:272–273) discusses a similar example to (29) in terms of his notion of "context-dependent entailment," but his treatment does little more than relabel the phenomenon, whereas ours offers a well-defined account of the im-plicature cancellation process.

Lauri Karttunen (personal communication) has drawn my attention to the fact that scalar implicatures, as defined, are language dependent in an interesting way. This is because the quantitative scales crucially depend on the lexical items available in the language. For example, consider truth-functional connectives. If a language has just conjunction and inclusive disjunction, then use of the latter, as we saw in Chapter 3, will typically be heard as exclusive. The couple $\langle \wedge, \vee \rangle$ constitutes the only relevant scale, $\varphi \vee \psi$ im-plicates $K \neg (\phi \wedge \psi)$, and $K \neg (\varphi \wedge \psi)$ and $\varphi \vee \psi$ together entail $\varphi \bar{\vee} \psi$. However, if any language were to have just conjunction and BOTH inclusive and exclusive disjunction, then the present theory predicts that use of the inclusive will never implicate the exclusive. This accords with Gricean commensense: Why use the inclusive to express the exclusive when the language is equipped to express the latter directly? Such a language would give rise to TWO relevant quantitative scales, $\langle \wedge, \vee \rangle$ and $\langle \bar{\vee}, \vee \rangle$, and hence two im-plicatures from $\varphi \vee \psi$, namely $K \neg (\varphi \wedge \psi)$ and $K \neg (\varphi \bar{\vee} \psi)$, but these two im-plicatures jointly lead to an inconsistency with $\varphi \wedge \psi$, hence both invariably get cancelled under (XVII). Thus the use of inclusive disjunction will never give rise to any scalar implicatures in such a language.

Presupposition Projection

In what follows I shall apply the apparatus developed above to a very large number of examples, a lot of them culled from the "presupposition" literature and many of them ones which constitute problems for, or counterexamples to, the treatments of presupposition already discussed. I shall draw examples from the previous chapter where appropriate, although they will be renumbered for the purposes of this one. In addition it should be noted that, except where the discussion makes it obvious that the assumption has been suspended, I shall assume that the context is neutral with respect to cancellation. Thus when it is claimed that some pre-supposition is also a presupposition, this claim should be understood as being qualified by an implicit claim to the effect that this is so just in case there is nothing in the context to prevent it. The same ceteris paribus clause is in operation when I treat some im-plicature as being an implicature in order to show its role in pre-supposition suspension. Note also that any locutions of the form SENTENCE ϕ DOES NOT PRESUPPOSE x are to be understood as elliptical for NO UTTERANCE OF ϕ CAN PRESUPPOSE x. See the list of symbols and typographical conventions on pages xiii–xv for exposition of the systematic sentence/proposition ambiguity to be found in certain other locutions.

Consider example (30) below. I shall exhibit the pre-supposition cancellation involved in this example in considerable detail so that it can stand as an illustration of the way this treatment of presupposition works. It will also help familiarize the reader with the mechanics of the approach and enable the reader to test whether putative counterexamples to the theory really are counterexamples. Subsequent examples will be dealt with more cursorily, that is, less formally, but in every case a similar detailed formal argument can be constructed to prove the point at issue.

(30)   *John doesn't regret killing his mother because he didn't kill her.*

(31)   *John killed his mother.*

We have that:

(32)   1. $[(30)] \subseteq [\neg(31)]$ *because* clauses
                                                  are entailed
        2. $[K(31)] \in e^{30}_p$ by (VI) and (XIV)
        3. $[K(30)] \in e^{30}_u$ by (XV)
        4. inc $\{[(30)],[(31)]\}$ from 1.
        5. inc $\{[K(30)],[K(31)]\}$ from 4.
        6. $[K(31)] \notin e^{30}_U$ from 5. by (XVII)
        7. $[K(31)] \notin e^{30}_U \cap e^{30}_p$ from 6.

Therefore

        8. Utterance of (30) does
            not presuppose $[K(31)]$.   from 7. by (XX)

A very similar proof can be given for why (33), given as (11) in the previous chapter, does not presuppose $[K(34)]$, only here we need to know that *passing the exam* entails *not failing the exam*:

(33)   *John doesn't regret having failed the exam because, in fact, he passed.*

(34)   *John failed the exam.*

The affirmative sentences corresponding to (30) and (33) entail their factive complements, which are thus not cancellable by (XVII). This predictably leads to the anomaly found in (35).

(35)   **John regrets having failed the exam because, in fact, he passed.*

Consider now examples (36) and (37), given as (134) and (135) in the previous chapter.

(36)   **For all I know Oedipus regrets killing his father although, in fact, he didn't kill him.*

(37)   *For all I know Oedipus regrets killing his father although, in fact, I don't know that he killed him.*

(38)   *Oedipus killed his father.*

For (36) we may reason as follows.

(39)   1. $[K(36)] \subseteq [(36)] \subseteq [P(38)]$ first conjunct entailment

        2. $[K(36)] \subseteq [K\neg(38)] \subseteq [\neg P(38)]$ second conjunct entailment

        3. inc $\{[\neg P(38)], [P(38)]\}$

        4. $[K(36)] = \Lambda$ from 1., 2., and 3.

        5. $[K(36)] \in e_u^{36}$ by (XV)

        6. inc e_u^{36} from 4. and 5.

The inconsistency inherent in e_u^{36} produces the anomaly. The second clause in (37) is of the form $\neg K(38)$ and this, unlike the form $\neg 38$ found in (36), does not lead to an inconsistency with the first clause. Thus (37) is not heard as anomalous.

Consider examples (40)–(43):

(40)   *The opposition claims that the Queen asked the Prime Minister to be more polite to the Duke of Edinburgh.*

(41)   *There is a Duke of Edinburgh.*

(42)   *Lord Avon didn't say that Churchill regretted resigning.*

(43)   *Churchill resigned.*

These pairs of examples [cf. (118)–(119) in the previous chapter] are predicted to be related presuppositionally by the system defined, since there are no grounds for cancellation. This prediction is contrary to that given by Karttunen's system. I leave it to the intuitions of the reader to decide which is right. On the other hand, although (44) pre-supposes (45), it does not PRESUPPOSE it in most contexts, since in most contexts it is known that there is no king of France:

(44)   *Strawson said that Russell was wrong about the king of France.*

(45)   *There is a king of France.*

The proof is as follows:

(46)   1. $[K(45)] \in e^{44}_p$ by (VI) and (XIV)
        2. $[K\neg(45)] \in e^{45}_2$ usual contextual
                                                 assumption
        3. $[K\neg(45)] \in e^{44}_u$ by (XV) from 2.
        4. inc $\{[K(45)], [K\neg(45)]\}$
        5. $[K(45)] \notin e^{44}_U$ from 4. by (XVII)
        6. $[K(45)] \notin e^{44}_U \cap e^{44}_p$ from 5.

Therefore

        7. Utterance of (44) does
            not presuppose $[K(45)]$ from 6. by (XX)

It will be apparent that the present theory offers a straightforward solution to the problem posed by sentences like (47) (discussed by, e.g., Biggs 1976:203, Katz 1972:141, 1977:98–99):

(47)   *The king of France does not exist.*

On a Strawsonian view of presupposition this sentence should appear paradoxical: It asserts the denial of its own presupposition. But (47) is not paradoxical or anomalous and the present account gives us no reason to think that it should be. Example (47) does indeed pre-suppose that there is a king of France but it can never presuppose that there is a king of France. The pre-supposition is invariably cancelled in the light of its inconsistency with the sentence itself. We thus have no reason to suppose that the logical form of (47) is any different from the logical form of (48) (cf. Kneale and Moore 1936).

(48)   *The king of France does not sing.*

Likewise our theory has no problem with the following example (due to Wilson 1975:123).

(49)   *What your generalization captures is exactly nothing.*

This entails (50) and pre-supposes K(51).

(50)   *Your generalization captures nothing.*
(51)   *Your generalization captures something.*

Since (50) and (51) are contradictory, it will never be possible to add the pre-supposition to e_u without an inconsistency arising, so the pre-supposition will always be cancelled.

The following examples (cf. Kiparsky and Kiparsky 1970:349, fn.a) are problematic for any account of presupposition that admits the univocality of negation but does not allow cancellation.

(52)   *Boris doesn't know that Maria is a secretary.*
(53)   *I don't know that Maria is a secretary.*
(54)   *Speaker knows that Maria is a secretary.*

Given that *know* is a factive verb, both (52) and (53) must pre-suppose (54). On the system defined above, (52) also presupposes [54] since con {[K(52)], [54]} but (53) cannot presuppose it, because inc{[K(53)], [54]} and cancellation is thus forced by (XVII). Semantic accounts of presupposition would presumably claim that both (52) and (53) were potentially ambiguous because of the two types of negation, but that only the nonpresuppositional reading was found in (53). Those pragmatic accounts that do not have two kinds of negation and do not allow cancellation could only claim that there were two senses of *know* involved, one of them exclusive to first-person negative sentences.

Unfortunately for any proponents of the latter position, exactly the same phenomenon appears in examples (55)–(57).

(55)   *She is not aware that she is allowed to use that area.*
(56)   *I am not aware that she is allowed to use that area.*
(57)   *Speaker knows that she is allowed to use that area.*

This is readily explained on the present account if we allow that A⌢*knows that*⌢φ entails that A⌢*is aware that*⌢φ. Modus tollens gives us (58) from (56) and cancellation of (57) follows automatically.

(58)   *I do not know that she is allowed to use that area.*

A rather more complex example is (50) below:[2]

(59)   *Nobody has yet discovered that protons are (in any way) influenced by the CIA.*
(60)   *Protons are influenced by the CIA.*
(61)   *Nobody knows that protons are influenced by the CIA.*

---

[2] I am indebted to Colin Biggs (personal communication, 1974) for this example.

If we allow that *Nobody has discovered that*$^\frown\phi$ entails *Nobody knows that*$^\frown\phi$, as all but the most ardent proponents of innate ideas or revelatory knowledge must, then (59) entails (61). But (61) entails that the SPEAKER does not know that (60), by universal instantiation, so we have the following.

(62)
1. $[K(59)] \subseteq [59] \subseteq [61] \subseteq [\neg K(60)]$
2. $[K(60)] \in e^{59}_p$ by (VI) and (XIV)
3. inc $\{[\neg K(60)], [K(60)]\}$
4. $[K(60)] \notin e^{59}_U$ and is thus not presupposed

Intuitions may vary with this example, partly because of the epistemological assumption necessary for the suspension, but largely because the quantifier *nobody* is usually used indexically to range over only some limited domain, for example, a domain that excludes speaker and addressee, or, say, a domain restricted to students, as in the following example.

(63)   *Nobody has yet discovered that all the questions in paper II are about Quine.*

In the event that either of the doubtful entailments assumed in (62.1) fail, no suspension takes place and (59) will presuppose [K(60)]. For another example, involving the verb *discover*, see (151).

We have seen above that appended clauses entailing the negation of a pre-supposition of a preceding part of the sentence have the effect of suspending it. This is also true of cases of lexical presupposition, as the following examples show (cf. Langendoen 1971:343, Stalnaker 1974:204).

(64)   *My cousins aren't boys anymore, they've had sex-change operations.*

(65)   *My cousins aren't boys anymore, they've grown into fine young men.*

In (64) the first clause entails that the cousins used to be boys and hence that they used to be male. The second clause, taken together with the entailment that they used to be male, itself entails that they are now female. This entailment is inconsistent with the pre-supposition (due to *boy*) that they are male and the latter is consequently suspended. In (65), of course, no such inconsistency arises. Examples (66) and (67) behave in a similar fashion.

(66)   *Hilary isn't a widow, **he**'s a widower.*

(67)   *Hilary isn't a widow, she's **divorced**.*

The cases of pre-supposition suspension that have attracted most attention in the literature are those involving logical connectives, where it appears to be partly dependent on the connective involved whether or not cancellation takes place. The behavior of such examples is quite straightforwardly predicted by the apparatus developed here, in which the implicatures of the sentence suspend the pre-suppositions of the sentence just in case the latter are inconsistent with the former. Consider the examples (68) and (69), which are similar to those discussed in Karttunen (1973a).

(68)   *If he was crying then he regrets killing his father.*
(69)   *If he killed his father then he regrets it* (= *killing his father*).
(70)   *He killed his father.*
(71)   *He was crying.*

K(70) is a pre–supposition of both (68) and (69) under (VI), but it is a presupposition only in the case of (68). The relevant difference between them lies in the implicatures deriving from the antecedent. Under (V), (68) will implicate $[P\neg(71)]$ whereas (69) will implicate $[P\neg(70)]$. The former implicature is consistent with the pre-supposition (i.e., con $\{[P\neg(71)], [K(70)]\}$) but the latter is not (i.e., inc$\{[P\neg(70)], [K(70)]\}$). The pre-supposition is cancelled by (XVII) in (69), but not in (68). The same proof applies to the suspension of the existence pre-supposition with definite descriptions.

(72)   *If he pulled the Fort Knox job, then the Godfather must be a very rich man.*
(73)   *If there is such a man, then the Godfather must be a very rich man.*
(74)   *There is a Godfather.*

A similar argument can be made in the case of disjunctions like (75) and (76).

(75)   *Either he wasn't crying or he regrets killing his father.*
(76)   *Either he didn't kill his father or he regrets killing him.*

Karttunen is forced to give a separate rule for disjunctions (see the discussion in the previous chapter), but in the present approach (V) enables a uniform treatment of disjunctions and conditionals [see (62) in Chapter 3].

Our analysis correctly predicts the presuppositional behavior of example (77), which Lakoff (1975:271) discusses informally in terms of Karttunen's "filters" and his own notion of implicature as context-dependent entailment.

(77)   *If Sam asks Professor Snurd to write him a recommendation*
         to graduate school, and Professor Snurd writes the
         recommendation, saying only that Sam has nice
         handwriting, then Sam will regret that Professor Snurd wrote
         him a bad recommendation.
(78)   *Professor Snurd will write Sam a bad recommendation.*
(79)   *Professor Snurd will write Sam a recommendation.*

Under (V), (77) will implicate $[P\neg(79)]$. But this is inconsistent with the pre-supposition that K(78), so the latter will be cancelled by (XVII). Since this alternative account is available, it can be seen that example (77) fails to provide, pace Lakoff, supporting evidence for a theory that equates implicature with entailment. Needless to say, in simple conjunctions there are no implicatures of this kind, since both conjuncts are entailed by the sentence as a whole. In more complex cases of logical compounding (V) still gives us the implicatures required to cancel pre-suppositions in accord with our intuitions. The following examples are due to Karttunen (1973c:16).

(80)   *If John is married and still living with his wife, then he is*
         probably not interested in becoming your room-mate.
(81)   *If no one has come out of that room, then either John never*
         went in or we all know that he is still in there.
(82)   *John has a wife.*
(83)   *John was in there.*

Example (80) pre-supposes K(82) but does not presuppose it, likewise (81) and K(83). Example (80) implicates that, for all the speaker knows, John is not married [under (V)] and this is inconsistent with [K(82)], so the latter cannot be presupposed. An analogous argument applies for (81) and [K(83)].

  Because Karttunen's original (1973a) account of *or* was asymmetrical, it made incorrect predictions in the following examples.

(84)   *Either all Bill's friends are keeping very quiet or he has no*
         friends.
(85)   *Bill has friends.*
(86)   *Either all of Jack's letters have been held up or he has not*
         written any.
(87)   *Jack's letters exist.*

Examples (84) and (86) pre-suppose, but do not presuppose, K(85) and K(87) respectively. Karttunen's (1973a) filters incorrectly predict that the presupposition was maintained in each case. Because (V) generates im-plicatures from the nonentailed clauses of compound sentences without reference to their linear position in the sentence, the system defined here correctly predicts the pre-supposition suspension that takes place. Proof is along lines of that given for (69). Similarly, the system makes the correct prediction with respect to Wilson's (1975:38) counterexample to the asymmetry of Karttunen's filter for conditionals. Example (88) pre-supposes, but does not presuppose, (89).

(88)   *If Nixon knows the war is over, the war is over.*
(89)   *The war is over.*

Another counterexample, (90), to Karttunen's filters, due to Wilson (1975:58), is equally susceptible to the present treatment although proof is a little more complicated.

(90)   *If all Bill's friends have encouraged him, he must have friends.*
(91)   *Bill must have friends.*
(92)   *Bill has friends.*

Example (90) pre-supposes, but does not presuppose K(92), contrary to Karttunen's predictions. If we accept Karttunen's (1972) arguments that *must* in sentences like (90) amounts to an epistemic necessity operator (i.e., K), then we have that [91] = [K(92)]. Under (V), we have that $[P\neg(91)]$ is an implicature of (90) but, given the equivalence just noted, this implicature is equivalent to $[P\neg K(92)]$. Furthermore, K(92) is pre-supposed by (90), but this pre-supposition is inconsistent with the implicature just established (i.e., $inc\{[P\neg K(92)], [K(92)]\}$) and is cancelled by (XVII).[3]

As we saw in the previous chapter in the discussion of (24) and (115), there exists a class of examples, discovered independently by Hausser and Wilson, which involve compound sentences having contradictory pre-suppositions, both of which, intuitively, get cancelled. Let us see how the present theory captures this intuition. Consider (93), which is due to Wilson (1975:73).

(93)   *Your teacher will be either a bachelor or a spinster.*
(94)   *Your teacher will be male.*
(95)   *Your teacher will be female.*

---

[3] The proof is as follows:

(1)	$P\neg Kp \in \mu$	assumption
(2)	$Kp \in \mu$	counterassumption
(3)	$\neg Kp \in \mu^*$	from (1) by C. P*
(4)	$Kp \in \mu^*$	from (2) by C.KK*

Example (93) pre-supposes both K(94) and K(95). But we have that inc{[K(94)], [K(95)]}, so, under the definition of ∪!, NEITHER pre-supposition will be allowed into e_U[93]. An identical analysis applies to Hausser's (1976:268) example given as (96) and the relation it bears to (97) and (98).

(96)   The liquid in this tank has either stopped fermenting or it has not yet begun to ferment.

(97)   In the past, the liquid was fermenting.

(98)   In the past, the liquid was not fermenting.

Likewise, Wilson's (1975:75) example, given as (99), causes no embarassment to the present theory.

(99)   If Sartre knows that Chomsky is alive, I'll be surprised, but if he knows that Chomsky is dead, I'll be amazed.

Consider also the following examples, which are due to Liberman (1973:350).

(100)   Maybe John used to beat his wife, but has now stopped doing so.

(101)   John used to beat his wife.

Example (100) pre-supposes, but does not presuppose, K(101). It contains an occurrence of (101), but this is not entailed by the matrix sentence, so under (V) we have [P¬(101)] as an implicature. This implicature is inconsistent with the pre-supposition K(101); the latter is thus cancelled. Exactly the same explanatory principle applies to (102) and (103) in respect to their cancelled pre-supposition given in (104) [cf. the discussion of (79)–(81) in Chapter 5].

(102)   Perhaps John has no children, but perhaps his children are away on vacation.

(103)   It is more likely that John has no children than that his children are away on vacation.

(104)   K(John has children)

Unlike Karttunen and Peter's theory, the present analysis correctly predicts that the pre-supposition will always be cancelled in any sentences of the form shown in (105).

(105) $possibly\,^\frown(not)\,^\frown\varphi\,^\frown \begin{Bmatrix} and \\ but \end{Bmatrix} possibly\,^\frown(not)\,^\frown\psi$ where φ

pre-supposes Kψ, or ψ pre-supposes Kφ.

In all such sentences the pre-supposition occurs also as a

non-pre-supposed clause that is not entailed by the sentence as a whole. This leads to the generation of a clausal implicature, which cancels the pre-supposition.

Unlike Karttunen and Peters's theory, the present analysis allows the relevant presuppositions to emerge unscathed (i.e., not turned into zany material conditionals) from sentences like the following (from Chapter 5).

(106)   *If I go to bed with her, then Maria's children get jealous.*
(107)   *If I torture him, Boris regrets laughing at me.*
(108)   *If I go to bed with Maria and her children get jealous, then I get to feeling maybe we should call the whole thing off.*

In these examples the clausal implicatures that arise are quite consistent with the pre-suppositions and no cancellation takes place. The same is true of the following complex counterexample to Karttunen and Peters' theory, given as (96) in Chapter 5.

(109)   *If John murdered his father, then he probably regrets killing him, but if he killed him accidentally, then he probably doesn't regret having killed him.*

In this case $P(110)$, $P\neg(110)$, $P(111)$, and $P\neg(111)$ are generated, inter alia, as clausal im-plicatures, and $K(112)$ is generated as a pre-supposition:

(110)   *John murdered his father.*
(111)   *John killed his father accidentally.*
(112)   *John killed his father.*

But $\{[P(110)], [P\neg(110)], [P(111)], [P\neg(111)], [K(112)]\}$ is a consistent set so no cancellation of the pre-supposition occurs.

Consider now the following examples, due to Thomason and given in Karttunen (1973c:5).

(113)   *Some member of the Harvard Philosophy Department has stopped beating his wife.* (take the nonspecific interpretation of *some member*)
(114)   *Either Quine has stopped beating his wife, or Putnam has stopped beating his wife, or Rawls has stopped beating his wife...* (and so on till we have enumerated every member of the Harvard Philosopy department).

The interesting thing about these examples is that they have exactly the same truth conditions, but they can have different presuppositions.[4]

---

[4] I am grateful to Hans Kamp for showing me that an early formulation of (XVI) foundered on these examples.

Thus (113) will presuppose [K(115)] but only (114) can presuppose [K(116)]:[5]

(115)   *Some member of the Harvard Philosophy Department used to beat his wife.*

(116)   *Quine used to beat his wife, Putnam used to beat his wife, Rawls used to beat his wife,...* (*i.e.*, EVERY member of the Harvard Philosophy Department used to beat his wife).

This result is correctly predicted by both the system developed here and by Karttunen's original filters. However, Karttunen used to think that presuppositions had something to do with truth conditions and so he could not accept the DIFFERENCE in presuppositions in view of the fact that (113) and (114) have the SAME truth conditions. He argued in Karttunen (1973c:6–9) that (114) was ambiguous between a reading which does presuppose [K(116)] and a "cleft" reading, glossed in (117), which does not presuppose [K(116)], but does presuppose [K(115)].

(117)   *Either it is Quine who has stopped beating his wife, or it is Putnam who . . .*

On my account there is no need to postulate an ambiguity, since in most contexts $[P\neg(116)]$ will be assumed and the pre-supposition will be cancelled anyway. The proposition [K(116)] could only emerge uncancelled among conversationalists who had a very low opinion of philosophers or of Harvard or of both.

Keenan (1971:52) gives a somewhat similar example, involving iterated cleft sentences, that constitutes a counterexample to the semantic account of presupposition.

(118)   *You say that someone in this room loves Mary. Well maybe so. But it certainly isn't Fred who loves Mary. And it certainly isn't John....* (We continue in this way until we have enumerated all the people in the room.) *Therefore no one in this room loves Mary.*

Because of the cleft construction, the third, fourth, and subsequent sentences (except the last) pre-suppose K(119). But clearly the text does not have this as a presupposition.

(119)   *Someone in this room loves Mary.*

Under (V), the first sentence implicates $[P\neg(119)]$. Once this sentence has entered the context, it will suffice to suspend the pre-supposition

---

[5] Note that both (113) and (114) entail (115). Strictly speaking, (114) does not presuppose [K(116)], but rather a set of propositions whose intersection is [K(116)].

K(119) of subsequent sentences, as it is carried along by the inductive context clause (XVIII).

Compound sentences which contain verbs of propositional attitude like *think*, *dream*, or *believe* cause problems for theories of presupposition projection [e.g., Karttunen (1973a:188–190) presages "Class II" verbs in Karttunen (1974:154)].

(120)   *Bill believed that Fred had been beating his wife and Harry hoped that Fred would stop beating her.*

(121)   *Fred had been beating his wife.*

Under (V), we will have [P¬(121)] as an implicature of (120), since (i) (121) occurs in (120); (ii) (121) is not entailed by (120); (iii) its negation is not entailed by (120); and (iv) if an arbitrary sentence is substituted for its occurrence, then that sentence is substituted for its occurrence, then that sentence is not pre-supposed by (120). This implicature cancels the pre-supposition K(121). The same explanation is available for the cancellation of K(123) from (122), an example which is originally due to Morgan (1969:171).

(122)   *I dreamed that I was a German and that I regretted being a German.*

(123)   *I was a German.*

So far we have mostly considered cases where the entailments of the sentence itself, or its implicatures, or both, suspend one of its pre-suppositions, but (118) showed that the context itself can suspend pre-suppositions. Heinämäki (1972) gives many examples where the context suspends the pre-supposition arising from sentences containing the word *before*. Although she has no formal solution to the problem this creates, her discussion is wide ranging and thorough and will not be paraphrased here. It will suffice to give a couple of examples and show how the formal system proposed here correctly predicts their presuppositional behavior.

(124)   *Max reread his diaries before he finished his autobiography.*

(125)   *Max died before he finished his autobiography.*

(126)   *Max finished his autobiography.*   (at time $t + 1$)

(127)   *Max died.*   (at time t)

The pre-supposition function f_p tells us that K(126) is a pre-supposition of both (124) and (125) and yet clearly it is a presupposition only of (124). But (125) has no relevant implicatures that could be involved in the suspension, nor is the first clause inconsistent with the second (i.e., con{[127], [126]}). However, if we assume that the contexts in which (124) and (125) are produced and evaluated contain a general principle or law of nature like (128), then we may derive the inconsistency required to suspend the pre-supposition.

(128)   *Nobody does anything after they have died.*

We now have that [128], [K(125)] $\in e_u^{125}$ and [K(126)] $\in e_p^{125}$, but since inc{[K(126)], [K(125)], [128]}, we may infer that [K(126)] $\notin e_u^{125}$ and thus that [K(126)] is not presupposed by (125). In contexts, such as a seance, in which (128) is not assumed, then (125) WILL presuppose [K(126)] unless there is some other contextual proposition operative (e.g., an assumption that spirits can not write or that they have total amnesia in respect of their earthly existence). Contextual components can REVERSE the most natural suspension pattern for sentences like (124) and (125), as the following examples show.

(129)   A: *Why didn't Max complete his autobiography?*
          B: *Because he made the mistake of rereading his diaries*
              before he finished it.
(130)   A: *What was it about the completion of Max's autobiog-*
              raphy that finally made you believe in life after death?
          B: *The fact that Max died **before** he finished it.*

Now that we have established that extralinguistic context is a partial determinant of pre-supposition suspension, we can move to a type of example, apparently first noted by J. D. McCawley (according to Karttunen 1973a:184) which has long haunted the presupposition literature. Compare (131) and (132).

(131)   *If Carter invites George Wallace's wife to the White House,*
          then the president will regret having invited a black
          militant to his residence.
(132)   *If Carter invites Angela Davis to the White House, then the*
          president will regret having invited a black militant to his
          residence.
(133)   *The president will have invited a black militant to his*
          residence.

Clearly, although K(133) is a pre-supposition of both (131) and (132), it is a presupposition only of the former. Examples (131) and (132) have among their implicatures [P⌐(134)] and [P⌐(135)] respectively:

(134)   *Carter will invite George Wallace's wife to the White House.*
(135)   *Carter will invite Angela Davis to the White House.*

Given a context containing real-world knowledge that Carter is the president and that the White House is his residence, we may deduce [P⌐(136)] and [P⌐(137)] from [P⌐(134)] and [P⌐(135)] respectively.

(136)   *The president will invite George Wallace's wife to his residence.*

(137)   *The president will invite Angela Davis to his residence.*

To prove the inconsistency necessary for suspension in (132) we need, in addition, contextually given propositions regarding the respective skin color and militancy of George Wallace's wife and Angela Davis, and a rule of anaphora for *a*.[6] It is no part of the present enterprise to provide such a rule, but clearly it will have to provide for the fact that (131) is an acceptable sentence even though *a black militant* cannot "refer" to Governor Wallace's wife, whereas the ceteris paribus interpretation of (132) is one in which *a black militant* does "refer" to Angela Davis. Given such a rule, the inconsistency required for pre-supposition suspension is derivable from the context and (132) but not from the context and (131). Note that *a black militant* does not HAVE TO "refer" to Angela Davis in (132), as the following text demonstrates.

(138)   *It's all very well for him to invite Huey Newton over but if Carter invites Angela Davis to the White House, then the president will regret having invited a black militant to his residence. Having more than one black militant about always causes trouble.*

In this case *a black militant* can "refer" to Huey Newton and if it does then no pre-suppositional inconsistency will arise. A similar analysis is available for the two contextual interpretations of the "drunken policeman" counterexample [(103) in Chapter 5] to Karttunen and Peters's theory.

We turn now to discussion of a number of complex examples of pre-supposition that are intended to show that the range of applicability of the system defined is greater than just the set of counterexamples to earlier theories that has been considered so far.

Observe that (139) entails (140) and, more interestingly, that (141) pre-supposes K(140).

(139)   *Oedipus regrets killing his father.*

(140)   *Oedipus knows that he killed his father.*

(141)   *Oedipus doesn't regret killing his father.*

Example (141) also pre-supposes K(142).

(142)   *Oedipus killed his father.*

and since $[K(140)] \subseteq [K(142)]$,[7] we might be inclined to treat K(140) as THE

---

[6] See Hawkins (1978) for one formulation of such a rule. I am using "refer" to refer to the anaphoric relation involved.

[7] For proof, see Hintikka (1962:61).

pre-supposition, having K(142) merely as a consequence. This would be mistaken, however, since K(140) can be cancelled quite independently of K(142), as the following examples show.

(143)   *Oedipus doesn't regret killing his father but then I don't know that he knows that he killed him.*

(144)   *Oedipus doesn't regret killing his father but then I know that he doesn't know that he killed him.*

(145)   *Oedipus doesn't regret killing his father because he doesn't know that he killed him.*

(146)   *Oedipus doesn't regret killing his father because he doesn't know that it was him that he killed.*

(147)   *Oedipus doesn't regret killing his father because he doesn't know that what he did proved fatal.*

All these five examples retain K(142) uncancelled, (146) and (147) have an interest over and beyond this noncancellability.

(148)   *Oedipus knows that he killed someone.*

(149)   *Oedipus knows that he did something to his father.*

Examples (148) and (149) are both entailed by (140), but in (146) and (147) it appears that they have been separately cancelled, each without affecting the other. That is, it seems at first sight as if K(140) itself could be broken down into two further pre-suppositions, each individually cancellable. This is not what is going on, however, since inspection will reveal that the cleft constructions in the second clauses of (146) and (147) lead to the pre-suppositions K(148) and K(149) respectively, quite independently of the contents of the first clause.[8]

Stalnaker (1974:207–210) has pointed out that Karttunen's (1971) distinction between two types of factive verb (FACTIVES including *regret, forget, resent*, etc. and SEMIFACTIVES including *realize, see, discover*, etc.), and his consequent need to distinguish two types of presupposition relation, is rendered otiose by the kind of pragmatic account provided in this book. We assumed this implicitly in considering examples (59) and (63) above. What follows is a demonstration that Stalnaker's informal findings can be proven within the formal framework defined here. Consider the following examples, due to Karttunen (1971).

(150)   *If I realize later that I have not told the truth then, I will confess it to everyone.*

---

[8] Embedded cleft constructions are like indirect questions with respect to this type of pre-supposition:
(i)   *Oedipus doesn't know who he killed.*
(ii)   *Oedipus doesn't know what he did to his father.*

(151)   *If I discover later that I have not told the truth, then I will*
         confess it to everyone.
(152)   *If I regret later that I have not told the truth, then I will*
         confess it to everyone.
(153)   *I have not told the truth.*

Although (150)–(152) all pre-suppose K(153), only (152) retains it as a presupposition. I take it that the following entailments hold by virtue of the meaning of the words involved.[9]

(154)   [A⌐knows that⌐φ]⊆[A⌐has realized that⌐φ]
(155)   [A⌐knows that⌐φ]⊆[A⌐has discovered that⌐φ]

But note that there is no entailment in (156).

(156)   [A⌐knows that⌐φ]⊄[A⌐has regretted that⌐φ]

From (154) and (155), (157) and (158) follow respectively by contraposition.

(157)   [A⌐has not realized that⌐φ]⊆[A⌐does not know that⌐φ]
(158)   [A⌐has not discovered that⌐φ]⊆[A⌐does not know that⌐φ]

Examples (150) and (151) implicate [P(159)] and [P(160)] respectively.

(159)   *I will not realize later that I have not told the truth.*
(160)   *I will not discover later that I have not told the truth.*
(161)   *I do not know that I have not told the truth.*

From either of these implicatures we may infer [P(161)] by virtue of the entailments given in (157) and (158).[10] Further, we have that inc{[K(153)], [P(161)]} so the pre-supposition gets cancelled in examples (150) and (151), but not in example (152), where no such inconsistency is provable by reference to (156).

Karttunen (1975:57–58) proposes that (162), (163), and (164) are truth-conditionally synonymous.

(162)   *I deprived Bill of 15 hours teaching.*
(163)   *I spared Bill 15 hours teaching.*
(164)   *I withheld 15 hours teaching from Bill.*

In his proposed analysis the meaning differences between them are at-

---

[9] See the discussion of example (59).

[10] This inference fudges the tense issue but not to so fudge it would make the proof even longer and more unwieldy than it is at present. For details of the complex interplay of pre-supposition and temporal matters, see Givón (1972).

tributed soley to the (different) presuppositions associated with *deprive* and *spare*. According to this analysis (165) is contradictory, just as (166) is.

(165)   *I spared, but did not deprive, Bill of 15 hours teaching.*
(166)   *I withheld, but did not withhold, 15 hours teaching from Bill.*

[Examples (165) and (166) are due, essentially, to Wilson (1975:149).] However, (165) is not contradictory, so Karttunen's proposed analysis is plainly incorrect. One approach to the problem posed by (165) is to abandon the claim that natural language negation is a truth-function. This is the tactic adopted by Wilson (1975:150–153). Until this very radical proposal is spelled out in sufficient detail to make testable predictions, I can see no reason for considering it further. An alternative approach, the one I shall adopt here, is to deny that (162)–(164) have the same truth-conditions (Kempson 1975:215–217 suggests this strategy, albeit incoherently.) (162) entails (167) but not (168), (163) entails (168) but not (167), and (164) entails neither (167) nor (168). Furthermore, (162) and (163) pre-suppose K(167) and K(168) respectively.

(167)   *There is some set of criteria under which Bill's doing the 15 hours teaching is deemed desirable.*

(168)   *There is some set of criteria under which Bill's doing the 15 hours teaching is deemed undesirable.*

According to this analysis, (165) is not a contradiction; (165) entails (164) and the negation of (167)—assuming that (167) and (164) together entail (162), as seems not unreasonable. Example (165) pre-supposes both K(167) and K(168). The former is already entailed by K(165) and hence by e_u, whereas the latter is inconsistent with K(165) and hence with e_u and is therefore cancelled. Note that the wording of (167) and (168), which is due, essentially, to Karttunen (1975:58), makes Wilson's objections to entailment analyses inapplicable, since (169) will not have contradictory entailments (or pre-suppositions).

(169)   *I both deprived and spared Bill 15 hours teaching.*

The advantage of the approach taken here, one which extends naturally to cover other Wilson examples (e.g., those involving such words as *credulous, trusting, gloating, rejoicing, reckless, daring*), is that it accounts automatically, given Π, for the fact that the implications that these words give rise to pattern in exactly the same way as the more familiar presuppositions due to factive verbs and definite descriptions. Thus they are, typically, maintained under negation and in compound sentences; they can also be suspended in sentences such as (170).

(170)   *If there really is some set of criteria under which Bill's doing*
         the 15 hours teaching is deemed desirable, then I have,
         indeed, deprived him of it (but I don't think he should be
         allowed near students).

In (170) the pre-supposition due to *deprive* is inconsistent with the clausal implicature arising from the antecedent and is consequently cancelled. The analysis also predicts, correctly, that (171) presupposes neither (167) nor (168).

(171)   *I either deprived, or spared, Bill of 15 hours teaching.*

The cancellation proof for (171), which requires some ingenuity, is left as an exercise for the reader. Note that it crucially relies on the assumption that (162) is logically equivalent to the conjunction of (164) and (167), and that (163) is logically equivalent to the conjunction of (164) and (168).

Counterexamples

The first category of counterexamples to the system defined above reflects a limitation on the consistency test employed.

(172)   *John doesn't realize that Zorn's Lemma is inconsistent with*
         the Axiom of Choice.
(173)   *Zorn's Lemma is inconsistent with the Axiom of Choice.*

Under the definitions of II, (172) can never presuppose its pre-supposition K(173) because there are no worlds in which K(173) is true. Hence for all ϕ, inc{[ϕ], [K(173)]}. But clearly (172) could be uttered by, say, a student, unwisely trying to demonstrate that he knows more set theory than John does, with the pre-supposition going uncancelled.

The solution to this problem is a less stringent consistency test, but this would enormously complicate the proofs of the fairly trivial inconsistencies present in all the other examples of pre-supposition suspension. This consistency problem is not particular to the system presented here, but is generally encountered in any attempt to do the semantics of propositional attitude. For example, most, if not all, doxastic logics have as a consequence that it is impossible to believe statements like (173). Yet clearly one can believe such statements and can even go on so believing them when the actual formulations referred to are substituted for the proper names referring to them. It is a serious problem in its own right but not an especially serious one for II.

The second category of counterexample is slightly more troublesome; examples (174)–(176) are due to Rohrer (1973:122).

(174)   *John dreamed that LBJ was a homosexual and that*
         everybody knew he was a homosexual.
(175)   *John dreamed that LBJ was a homosexual and that*
         everybody knew that he waited for boys in the restroom of the
         Y.M.C.A.
(176)   *John dreamed that LBJ was a homosexual and that*
         everybody knew his foreign policy was a failure.

As we should wish, the pre-supposition of the factive complement is cancelled straightforwardly in example (174) in the same way as in example (122) considered above. On the other hand, no cancellation takes place in the example (176) and this too accords with intuition. Unfortunately II predicts that no cancellation will take place in (175) either and thus that the sentence will presuppose [K(177)].

(177)   *LBJ waited for boys in the restroom of the Y.M.C.A.*

Rohrer (1973:122) thinks that the solution to this problem—which is a problem for ANY current theory—lies in the establishment of an inferential link between the two embedded conjuncts of the sentence, and he cites Lakoff (1971b) as providing independent motivation for the role of inference. Rohrer may well be right, but the notion of inference required is going to be rather special, since the simple logical modes of inference (e.g., modus ponens or universal instantiation) are inadequate to the task.

(178)   *If one hangs around Y.M.C.A. restrooms then one is*
         homosexual.
(179)   *All persons who hang around Y.M.C.A. restrooms are*
         homosexual.

The claims made by (178) and (179) are both clearly false and it is not the case that one has to assume either of them to get pre-supposition cancellation in (175). For the moment we have no formal solution to this problem and can only suggest that what is involved is a species of PARTICULARIZED CONVERSATIONAL IMPLICATURE deriving from Grice's maxim of RELEVANCE. But in view of how little has been said, in this book and elsewhere, about either of those concepts, this suggestion may do no more than label the problem.

Sentence-Meaning

Stalnaker (1972, 1974) has proposed that the MEANING of a sentence be identified with a function from contexts into propositions. Such functions can be straightforwardly defined given the formal system provided in this chapter. It should be noted, however, that the restrictions pertaining to Π (e.g., the exclusion from consideration of illocutionary force) apply equally to the definitions given below. Nevertheless the fact that we can go part of the way towards formalizing Stalnaker's proposal strikes me as being of some interest and importance. The MEANING of a sentence ϕ (written as $[\![\phi]\!]$) is defined as follows.

(XXII) $[\![\phi]\!] = \lambda X[cc(\langle 0,\phi,X\rangle)]$
(We can let $e_0 = 0$ here because
$(n \in N) \, (\phi \in D) \, (X \in M)[cc(\langle 0,\phi,X\rangle) = cc(\langle n,\phi,X\rangle)]$

Consider (180) and (181).

(180)   *Either Mary is pregnant or she isn't pregnant.*
(181)   *If Mary's husband is pregnant then Mary's husband is pregnant.*

Intuitively, (180) and (181) do not mean the same thing, but we have that [180] = [181], since they are both tautologies and thus denote the set of all possible worlds. So the function [ ] fails to predict our intuitions respecting sameness of meaning. On the other hand, we have that $[\![180]\!] \neq [\![181]\!]$, because in some contexts (181) will presuppose that Mary has a husband and will implicate that Mary's husband may be pregnant. Example (180) cannot have this implicature or this presupposition.

The function $[\![\ ]\!]$ also makes the distinctions of meaning that our intuitions require in the case of truth-conditionally synonymous sentences which are not tautologies.

(182)   *John went out or Mary went out.*
(183)   *John went out or Mary went out or both of them went out.*

It will be obvious, in light of our earlier discussion, that $[\![\phi \lor \psi]\!] \neq [\![\phi \lor \psi \lor (\phi \land \psi)]\!]$, even though $[\phi \lor \psi] = [\phi \lor \psi \lor (\phi \land \psi)]$.

(184)   *John stole the money and went to the bank.*
(185)   *John went to the bank and stole the money.*

If we had integrated the conversational implicatures arising from Grice's "Be orderly!" maxim into our account, then we would have been able to show that $[\![\phi \widehat{\ } and \widehat{\ } \psi]\!] \neq [\![\psi \widehat{\ } and \widehat{\ } \phi]\!]$ despite the fact that $[\phi \widehat{\ } and \widehat{\ } \psi] = [\psi \widehat{\ } and \widehat{\ } \phi]$.

(186) $\left\{\begin{array}{l}\textit{For all John knows,} \\ \textit{It is compatible with all John knows, that}\end{array}\right\}$ *Mary is pregnant.*

(187)   *John doesn't know that Mary isn't pregnant.*

If we continue to assume the plausibility of the Hintikka paraphrases, then we have that [186] = [187] (because $[P_j\phi] = [\neg K_j \neg \phi]$) but we do NOT get that $[\![186]\!] = [\![187]\!]$, because the English expression corresponding to K_j is factive whereas those corresponding to P_j are not factive.

(188)   *For all I know, Mary is pregnant.*

Another intuitively satisfying result is that, for any context X in which (188) can be informatively uttered, we have that $[\![180]\!](X) = [\![188]\!](X)$. The property of "being informative" can be defined in an obvious way.

(XXIII)   A sentence ϕ is **informative with respect to** a context X iff $[\![\phi]\!](X) \subset W$.

Under this definition the utterance of complex mathematical theorems will not be informative. This is a standard defect of such definitions, but see Hintikka (1973) for one way out of the problem. Definition (XXIII) DOES allow (180) and (181) to be informative on some occasions of utterance. Note that, given the way contexts are defined, ϕ cannot be uttered AT ALL if it would lead to inconsistency in the resulting context. The present formulation of Stalnaker's proposal allows us to go some way towards capturing the distinction that some (e.g., Gordon and Lakoff 1971, Searle 1975) have wished to make between "literal" and "conveyed" meaning. The literal meaning of ϕ is $[\phi]$ but the meaning it conveys in a context X is $[\![\phi]\!](X)$.

7

PRAGMATICS AND SEMANTICS

"Garden Variety Semantics"

> What we have done is to largely, if not
> entirely, eliminate pragmatics, reducing it
> to garden variety semantics
> [G. Lakoff 1972:655].

The claim that Lakoff was making can be stated in a more precise, though less stylish, manner as follows:

(1)   Most, if not all, putative pragmatic relations between utterances and contexts can be reduced to a relation of entailment holding between sentences.

There is a trivial sense in which (1) is true: We can define CONSISTENCY along the lines shown in (2) and then do everything that this book has done in terms of that notion of consistency, rather than the one given in (70) of Chapter 5.

(2)   A sentence ϕ is **consistent with** a set of sentences Γ iff it is not the case that $T \Vdash \neg \phi$.

This is not what Lakoff had in mind, however. He was claiming that relations such as those which map into felicity conditions, presuppositions and implicatures could be stated directly in terms of the familiar notion of semantic entailment. The preceding chapters of this book have shown that Lakoff was mistaken: These relations cannot be handled semantically in any straightforward way. Let me recapitulate.

The claim that ILLOCUTIONARY FORCE can be given a semantic analyzans crucially depends on two subsidiary claims: (i) Every sentence used with illocutionary force has an underlying performative verb representing that force, and (ii) performative sentences ENTAIL (or semantically presuppose) the felicity conditions appropriate to their illocutionary force. Chapter 2 of this book was devoted to showing that (i) is false, at the same time it was shown that (ii) is false, for it predicts incorrectly that both (3) and (4) are contradictory.[1]

(3)   *Henry requested Jill that she take her clothes off, but he was only attempting to shock her.*

(4)   *Sam ordered Harry to get out of the bar but Harry reminded him that he didn't have the authority.*

The claim that PRESUPPOSITION can be defined semantically requires an unmotivated attribution of ambiguity to natural language negation. It also fails to offer an explanation for the presupposition in sentences like (5).[2]

(5)   *It is possible that John regrets that he passed.*

It further fails to offer an explanation for the presuppositional asymmetry existing between (6) and (7).

(6)   *I don't know that John passed.*

(7)   *John doesn't know that I passed.*

And it fails to offer an explanation for the presuppositional behavior of compound sentences. Still further inadequacies are exposed by Boer and Lycan (1976), Kempson (1975), and Wilson (1975). There is just no way that presupposition can be handled with garden variety semantics.

The long sad history of attempts to treat CONVERSATIONAL IMPLICATURE as entailment is recounted in Horn (1973). It can not be done, for the reasons adduced there and in Chapter 3 of this book. Informal suggestions, such as that of Lehrer (1975),[3] that conversational implicature should be identified with "fuzzy" entailment merely obfuscate the central issue which is how to handle cancellability. Fuzzy logic, of itself,

---

[1] Given as examples (60) and (61), respectively, in Chapter 2.

[2] Given as example (3) in Chapter 5.

[3] I find Lehrer's paper very puzzling. She begins by showing that a semantic treatment, of the implications of adverbs like *foolishly* would involve introducing unmotivated ambiguities into linguistic description. She then provides a sensible, albeit partial and informal,

offers no purchase on context-sensitivity. Lakoff's (1975) conjecture that conversational implicature can be treated as a species of context-dependent entailment stands in need of clarification. I suspect that it will either fall victim to the circularity associated with Thomason's definition[4] or else turn out to be formally equivalent to the pragmatic theory defined in Chapters 3 and 6 of this book. Both the bits of data that Lakoff mentions in connection with his conjecture are accounted for very simply by that theory.[5] The motivated exclusion of entailment based analyses of illocutionary force, implicature, and presupposition allows us to cultivate a much tidier semantic garden than would be possible were they included. Consider first the case of NEGATION. We have seen that a semantic account of presupposition either requires two distinct underlying negation operators and a nonbivalent semantics on which to define them (which complicates the semantics) or one negation operator that occurs in different positions in underlying structure, together with transformations to move it into one position in surface structure (which complicates the syntax). Note also, in this connection, Martin's (1975) demonstration that the semantic account of presupposition needs to escalate into two dimensions and four values, if it is to account for the fact that *possible* and its ilk are holes. The pragmatic theory of presupposition developed in Chapter 6 of this book obviates the need for any of these complications.

Consider next the case of coordinating CONNECTIVES. The theory of implicature developed in this book allows us to treat them semantically as truth-functions. The theory of presupposition allows us to treat them as BIVALENTLY truth-functional and free of the elaborate filtering conditions that would have to be associated with them in a semantic theory of presupposition. Given the present pragmatic framework, the semantics of CONJUNCTION need make no reference to the linear order of the conjuncts and the semantics of DISJUNCTION need postulate no inclusive/exclusive ambiguity. The present framework, taken together with pragmatic arguments due to Givón, Grice, and Horn, allows a very strong claim to be made about the underlying truth-functional structure of natural language: there are just two set-taking TFC's: conjunction and disjunction.

Gricean explanation for these implications. But she concludes (175:248) that "to treat some implications as semantic while similar ones are pragmatic is *ad hoc*, or unnatural."

The remedy she suggests is to treat all forms of implication as more or less fuzzy entailment, in other words to treat all pragmatic relations as essentially semantic. Until she spells this out formally and demonstrates that fuzzy logic can be made to handle at least one case of implicature, I see no reason to take her suggestion seriously. As Sadock (1977:550) pertinently remarks, "the easy way out is to mumble something about fuzziness."

[4] See the discussion of (13)–(16) in Chapter 3.

[5] See the discussion of (29) and (77) in Chapter 6.

The semantics is trivially simple (intersection and union, respectively) and the syntax is also simplified. For example, there is no longer any need to generate the structurally ambiguous sentences that binary connectives force upon one [McCawley's (1972) original proposal was, it will be remembered, SYNTACTICALLY motivated]. It seems, then, that Thomason (1977:165) was right when he wrote that "an account of implicature . . . would make possible a much simpler syntax and semantics than we could otherwise be content with." There is a methodological moral that can be drawn from our previous discussion, one which Bar-Hillel (1971:405) drew some years ago: "Be careful with forcing bits and pieces you find in the pragmatic wastebasket into your favorite syntactico-semantic theory. It would perhaps be preferable to first bring some order into the contents of this wastebasket."

The Semantic-Autonomy Hypothesis

Let me conclude this book by examining briefly an issue which, given the extreme passions evoked in linguists by the word "autonomy," looks like providing a fertile breeding ground for controversy in the next few years. Is semantics autonomous with respect to pragmatics? That is, can one recursively enumerate the truth conditions of the sentences of a natural language without referring to pragmatic properties and relations such as presupposition, implicature, and illocutionary force? To answer affirmatively is to adopt the semantic-autonomy hypothesis.

It should be noted initially that the present work has implicitly assumed this hypothesis. If the definition of [ ] refers to, for example, presuppositions and implicatures, then our definitions of presupposition and implicature, which crucially depend on [ ], become mutually recursive, or, worse, circular. Furthermore, there has been little in this book, so far, to suggest that the hypothesis should be rejected. Conversational implicatures and presuppositions were both defined in a way which appears to make them irrelevant to determinimg the truth conditions of sentences. However, recent work, done on some of the semantico–pragmatic topics that this book has had little to say about (i.e., illocutionary force, and stress), seems to show that the semantic-autonomy hypothesis cannot be maintained.

Let us be clear what the semantic-autonomy hypothesis claims. The only writer to have formulated it explicitly is Kamp (1976); I shall adopt his formulation here. Our overall semantico–pragmatic theory $\mathcal{T}$ employs a set of terms $\mathcal{S}_1 \ldots \mathcal{S}_n$ which are agreed to be semantic in character (TRUTH, SATISFACTION, VALIDITY, CONSEQUENCE, etc.) and another set $\mathcal{P}_1$

. . . . . .$\mathscr{P}_m$ which are agreed to be pragmatic (IMPLICATURE, ILLOCUTIONARY FORCE, TOPIC, etc.). Then we can say that the semantic component of $\mathscr{T}$ is autonomous with respect to the pragmatics if and only if there is some $\mathscr{T}' \subset \mathscr{T}$ which does not involve $\mathscr{P}_1 \ldots \mathscr{P}_m$ and which is such that if Σ is a sentence not involving $\mathscr{P}_1 \ldots \mathscr{P}_m$ then $\mathscr{T}' \Vdash \Sigma \leftrightarrow \mathscr{T} \Vdash \Sigma$.

Kamp (1976) argues against the semantic-autonomy hypothesis on the basis of compound sentences containing sentences which can be used for the speech act of PERMISSION. His argument, which I shall oversimplify and abbreviate radically, runs as follows.

(8)   *Inmates may smoke or drink.*

Given the standard assumption as to the semantics of disjunction (that it amounts to set-theoretic union), the truth conditions of the assertion of (8) cannot be determined by reference to the truth conditions of (9) and (10).

(9)   *Inmates may smoke.*
(10)   *Inmates may drink.*

However, the truth conditions of the assertion of (8) can be determined by reference to the pragmatic effects that would result from the use of sentence (8) as a permission. Roughly speaking, (8) is true if and only if the range of options open to inmates includes those that would have been opened for them, had (8) been uttered as a permission. The pragmatic effects of using (8) as a permission can be determined from the union of the pragmatic effects that result from the use of (9) as a permission with those that result from the use of (10) as a permission. Roughly speaking, the options opened by the permissive use of (8) are exactly those in the union of those opened by the permissive use of (9) and (10). This analysis preserves the intuition that disjunction always amounts to union. The pragmatic effects of the use of (9) and (10) as permissions depends in turn on the truth conditions of (11) and (12), respectively.

(11)   *Inmates smoke.*
(12)   *Inmates drink.*

Thus we see that, to arrive at the truth conditions of a sentence like (8), we must make reference to pragmatic conditions which themselves make reference to truth conditions. If the analysis is correct then the autonomy hypothesis is refuted.

Dretske (1972) presents an argument against the semantic-autonomy hypothesis that has a similar structure to Kamp's but which depends on contrastive stress data.

(13)   **Clyde** gave me the tickets.
(14)   Clyde gave **me** the tickets.
(15)   Clyde gave me **the tickets**.

These three sentences are truth–conditionally equivalent, which gives us prima facie grounds for not supposing that the (written) sentence (16) has (at least) three semantic representations.

(16)   Clyde gave me the tickets.

And there are no obvious syntactic grounds for supposing that (16) is like (17) and has two truth-conditionally equivalent but structurally distinct semantic representations.

(17)   We are visiting relatives.

Postal (1971:230–239) did once propose that sentences like (13), (14), and (15) had different semantic representations.[6] Thus (13), for example, was to be derived from (18).

(18)   The one who gave me the tickets was Clyde.

This proposal was attacked by Hasegawa (1972:158), who pointed out that it could not provide underlying structures for cases of contrastive stress NOT involving NPs. Thus there would be no plausible sources for (19) and (20).

(19)   Clyde gave me **those** tickets.
(20)   Clyde **gave** me those tickets.

McCawley (1973:236) in his discussion of Hasegawa's paper, makes the following comment: "I think that the rule Postal proposes is irremediably wrong." Hasegawa and McCawley show that the rule which Postal (1971:235) needs to get (13) from (18) is quite unlike any well-established transformation, and even violates certain plausible constraints on such rules.

   Furthermore, we have good methodological grounds for not assigning a distinct semantic representation to each stress variant of a sentence (even supposing that we could see how to do this): To do so would make every well-formed string of morphemes massively ambiguous, and the extent of this ambiguity would be some kind of geometric function of the length of the string. So we may conclude that (13), (14), and (15) share the same semantic representation. The difference between them is pragmatic. This conclusion is hardly controversial but it has, as Dretske shows, a very important corollary.

   [6] Geoff Pullum (personal communication, 1976) informs me that Postal (personal communication) no longer wishes to maintain this analysis.

(21)   *Clyde gave me **the tickets** by mistake.*
(22)   *Clyde gave **me** the tickets by mistake.*

Sentences (21) and (22) have different truth-conditions, as Dretske (1972:413) points out: "If Clyde is instructed to give the tickets to Harry, but gives them to me by mistake, (21) is false and (22) is true. Since, therefore, there are circumstances in which they differ in truth value, (21) and (22) are not logically equivalent. They differ semantically." We have here a case, just like Kamp's, where the truth conditions of a compound sentence are dependent on the pragmatic properties of an embedded sentence.

Consider the following examples.[7]

(23)   *The professors didn't sign* [ə] *petition.*
(24)   *The professors didn't sign* [éj] *petition.*

It would not be unreasonable to maintain that (23) and (24) have different truth conditions. If the professors signed two petitions, then one might claim that (24) was true, whereas (23) was false. This putative difference in truth conditions cannot be ascribed to differing scope relations holding between the negation and the article, since (24) is NOT synonymous with (25).

(25)   *There is some petition such that it was not signed by the professors.*

The difference must be ascribed to the pragmatic effect of stressing the article. What is denied in (24) is not some entailment of the corresponding affirmative sentence, but rather an implicature of the corresponding affirmative caused by the stressed article (namely that the professors signed no more than one petition). If it is accepted that (23) and (24) have different truth conditions, then the only alternative that I can see to the analysis just suggested would involve an otherwise unmotivated rule of *only*-deletion applying in (24). Thus (24) looks as if it provides another plausible candidate for the status of counterexample to the semantic-autonomy hypothesis.

As was noted in Chapter 4, Cohen (1971:58) has claimed that (26) and (27) have different truth conditions.

(26)   *If the old king has died of a heart attack and a republic has been declared, then Tom will be quite content.*

(27)   *If a republic has been declared and the old king has died of a heart attack, then Tom will be quite content.*

---

[7] Example (24) is due to Schachter (1973:41).

If Cohen is correct, and if the commutative truth–functional analysis of
and given in Chapter 4 is also correct, then it follows the truth conditions
of conditionals can make reference to pragmatic properties of their antecedent clauses (in these examples, implicatures arising from Grice's "Be
orderly!" maxim). Wilson (1975:151) provides an example which makes
the same point with respect to comparatives.

(28)   *To have a child and get married is worse than getting married
         and having a child.*

For (28) to be even possibly true it is necessary, given our assumption
regarding *and*, that the truth conditions of the comparative construction
make reference to the pragmatic properties of its constituent clauses.
Clearly (26), (27), and (28) are at least potential counterexamples to the
semantic autonomy hypothesis.

REFERENCES

Adams, E. W. (1975) *The logic of conditionals*. Dordrecht: Reidel.

Adato, A. (1971) *On the sociology of topics in ordinary conversation*. Ph.D. thesis, University of California, Los Angeles.

Allwood, J. (1972) Negation and the strength of presuppositions. Gothenburg: *Logical Grammar Report* 2.

Anderson, S. R. (1971) On the linguistic status of the performative/constative distinction. Mimeograph, Indiana University Linguistics Club.

Anderson, S. R. & P. Kiparsky, (Eds.). (1973) *A Festschrift for Morris Halle*. New York: Holt.

Aqvist, L. (1972) *Performatives and verifiability by the use of language*. Uppsala: Filosofiska Studier 14.

Atlas, J. D. (1975) Presupposition: A semantico-pragmatic account. *Pragmatics Microfiche* 1.2, D13–G8.

Atlas, J. D. & S. C. Levinson (1973) What is an implicature? Mimeograph, University of California, Berkeley.

Austin, J. L. (1962) *How to do things with words*. Oxford: Oxford University Press.

Bach, E. (1974) *Syntactic theory*. New York: Holt.

Bach, E. (1975) Order in base structure. In Li, C. (Ed.), *Word order and word order change*. Austin: University of Texas Press. Pp. 307–345.

Bach, K. (1975) Performatives are statements too. *Philosophical Studies* 28, 229–236.

Bacon, J. (1973) The semantics of generic *the*. *Journal of Philosophical Logic* 2, 323–39.

Bar–Hillel, Y. (1954) Indexical expressions. *Mind* 63, 359–379.

Bar–Hillel. Y. (1964) *Language and information*. Reading, Mass.: Addison-Wesley.

Bar–Hillel. Y. (1971a) Out of the pragmatic wastebasket. *Linguistic Inquiry* 2, 401–407.

Bar–Hillel, Y. (Ed) (1971b) *Pragmatics of natural language*. Dordrect: Reidel.

Barrett, R. B. & A. J. Stenner (1971) The myth of exclusive *or*. *Mind* 80, 116–121.

Bartsch, R. (forthcoming) The syntax and semantics of subordinate clause constructions and pronominal references. In Heny F. & H. S. Schnelle (Eds.) (forthcoming). *Syntax and semantics 10*. New York: Academic Press.

Bartsch, R. & T. Venneman (1972) *Semantic structures*. Frankfurt: Athenaum.

Bever, T. G., J. J. Katz, & D. T. Langendoen (Eds.) (1976) *An integrated theory of linguistic ability*. New York: Crowell.

Biggs, C. (1976) *Reference, and its role in grammars of natural languages*. Ph.D. thesis, Cambridge University.

Blackburn, S. (Ed.) (1975) *Meaning, reference and necessity*. Cambridge: Cambridge University Press.

Boer, S. E. & W. G. Lycan (1973) Invited inferences and other unwelcome guests. *Papers in Linguistics 6*, 3–4.

Boer, S. E. & W. G. Lycan. (1976) The myth of semantic presupposition. Mimeograph, Indiana University Linguistics Club.

Boer, S. E. & W. G. Lycan (1978) A performadox in truth-conditional semantics. *Pragmatics Microfiche 3.3*, A3–C12.

Bolinger, D. L. (Ed.) (1972) *Intonation*. Harmondsworth: Penguin.

Borowski, E. J. (1976) English and truth–functions. *Analysis 36*, 96–100.

Boyd, J. & J. P. Thorne. (1969) The semantics of modal verbs. *Journal of Linguistics 5*, 57–74.

Carden, G. (1977) Performatives and quantifiers. *Linguistic Inquiry 8*, 163–167.

Carnap, R. (1938) Foundations of logic and mathematics. In Neurath, O. (1938) *International encyclopedia of unified science 1*. Chicago: University of Chicago Press. Pp. 139–214.

Carnap, R. (1955) On some concepts of pragmatics. *Philosophical Studies 6*, 89–91.

Carnap, R. & Y. Bar–Hillel (1952) An outline of a theory of semantic information. In Bar–Hillel, Y. (1964) *Language and information*. Reading, Mass.: Addison-Wesley. Pp. 221–274.

Caton, C. E. (1966) Epistemic qualification of things said in English. *Foundations of Language 2*, 37–66.

Chomsky, N. (1957) *Syntactic structures*. The Hague: Mouton.

Chomsky, N. (1964) *Current issues in linguistic theory*. The Hague: Mouton.

Chomsky, N. (1965) *Aspects of the theory of syntax*. Cambridge, Mass.: M.I.T. Press.

Chomsky, N. (1976) *Reflections on language*. London: Temple Smith.

Clark, E. (1973) What's in a word? In Moore, T. (Ed.), *Cognitive development and the acquisition of language*. New York: Academic Press. Pp. 65–110.

Clark, H. (1969) Linguistic processes in deductive reasoning. *Psychological Review 76*, 387–404.

Clark, H. (1971) The chronometric study of meaning components. *Colloques Internationaux du CRNS 206*, 489–506.

Clark, H. (1974) Semantics and comprehension. In Sebeok, T. (1974) *Current trends in linguistics 12*. The Hague: Mouton. Pp. 1291–1428.

Clark, H. & P. Lucy (1975) Understanding what is meant from what is said: a study in conversationally conveyed requests. *Journal of Verbal Learning and Verbal Behavior 14*, 56–72.

Clark, M. (1971) Ifs and hooks. *Analysis 32*, 33–39.

Cohen, D. & J. R. Wirth. (1975) *Testing linguistic hypotheses*. Washington, D.C.: Hemisphere.

Cohen, L. J. (1971) The logical particles of natural language. In Bar–Hillel, Y. (Ed.) (1971b) *Pragmatics of natural language*. Dordrecht: Reidel. Pp. 50–68.

Cole, P. (1975) The synchronic and diachronic status of conversational implicature. In Cole P. & J. L. Morgan (Eds.) (1975) *Syntax and semantics 3: Speech acts*. New York: Academic Press. Pp. 257–288.

Cole, P. (Ed.) (1978) *Syntax and semantics 9: Pragmatics.* New York: Academic Press.

Cole, P. & J. L. Morgan (Eds.) (1975) *Syntax and semantics 3: Speech acts.* New York: Academic Press.

Cole, P. & J. M. Sadock (Eds.) (1976) *Syntax and semantics 8: Grammatical relations.* New York: Academic Press.

Collinson, W. E. (1948) Some recent trends in linguistic theory with special reference to syntactics. *Lingua 1*, 306–332.

Comrie, B. (1976) Linguistic politeness axes: Speaker–addressee, speaker–referent, speaker–bystander. *Pragmatics Microfiche 1.7*, A3–B1.

Cooper, R. & T. Parsons (1976) Montague grammar, generative semantics and interpretive semantics. In Partee, B. H. (Ed.) (1976) *Montague grammar.* New York: Academic Press. Pp. 311–362.

Cooper, W. S. (1968) The propositional logic of ordinary discourse. *Inquiry 11*, 295–320.

Dahl, O. (1972) Review of Lakoff (1972). *Gothenburg Papers in Theoretical Linguistics 10.*

Dahl, O. (1974) Operational grammars. Gothenburg: *Logical Grammar Report 8.*

Danielsson, S. (1965) Definitions of 'performative.' *Theoria 31*, 20–31.

Davidson, D. & G. Harman (Eds.) (1972) *Semantics of natural language.* Dordrecht: Reidel.

Davison, A. (1973) *Performative verbs, felicity conditions and adverbs.* Ph.D. thesis, University of Chicago.

Dixon, R. M. W. (1972) *The Dyirbal language of North Queensland.* Cambridge: Cambridge University Press.

Downing, P. (1975) Conditionals, impossibilities and material implications. *Analysis 35*, 84–91.

Dretske, F. I. (1972) Contrastive statements. *Philosophical Review 81*, 411–437.

Edwards, P. (1967) *Encyclopedia of philosophy VII.* New York: Collier-Macmillan.

Eid, M. (1974) Disjunctions and alternative questions in Arabic. Mimeograph, Indiana University Linguistics Club.

Fauconnier, G. (1975a) Pragmatic scales and logical structure. *Linguistic Inquiry 6*, 353–375.

Fauconnier, G. (1975b) Polarity and the scale principle. *Papers from the 11th Regional Meeting, Chicago Linguistic Society*, 188–199.

Ferguson, C. & D. Slobin (Eds.) (1973) *Studies in child language development.* New York: Holt.

Fillmore, C. J. & D. T. Langendoen (Eds.) (1971) *Studies in linguistic semantics.* New York: Holt.

Fodor, J. A. & J. J. Katz (Eds.) (1964) *The structure of language.* Englewood Cliffs, N.J.: Prentice-Hall.

Fogelin, R. (1967) *Evidence and meaning.* New York: Humanities Press.

Forman, D. (1974) The speaker knows best principle. *Papers from the 10th Regional Meeting, Chicago Linguistic Society*, 162–77.

Fox, S. E., W. A. Beach, & S. Philosoph (Eds.) (1977) *The CLS book of squibs.* Chicago: Chicago Linguistic Society.

Fraser, B. (1971) An examination of the performative analysis. Mimeograph, Indiana University Linguistics Club.

Fraser, B. (1974) An analysis of vernacular performative verbs. In Shuy, R. W. & C.-J. N. Bailey (Eds.) (1974) *Towards tomorrow's linguistics.* Washington, D.C.: Georgetown University Press. Pp. 139–158.

Freudenthal, H. (Ed.) (1961) *The concept and the role of the model in mathematics and natural and social sciences.* Dordrecht: Reidel.

Garcia, E. (1975) Other than ambiguity. Mimeograph, City University of New York.

Gazdar, G. J. M. (1976) On performative sentences. *Semantikos 1*, 37–62.

Gazdar, G. J. M. (1977a) Implicature, presupposition and logical form. Mimeograph, Indiana University Linguistics Club.

Gazdar, G. J. M. (1977b) Univocal *or*. In Fox, S. E., W. A. Beach, & S. Philosoph (Eds.) (1977) *The CLS book of squibs*. Chicago: Chicago Linguistic Society. Pp. 44–45.

Gazdar, G. J. M. (1977c) Conversational analysis and conventional sociolinguistics. *Analytical Sociology 1*, D8–F9.

Gazdar, G. J. M. (1978) Heavy parentheses wipe-out rules, okay? *Linguistics and Philosophy 2*, 281–289.

Gazdar, G. J. M. & E. L. Keenan (1975) Review of Shuy (1973) *Some new directions in linguistics*. *Language in Society 4*, 377–384.

Gazdar, G. J. M. & E. H. Klein (1977) Context-sensitive transderivational constraints and conventional implicature. *Papers from the 13th Regional Meeting, Chicago Linguistic Society 13*, 137–146.

Gazdar, G. J. M. & G. K. Pullum (1976) Truth-functional connectives in natural language. *Papers from the 12th Regional Meeting, Chicago Linguistic Society*, 220–234.

Geach, P. (1965) Logical procedures and the identity of expressions. *Ratio 7*, 199–205.

Geis, M. (1973) *If* and *unless*. In Kachru, B. B., R. B. Lees, Y. Malkiel, A. Pietrangeli, & S. Saporta (Eds.) (1973) *Issues in linguistics: Papers in honor of Henry and Renee Kahane*. Urbana: University of Illinois Press. Pp. 231–253.

Geis, M. & A. M. Zwicky (1971) On invited inferences. *Linguistic Inquiry*, 561–566.

Givón, T. (1972) Forward implications, backward presuppositions and the time-axis of verbs. In Kimball, J. P. (Ed.) (1972) *Syntax and semantics 1*. New York: Seminar Press. Pp. 29–50.

Givón, T. (1975) Negation in language: Pragmatics, function and ontology. *Pragmatics Microfiche 1.2*, A2–G14.

Gordon, D. & G. Lakoff (1971) Conversational postulates. *Papers from the 7th Regional Meeting, Chicago Linguistic Society*, 63–84.

Green, G. M. (1968) On *too* and *either* and not just *too* and *either* either. *Papers from the 4th Regional Meeting, Chicago Linguistics Society CLS 4*, 22–39.

Green, G. M. (1973a) How to get people to do things with words. In P. Cole & J. L. Morgan (Eds.) (1975) *Syntax and semantics 3: Speech acts*. New York: Academic Press. Pp. 107–142.

Green, G. M. (1973b) The lexical expression of emphatic conjunction: Theoretical implications. *Foundations of Language 10*, 197–248.

Grice, H. P. (1967) *Logic and conversation*. Unpublished manuscript of the William James Lectures, Harvard University.

Grice, H. P. (1975) Logic and conversation. In P. Cole & J. L. Morgan (Eds.) *Syntax and semantics 3: Speech acts*. New York: Academic Press. Pp. 41–58.

Groenendijk, J. & M. Stokhof (1976) *Proceedings of the Amsterdam Colloquium on Montague Grammar and Related Topics*. Amsterdam Papers in Formal Grammar (Vol. 1). Amsterdam: Centrale interfaculteit, Universiteit van Amsterdam.

Grossman, R. E., L. J. San, & T. J. Vance (Eds.) (1975) *Papers from the parasession on functionalism*. Chicago: Chicago Linguistic Society.

Gunter, R. (1972) Intonation and relevance. In Bolinger, D. L. (Ed.). *Intonation*. Harmondsworth, U. K.: Penguin. Pp. 194–215.

Halbasch, K. (1975) An observation on English truth-functions. *Analysis 35*, 109–110.

Hamblin, C. L. (1970) *Fallacies*. London: Methuen.

Hamblin, C. L. (1971) Mathematical models of dialogue. *Theoria 37*, 130–155.

Hamblin, C. L. (1973) Questions in Montague English. *Foundations of Language 10*, 41–53.

Hankamer, J. (1973) Unacceptable ambiguity. *Linguistic Inquiry* 4, 17–68.

Harman, G. (1974a) *On Noam Chomsky: Critical essays*. New York: Doubleday.

Harman, G. (1974b) Meaning and semantics. In Munitz, M. K. & P. K. Unger (Eds.) (1974) *Semantics and philosophy*. New York: New York University Press. Pp. 1–16.

Harman, G. (1975) *If* and modus ponens. Mimeograph, Indiana University Linguistics Club.

Harnish, R. M. (1975) The argument from *lurk*. *Linguistic Inquiry* 6, 145–154.

Harnish, R. M. (1976) Logical form and implicature. In T. G. Bever, J. J. Katz & D. T. Langendoen (Eds.) (1976) *An integrated theory of linguistic ability*. New York: Crowell. Pp. 313–391.

Harris, R. J. (1974) Memory for presuppositions and implications: a case study of 12 verbs of motion and inception-termination. *Journal of Experimental Psychology* 103, 594–597.

Hasegawa, K. (1972) Transformations and semantic interpretation. *Linguistic Inquiry* 3, 141–159.

Hausser, R. R. (1973) Presuppositions and quantifiers. *Papers from the 9th Regional Meeting, Chicago Linguistic Society*, 192–204.

Hausser, R. R. (1976) Presupposition in Montague Grammar. *Theoretical Linguistics* 3, 245–280.

Hawkins, J. A. (1978) *Definiteness and indefiniteness*. London: Croom Helm.

Hedenius, I. (1963) Performatives. *Theoria* 29, 115–136.

Heinamaki, O. (1972) Before. *Papers from the 8th Regional Meeting, Chicago Linguistic Society* 139–151.

Heny, F. & H. S. Schnelle (Eds.) (forthcoming) *Syntax and semantics 10*. New York: Academic Press.

Heringer, J. T. (1972) Some grammatical correlates of felicity conditions and presuppositions. Mimeograph, Indiana University Linguistics Club.

Heringer, J. T. (1977) Pre-sequences and indirect speech acts. *Southern California Occasional Papers in Linguistics* 5, 169–179. Los Angeles: Department of Linguistics, University of Southern California.

Herzberger, H. O. (1971) Some results on presupposition and modality. Mimeograph, University of Toronto.

Hintikka, J. (1962) *Knowledge and belief*. Ithaca, N.Y.: Cornell University Press.

Hintikka, J. (1973) *Logic, language games and information*. Oxford: Oxford University Press.

Hintikka, J., J. Moravesik & P. Suppes (Eds.) (1973) *Approaches to natural language*. Dordrecht: Reidel.

Hiz, H. (forthcoming) On some general principles of semantics of a natural language. In Heny F. & H. S. Schnelle (forthcoming). *Syntax and semantics 10*. New York: Academic Press.

Hoosain, R. (1973) The processing of negation. *Journal of Verbal Learning and Verbal Behavior* 12, 618–626.

Horn, L. R. (1972) *On the semantic properties of logical operators in English*. Ph.D. thesis, University of California, Los Angeles.

Horn, L. R. (1973) Greek Grice. *Papers from the 9th Regional Meeting, Chicago Linguistics Society*, 205–214.

Huddleston, R. (1976) *An introduction to English transformational syntax*. London: Longmans.

Hudson, G. (1972) Is deep structure linear? *UCLA Papers in Syntax* 2, 51–77.

Humberstone, I. L. (1975) Review of Davidson, D. & G. Harman (Eds.) (1972). *Semantics of natural language*. *York Papers in Linguistics* 5, 195–224.

Hurford, J. R. (1974) Exclusive or inclusive disjunction. *Foundations of Language 11*, 409–411.

Hurford, J. R. (1976) The significance of linguistic generalizations. Mimeograph, University of Lancaster.

Jacobs, R. A. & P. S. Rosenbaum (1970) *Readings in English transformational grammar*. Waltham: Ginn.

Jespersen, O. (1917) Negation in English and other languages. In Jespersen, O. (1962) *Selected writings*. London: Allen & Unwin. Pp. 3–152.

Jespersen, O. (1962) *Selected writings*. London: Allen & Unwin.

Johnson, D. E. (1974) *Toward a theory of relationally based grammar*. Ph.D. thesis, University of Illinois.

Just, M. A. & H. Clark (1973) Drawing inferences from the presuppositions and implications of affirmative and negative sentences. *Journal of Verbal Learning and Verbal Behavior 12*, 21–31.

Kachru, B. B., R. B. Lees, Y. Malkiel, A. Pietrangeli, & S. Saporta (Eds.) (1973) *Issues in linguistics: Papers in honor of Henry and Renee Kahane*. Urbana: University of Illinois Press.

Kalish, D. (1967) Semantics. In Edwards, D. (1967) *Encyclopedia of philosophy VII*. New York: Collier–MacMillan. Pp. 348–358.

Kamp, J. A. W. (1973) Free choice permission. *Aristotelian Society Proceedings 74*, 57–74.

Kamp, J. A. W. (1976) The formal semantics and pragmatics of non-indicative speech acts. Paper presented to the 3rd Groningen Round Table, Mathematical Linguistics: Semantics for Natural Languages, Groningen.

Karttunen, L. (no date) Presuppositional phenomena. Mimeograph, Texas.

Karttunen, L. (1971) Some observations on factivity. *Papers in Linguistics 4*, 55–69.

Karttunen, L. (1972) Possible and must. In Kimball, J. P. (Ed.) (1972) *Syntax and semantics 1*. New York: Seminar Press. Pp. 1–20.

Karttunen, L. (1973a) Presuppositions of compound sentences. *Linguistic Inquiry 4*, 169–193.

Karttunen, L. (1973b) The last word. Mimeograph, Texas.

Karttunen, L. (1973c) Remarks on presuppositions. Mimeograph, Texas.

Karttunen, L. (1974) Presupposition and linguistic context. *Theoretical Linguistics 1*, 181–194. [Reprinted in Rogers, A., R. Wall, & J. P. Murphy (1977). *Proceedings of the Texas conference on performatives, presuppositions and implicatures*. Arlington, Va.: Center for Applied Linguistics. Pp. 149–160. (Page numbers given refer to this version.)]

Karttunen, L. (1975) On pragmatic and semantic aspects of meaning. *Texas Linguistic Forum 1*, 51–64.

Karttunen, L. (1976) Discourse referents. In McCawley, J. D. (Ed.) (1976). *Syntax and semantics 7: Notes from the linguistic underground*. New York. Academic Press. Pp. 363–385.

Karttunen, L. & P. S. Peters (1975) Conventional implicature in Montague grammar. *Proceedings of the First Annual Meeting of the Berkeley Linguistics Society*, 266–278.

Karttunen, L. & P. S. Peters (1977) Conventional implicature. Mimeograph, University of Texas. [Revised version to appear in C.K. Oh (forthcoming), *Syntax and semantics 11: Presupposition*. New York: Academic Press.]

Kasher, A. (1974) Mood implicatures: A logical way of doing generative pragmatics. *Theoretical Linguistics 1*, 6–38.

Katz, J. J. (1972) *Semantic theory*. New York: Harper & Row.

Katz, J. J. (1977) *Propositional structure and illocutionary force*. New York: Crowell.

Katz, J. J. & D. T. Langendoen (1976) Pragmatics and presupposition. *Language 52*, 1–17.

Katz, J. J. & P. M. Postal (1964) *An integrated theory of linguistic descriptions*. Cambridge, Mass.: M.I.T. Press.

Keenan, E. L. (1969) *A logical base for a transformational grammar of English*. Ph.D. thesis, University of Pennsylvania.

Keenan, E. L. (1971) Two kinds of presupposition in natural language. In Fillmore, C. J. & D. T. Langendoen (Eds.) (1971) *Studies in linguistic semantics*. New York: Holt. Pp. 45–54.

Keenan, E. L. (1972) On semantically based grammar. *Linguistic Inquiry 3*, 413–461.

Keenan, E. L. (Ed.) (1975) *Formal semantics of natural language*. Cambridge: Cambridge University Press.

Keenan, E. O. (1976) On the universality of conversational implicatures. *Language in Society 5*, 67–80.

Kempson, R. M. (1975) *Presupposition and the delimitation of semantics*. Cambridge: Cambridge University Press.

Kenny, A. J. (1966) Practical inference. *Analysis 26*, 65–75.

Kimball, J. P. (Ed.) (1972) *Syntax and semantics 1*. New York: Seminar Press.

Kimball, J. P. (Ed.) (1975) *Syntax and semantics 4*. New York: Academic Press.

Kiparsky, P. & C. Kiparsky (1970) Fact. In Steinberg, D. D. & L. A. Jakobovits (Eds.) (1971). *Semantics: An interdisciplinary reader*. Cambridge: Cambridge University Press.

Kleene, S. C. (1967) *Mathematical Logic*. New York: Wiley.

Klein, E. H. (1975) Two sorts of factive predicate. *Pragmatics Microfiche 1.1*, B5–C14.

Klima, E. S. (1964) Negation in English. In Fodor, J. A. & J. J. Katz (Eds.) (1964) *The structure of language*. Englewood Cliffs, N. J.: Prentice–Hall. Pp. 246–323.

Klima, E. S. & U. Bellugi (1973) Syntactic regularities in the speech of children. In Ferguson, C. & D. Slobin (Eds.) (1973) *Studies in child language development*. New York: Holt. Pp. 333–353.

Kneale, W. & G. E. Moore (1936) Is existence a predicate? (symposium). *Aristotelian Society Supplementary Volume 15*, 154–188.

Kroch, A. (1972) Lexical and inferred meanings for some time adverbs. *Quarterly Progress Report of the Research Laboratory of Electronics 104*, Massachusetts Institute of Technology.

Kuno, S. (1972) Pronominalization, reflexivization and direct discourse. *Linguistic Inquiry 3*, 161–195.

Kuroda, S.-Y. (1976) Headless relative clauses in modern Japanese and the relevancy condition. *Proceedings of the Second Annual Meeting of the Berkeley Linguistics Society*, 269–279.

Lakoff, G. (1968) Instrumental adverbs and the concept of deep structure. *Foundations of Language 4*, 4–29.

Lakoff, G. (1971a) On generative semantics. In Steinberg, D. D. & L. A. Jakobovits (Eds.) (1971) *Semantics: An interdisciplinary reader*. Cambridge: Cambridge University Press. Pp. 232–296.

Lakoff, G. (1971b) The role of deduction in grammar. In Fillmore, C. J. & D. T. Langendoen (Eds.) (1971) *Studies in linguistic semantics*. New York: Holt. Pp. 63–72.

Lakoff, G. (1972) Linguistics and natural logic. In Davidson, D. & G. Harman (Eds.) (1972) *Semantics of natural language*. Dordrecht: Reidel.

Lakoff, G. (1975) Pragmatics in natural logic. In Keenan, E. L. (Ed.) (1975) *Formal semantics of natural language*. Cambridge: Cambridge University Press. Pp. 253–286. Reprinted in Rogers, A. *et al.* (1977) *Proceedings of the Texas conference performatives, presuppositions and implicatures*. Arlington, Va.: Center for Applied Linguistics. Pp. 107–134.

Lakoff, G. & H. Thompson (1975a) Introducing cognitive grammar. *Proceedings of the First Annual Meeting of the Berkeley Linguistics Society*, 295–313.

Lakoff, G. & H. Thompson (1975b) Dative questions in cognitive grammar. In Grossman, R. E. *et al.* (Eds.) (1975) *Papers from the parasession on functionalism.* Chicago: Chicago Linguistic Society. Pp. 337–350.

Lakoff, R. (1968) *Abstract syntax and Latin complementation.* Cambridge: M.I.T. Press.

Lakoff, R. (1970) Tense and its relation to participants. *Language 46*, 838–850.

Lakoff, R. (1971) If's, and's and but's about conjunction. In Fillmore, C. J. & D. T. Langendoen (Eds.) (1971) *Studies in linguistic semantics.* New York: Holt. Pp. 115–150.

Lakoff, R. (1972) The pragmatics of modality. *Papers from the 8th Regional Meeting, Chicago Linguistic Society* 229–246.

Lakoff, R. (1973) Questionable answers and answerable questions. In Kachru, B. B. *et al.* (Eds.) (1973) *Issues in linguistics: Papers in honor of Henry and Renee Kahane.* Urbana: University of Illinois Press. Pp. 453–467.

Lakoff, R. (1977) What you can do with words: Politeness, pragmatics and performatives. In Rogers, A. *et al.* (Eds.) (1977) *Proceedings of the Texas conference on performatives, presuppositions and implicatures.* Arlington, Va.: Center for Applied Linguistics. Pp. 79–105.

Lambert, K. (1969) *The logical way of doing things.* New Haven: Yale University Press.

Langendoen, D. T. (1971) Presupposition and assertion in semantic analysis. In Steinberg, D. D. & L. A. Jakobovits (Eds.) (1971) *Semantics: An interdisciplinary reader.* Cambridge: Cambridge University Press. Pp. 341–344.

Langendoen, D. T. (1975) Acceptable conclusions from unacceptable ambiguity. In Cohen, D. & J. R. Wirth (Eds.) (1975) *Testing linguistic hypotheses.* Washington, D.C.: Hemisphere. Pp. 111–128.

Langendoen, D. T. & H. B. Savin (1971) The projection problem for presuppositions. In Fillmore, C. J. & D. T. Langendoen (Eds.) (1971) *Studies in linguistic semantics.* New York: Holt. Pp. 55–62.

Lehrer, A. (1975) Interpreting certain adverbs: Semantics or pragmatics? *Journal of Linguistics 11*, 239–248.

Lemmon, E. J. (1962) On sentences verifiable by their use. *Analysis 22*, 86–89.

Lewis, D. (1969) *Convention.* Cambridge, Mass.: Harvard University Press.

Lewis, D. (1972) General semantics. In Davidson, D. & G. Harman (Eds.) (1972) *Semantics of natural language.* Dordrecht: Reidel. Pp. 169–218.

Lewis, D. (1973) *Counterfactuals.* Oxford: Blackwell.

Li, C. (Ed.) (1975) *Word order and word order change.* Austin: University of Texas Press.

Liberman, M. (1973) Alternatives. *Papers from the 9th Regional Meeting, Chicago Linguistic Society*, 356–368.

Linde, C. (1976) Constraints on the ordering of if-clauses. *Proceedings of the Second Annual Meeting of the Berkeley Linguistics Society*, 280–285.

Linde, C. & W. Labov (1975) Spatial networks as a site for the study of language and thought. *Language 51*, 924–939.

Loetscher, A. (1973) On the role of NRRCs in discourse. *Papers from the 9th Regional Meeting, Chicago Linguistics Society*, 356–368.

Lyons, J. (1977) *Semantics 1.* Cambridge: Cambridge University Press.

McCawley, J. D. (1972) A program for logic. In Davidson, D. G. & Harman (Eds.) (1972) *Semantics of natural language.* Dordrecht: Reidel. Pp. 498–544.

McCawley J. D. (1973) External NPs versus annotated deep structures. *Linguistic Inquiry 4*, 221–240.

McCawley, J. D. (1974) If and only if. *Linguistic Inquiry 5*, 632–635.

McCawley, J. D. (Ed.) (1976) *Syntax and semantics 7: Notes from the linguistic underground*. New York: Academic Press.

Mackie, J. L. (1973) *Truth, probability and paradox*. Oxford: Oxford University Press.

Mandel, M. (1974) When things don't happen. *Berkeley Studies in Syntax and Semantics 1*, XIX 1–3.

Martin, J. N. (1975) Karttunen on possibility. *Linguistic Inquiry 6*, 339–341.

Martin, R. M. (1959) *Towards a systematic pragmatics*. Amsterdam: North Holland.

Martin, R. M. (1963) *Intension and decision*. Englewood Cliffs, N.J.: Prentice–Hall.

Matthews, P. H. (1967) Review of Chomsky (1965) *Aspects of the theory of syntax*. *Journal of Linguistics 3*, 119–152.

Matthews, P. H. (1972) Review of Jacobs & Rosenbaum (1970) *Readings in English transformational grammar*. *Journal of Linguistics 8*, 125–136.

Matthews, P. H. (1976) Review of Sadock (1974) *Toward a linguistic theory of speech acts*. *General Linguistics 16*, 236–242.

Mittwoch, A. (1977) How to refer to one's own words: Speech–act modifying adverbials and the performative analysis. *Journal of Linguistics 13*, 177–189.

Montague, R. (1974) *Formal philosophy: Selected papers* (R. H. Thompson, Ed.). New Haven: Yale University Press.

Moore, T. (1973) *Cognitive development and the acquisition of language*. New York: Academic Press.

Moore, T. (1976) Languages are clouds and clocks. *York Papers in Linguistics 6*, 21–32.

Morgan, J. L. (1969) On the treatment of presupposition in transformational grammar. *Papers from the 5th Regional Meeting, Chicago Linguistics Society*, 167–177.

Morgan, J. L. *et al.* (1976) Topics in relational grammar. *Studies in the Linguistic Sciences 6.1*, 47–248.

Morris, C. (1938) Foundations of the theory of signs. In Neurath, O. (1938) *International encyclopedia of unified science 1*. Chicago: University of Chicago Press. Pp. 77–138.

Munitz, M. K. & P. K. Unger (Eds.) (1974) *Semantics and philosophy*. New York: New York University Press.

Neurath, O. (1938) *International encyclopedia of unified science 1*. Chicago: University of Chicago Press.

Nunberg, G. & C. Pan (1975) Inferring quantification in generic sentences. *Papers from the 11th Regional Meeting, Chicago Linguistic Society*, 412–422.

Oh, C.-K. (Ed.) (forthcoming) *Syntax and semantics 11: Presupposition*. New York: Academic Press.

Palmer, F. R. (1971) *Grammar*. Harmondsworth U. K.: Penguin.

Partee, B. H. (1971) Linguistic metatheory. In Harman, G. (Ed.) (1974a) *On Noam Chomsky: Critical essays*. New York: Doubleday. Pp. 303–315.

Partee, B. H. (1973) Some transformational extensions of Montague Grammar. *Journal of Philosophical Logic 2*, 509–534.

Partee, B. H. (Ed.) (1976) *Montague grammar*. New York: Academic Press.

Pelletier, F. J. (1977) Or *Theoretical Linguistics 4*, 61–74.

Peters, P. S. (1975) Presuppositions and conversation. *Texas Linguistic Forum 2*, 122–134.

Peters, P. S. (1977) A truth-conditional formulation of Karttunen's account of presupposition. *Texas Linguistic Forum 6*, 137–149.

Peters, P. S. & R. W. Ritchie (1969) A note on the universal base hypothesis. *Journal of Linguistics 5*, 150–152.

Peters, P. S. & R. W. Ritchie (1973a) On the generative power of transformational grammars. *Information Sciences 6*, 49–83.

Peters, P. S. & R. W. Ritchie (1973b) Nonfiltering and local–filtering transformational grammars. In Hintikka, J. *et al.* (Eds.) (1973) *Approaches to natural language.* Dordrecht: Reidel. Pp. 180–194.

Peterson, T. (1971) Multi-ordered base structures in generative grammar. *Papers from the 7th Regional Meeting, Chicago Linguistic Society,* 181–192.

Postal, P. M. (1971) *Cross-over phenomena.* New York: Holt.

Postal, P. M. (1977) About a "nonargument" for Raising. *Linguistic Inquiry* 8, 141–154.

Pullum, G. K. (1974) General conditions on reduced coordinations. Paper presented to the Spring 1974 meeting of the Linguistics Association of Great Britain, Hatfield.

Pullum, G. K. (1976a) *Rule interaction and the organization of a grammar.* Ph.D. thesis. University of London.

Pullum, G. K. (1976b) Word order universals and grammatical relations. In Cole, P. & J. M. Sadock (1976) *Syntax and Semantics 8: Grammatical relations.* New York: Academic Press. Pp. 249–278.

Quasthoff, U. (Ed.) (1977) *Sprachstruktur-Sozialstruktur.* Kronberg: West Germany, Scriptor Verlag.

Quine, W. V. O. (1941) *Elementary Logic.* New York: Harper & Row.

Radford, A. (1975) *Bidirectionality in raising.* Ph.D. thesis, Cambridge University.

Reis, M. (1974) Further and's and but's about conjunction. *Papers from the 10th Regional Meeting, Chicago Linguistic Society,* 539–550.

Rescher, N. (1968) *Studies in logical theory.* Oxford: Blackwell.

Rodman, R. (Ed.) (1972) *Papers in Montague grammar. UCLA Occasional Papers in Linguistics 2.*

Rodman, R., R. Nolan & S. Munsat (1977) Some remarks on pragmatics and presupposition. Mimeograph, University of North Carolina, Chapel Hill.

Rogers, A., R. Wall & J. P. Murphy (Eds.) (1977) *Proceedings of the Texas conference on performatives, presuppositions and implicatures.* Arlington, Va.: Center for Applied Linguistics.

Rohrer, C. (1973) Le systeme de Montague et les presuppositions. *Langages* 30, 111–124.

Ross, J. R. (1967) *Constraints on variables in syntax.* Ph.D. thesis, M.I.T.

Ross, J. R. (1970) On declarative sentences. In Jacobs, R. A. & P. S. Rosenbaum (Eds.) (1970) *Readings in English transformational grammar.* Waltham, Mass.: Ginn. Pp. 222–272.

Ross, J. R. (1975) Where to do things with words. In Cole P. & J. L. Morgan (Eds.) (1975) *Syntax and semantics 3: Speech acts.* New York: Academic Press Pp. 233–256. Reprinted in Rogers A. *et al.* (1977) *Proceedings of the Texas conference on performatives, presuppositions and implicatures.* Arlington, Va.: Center for Applied Linguistics. Pp. 47–66.

Russell, B. (1905) On denoting. *Mind* 14, 479–93.

Sacks, H. (1968) Lecture (May 29th). Mimeograph, University of California, Irvine.

Sacks, H. (1976) Paradoxes, pre–sequences and pronouns. *Pragmatics Microfiche 1.8,* E6–G12.

Sacks, H. & E. A. Schegloff (1977) Two preferences in the organization of reference to persons in conversation and their interaction. In Quasthoff, U. (1977) *Sprachestrukur–Sozialstruklur.* Kronberg, West Germany: Scriptor Verlag.

Sadock, J. M. (1969a) Hypersentences. *Papers in Linguistics 1,* 283–370.

Sadock, J. M. (1969b) Super–hypersentences. *Papers in Linguistics 1,* 1–15.

Sadock, J. M. (1970) Whimperatives. In Sadock, J. M. & A. L. Vanek (Eds.) (1970) *Studies presented to R. B. Lees.* Edmonton, Canada: Linguistics Research Incorporated. Pp. 223–237.

Sadock, J. M. (1971) Quedeclaratives. *Papers from the 7th Regional Meeting, Chicago Linguistic Society,* 223–231.

Sadock, J. M. (1972) Speech act idioms. *Papers from the 8th Regional Meeting, Chicago Linguistic Society*, 329–339.

Sadock, J. M. (1974) *Toward a linguistic theory of speech acts*. New York: Academic Press.

Sadock, J. M. (1975) Larry scores a point. *Pragmatics Microfiche 1.4*, G10–G14.

Sadock, J. M. (1977) Aspects of linguistic pragmatics. In Rogers, A. *et al.* (Eds.) (1977) *Proceedings of the Texas conference on performatives, presuppositions and implicatures*. Arlington, Va.: Center for Applied Linguistics. Pp. 67–78.

Sadock, J. M. (1977) Modus brevis: The truncated argument. *Papers from the 13th Regional Meeting, Chicago Linguistic Society*, 545–554.

Sadock, J. M. ₁ (1978) On testing for conversational implicature. In Cole, P. (Ed.) (1978) *Syntax and semantics 9: Pragmatics*. New York: Academic Press.

Sadock, J. M. & A. L. Vanek (Eds.) (1970) *Studies presented to R. B. Lees*. Edmonton, Canada: Linguistics Research Incorporated.

Sanders, G. (1970) Constraints on constituent ordering. *Papers in Linguistics 2*, 460–502.

Sayward, C. (1974) The received distinction between pragmatics, semantics and syntax. *Foundations of Language 11*, 97–104.

Sayward, C. (1975) Pragmatics and indexicality. *Pragmatics Microfiche 1.3*, D5–D12.

Schachter, P. (1973) On syntactic categories. Mimeograph, Indiana University Linguistics Club.

Schmerling, S. F. (1975) Asymmetric conjunction and rules of conversation. In Cole, P. & J. L. Morgan (1975) *Syntax and semantics 3: Speech acts*. New York. Academic Press. Pp. 211–232.

Schmerling, S. F. (1978) Synonymy judgments as syntactic evidence. In Cole, P. (Ed.) (1978). *Syntax and semantics 9: Pragmatics*. New York: Academic Press.

Searle, J. R. (1969) *Speech acts*. Cambridge: Cambridge University Press.

Searle, J. R. (1975) Indirect speech acts. In Cole, P. & J. L. Morgan (Eds.) (1975) *Syntax and semantics 3: Speech acts*. New York: Academic Press. Pp. 59–82.

Sebeok, T. (Ed.) (1974) *Current trends in linguistics 12*. The Hague: Mouton.

Shuy, R. W. (Ed.) (1973) *Some new directions in linguistics*. Washington, D.C.: Georgetown University Press.

Shuy, R. W. & C.-J. N. Bailey (Eds.) (1974) *Towards tomorrow's linguistics*. Washington, D.C.: Georgetown University Press.

Sperber, D. & D. Wilson (1977) Pragmatics and rhetoric. MS.

Stalnaker, R. C. (1968) A theory of conditionals. In Rescher (1968) *Studies in logical theory*. Oxford: Blackwell. Pp. 98–112.

Stalnaker, R. C. (1972) Pragmatics. In Davidson, D. & G. Harman (Eds.) (1972) *Semantics of natural language*. Dordecht: Reidel.

Stalnaker, R. C. (1973) Presuppositions. *Journal of Philosophical Logic 2*, 447–457.

Stalnaker, R. C. (1974a) Pragmatic presuppositions. In Munitz, M. K. & D. K. Unger (Eds.) (1974) *Semantics and philosophy*. New York: New York University Press. Pp. 197–213. Reprinted in Rogers, A. *et al.* (Eds.) (1977) *Proceedings of the Texas conference on performatives, presuppositions and implicatures*. Arlington, Va.: Center for Applied Linguistics. Pp. 135–147.

Stalnaker, R. C. (1974b) Contexts and possible worlds. Mimeograph, Cornell University.

Stalnaker, R. C. (1975) Indicative conditionals. *Philosphia 5*, 269–286.

Stalnaker, R. C. (1978) Assertion. In P. Cole (Ed.) *Syntax and semantics 9: Pragmatics*. New York: Academic Press.

Stalnaker, R. C. & R. H. Thomason (1970) A semantic analysis of conditional logic. *Theoria 36*, 23–42.

Staal, J. F. (1967) *Word order in Sanskrit and universal grammar*. Dordrecht: Reidel.

Steinberg, D. D. & L. A. Jakobovits (Eds.) (1971) *Semantics: An interdisciplinary reader*. Cambridge: Cambridge University Press.

Stockwell, R. P., P. Schachter, & B. H. Partee (1973) *The major syntactic structures of English*. New York: Holt.

Strawson, P. F. (1950) On referring. *Mind 59*, 320–44.

Strawson, P. F. (1967) If and ⊃. Mimeograph, Oxford University.

Suppes, P. (1960) *Axiomatic set theory*. New York: Dover.

Suppes, P. (1961) A comparison of the meaning and uses of models in mathematics and the empirical sciences. In Freudenthal, H. (Ed.) (1961) *The concept and the role of the model in mathematics and natural and social sciences*. Dordrecht: Reidel. Pp. 163–177.

Suppes, P. (1973) Semantics of context-free fragments of natural languages. In Hintikka *et al*. (Eds.) (1973) *Approaches to natural language*. Dordrecht: Reidel. Pp. 370–394.

Tedeschi, P. J. (1977) Complementizers and conditionals. *Papers from the 13th Regional Meeting, Chicago Linguistic Society*, 629–639.

Thomason, R. H. (1970) A Fitch-style formulation of conditional logic. *Logique et Analyse 52*, 397–412.

Thomason, R. H. (1973) Semantics, pragmatics, conversation and presupposition. Mimeograph, University of Pittsburgh.

Thomason, R. H. (1976) On the semantic interpretation of the Thomason 1972 fragment. Mimeograph, University of Pittsburgh.

Thomason, R. H. (1977) Where pragmatics fits in. In Rogers, A. *et al*. (Eds.) (1977) *Proceedings of the Texas conference on performatives, presuppositions and implicatures*. Arlington, Va.: Center for Applied Linguistics. Pp. 161–166.

Thompson, H. & J. Wright (1975) Speaker alignment and embedded performatives. *Proceedings of the First Annual Meeting, of the Berkeley Linguistics Society*, 438–444.

Van Fraassen, B. C. (1968) Presupposition, implication and self reference. *Journal of Philosophy 65*, 136–152.

Van Fraassen, B. C. (1969) Presuppositions, supervaluations and free logic. In Lambert, K. (Ed.) *The logical way of doing things*. New Haven: Yale University Press. Pp. 67–92.

Van Fraassen, B. C. (1971) *Formal semantics and logic*. New York: Macmillan.

Von Wright, G. H. (1969) *An essay in deontic logic and the theory of action*. Amsterdam: North Holland.

Walker, R. C. S. (1975) Conversational implicatures. In Blackburn S. (Ed.) (1975) *Meaning, reference and necessity*. Cambridge: Cambridge University Press. Pp. 133–181.

Wall, R. (1972) *Introduction to mathematical linguistics*. Englewood Cliffs, N.J.: Prentice–Hall.

Wason, P. C. (1959) The processing of positive and negative information. *Quarterly Journal of Experimental Psychology 11*, 92–107.

Wason, P. C. (1961) Response to affirmative and negative binary statements. *British Journal of Psychology 52*, 133–142.

Wason, P. C. & P. N. Johnson–Laird (1972) *Psychology of reasoning*. London: Batsford.

Watson, R. (1975) Interactional uses of pronouns. *Pragmatics Microfiche 1.3*, A3–C1.

Weiser, A. (1974) Deliberate ambiguity *Papers from the 10th Regional Meeting, Chicago Linguistics Society*, 723–731.

Wilson, D. M. (1975) *Presupposition and non–truth-conditional semantics*. London: Academic Press.

Young, J. (1972) Ifs and hooks: a defence of the orthodox view. *Analysis 33*, 56–63.

Zwicky, A. M. (1973) Linguistics as chemistry: the substance theory of linguistic primes. In Anderson, S. P. & P. Kiparsky (1973) *A Festschrift for Morris Halle*. New York: Holt. Pp. 467–485.

Zwicky, A. M. & J. M. Sadock (1975) Ambiguity tests and how to fail them. In Kimball, J. P. (Ed.) (1975) *Syntax and semantics 1*. New York: Seminar Press. Pp. 1–36.

INDEX